Unfinished Revolution

South Tyneside 1969–1976

To Shirley,

With best wishes

Jack Grassby

Oct. 2002,

Jack Grassby

©Jack Grassby 1999
ISBN: 1 901237 11 7

Cover and book typeset and designed
by Lee Foster at

Thanks to the following:

Shields Gazette
Newcastle Evening Chronicle
Newcastle Journal
Sunday Sun
Daily Mirror
The Guardian
South Shields Central Library
and
The Lipman – Miliband Trust

Printed and Published by TUPS Books
30 Lime Street, Newcastle, NE1 2PQ. T:0191 2330990

*This book is dedicated
to the people of South Shields*

Contents

Preface

The period around the mid-60s to mid-70s has been recognised as a time of radical change in the arts and in society, colourfully, if misleadingly, identified by the phrase 'drugs, sex and rock 'n' roll'.

The period was also one of world-wide grass-root political action involving workers, students, and community groups. The anti-Vietnam war demonstrations and civil rights movements in America; the 1968 students' demonstrations and general strike in France; the 1972 and 1974 miners' strikes in the UK, typified such events. For a brief few years, confidently, and in retrospect incredibly, 'we the people' could change the world.

As well as demonstrations and strikes the events included factory and college occupations, lock-outs, sit-downs, teach-ins and other more innovative actions. In all cases the events were characterised by grass-root direct action to confront the establishment.

Around 1969–1976 South Tyneside, and in particular South Shields, was the unlikely centre for some of these events, concentrated largely on the South Shields Trades Union Council.

Many of those involved were seeking a radical change in the social and political structures. Some viewed them with a clearly revolutionary perspective. Others, fearing a charge of what Lenin might have called 'left-wing adventurism', would describe the actions as 'pre-revolutionary'.

This book is an attempt to record some of these events in a (fairly) objective manner by reproducing contemporary documents, pamphlets and press reports. The political/social significance is left

The Unfinished Revolution　　　　　　　　　　　　　　　　　　　**1**

largely to the reader – except for my own comments where the reader will need to set my prejudices against their own political sensibilities.

The Introduction sets out the social and political background against which the events occurred. Each chapter is introduced by a brief description of the events covered, and these introductions, read by themselves, will give the reader an overview of the book's narrative. The reproduced documents are accompanied by a running commentary and are intended to give some detail of the events and a feel of the period.

The Epilogue briefly considers the impact of these events (and others like them) from a longer perspective.

The book is not intended simply as an exercise in nostalgia but rather with the hope that it will interest and hopefully inspire contemporary political/social activists.

All the original source material is held by South Tyneside Central Library.

Jack Grassby
South Shields, June 1999

Introduction

South Shields is a medium sized, northern, industrial town at the mouth of the Tyne, with a population of around 100,000. Its main industries, shipyards, seafaring, mining and other heavy industry are now largely gone. It is bounded on one side by the Tyne and another by the North Sea and it has a strong sense of local community.

The town's unemployment rate in the late 60s was around 12% – the rate has usually been about twice the national average.

The South Shields Trades Council was formed in 1872 – one of the first in the country. From around 1900 it co-operated in various ways with the Labour movement and in 1919 it formed a joint organisation with the constituency Labour Party.

In 1970, the Trades Council separated from the Labour Party, in accordance with the official Trades Union Congress (TUC) and Labour Party policy, to become the South Shields Trades Union Council (SSTUC). The separation was not without reservations (and recriminations) – even though this was one of the last organisations in England to split in this way.

The first President (Chair) of the Trades Union Council was Jim Florence, an ex-Labour Councillor and experienced trade unionist. He gave early gravitas and credibility to the Council.

The SSTUC was affiliated to the national TUC and as such was the TUC's official local representative, dealing with matters of joint trade union interest in the area.

In 1970, the SSTUC consisted of:
89 affiliated trade union branches, sending
140 delegates, representing some
10,000 local trade unionists.

The affiliated unions ranged from unskilled manual workers to professional 'white-collar' workers.

The national TUC reluctantly accepted a SSTUC constitution which allowed affiliated 'observer' status to:

Pensioners Groups;
Students Unions;
Shop Stewards;
Unemployed;
Social Security Claimants.

By far the most influential of this group was the South Shields Claimants' Union (SSCU). This was part of a loose national federation of Claimants Unions (CUs), based in some 80 major conurbations, and run by and for social security claimants on a unique open democratic basis (but that is another story!).

The SSTUC met monthly with an average attendance of around 50 delegates. Sub-committees were set up on an ad-hoc basis to deal with individual issues, and it was these sub-committees which initiated and promoted the various campaigns and projects.

Significantly, the sub-committee structure allowed for the co-option of a range of activists from the 'observer' groups. These activists included members from a spectrum of political organisations, predominantly Labour Party (and Labour Party Young Socialists), but including self-proclaimed international revolutionaries:–

Communist Party;
Workers Revolutionary Party;
International Marxist Group;
Unemployed Workers Union;
International Socialists.

It is interesting that these notoriously warring factions were prepared to sink their ideological differences in favour of (what one member described as) the 'dynamic of existential action'.

Certainly, while the Trades Union Council was evowedly non-party political, it was from this wide representation of interests that the dynamic for action developed.

The background against which the SSTUC operated was a Labour-dominated local council (pragmatically right-wing rather than 'Old Labour') and a regional Labour Party~trade union Mafia – the time of T. Dan Smith, John Poulson and Andy Cunningham.

The Trades Union Council received more than one visit from Andy Cunningham who sought, like his more famous son, (Jack Cunningham, the current cabinet 'enforcer') to bring unruly elements into more conformative ways.

Nationally there was a failed Tory government under Edward Heath and, in 1974, a struggling minority Labour government under Harold Wilson, in power with Liberal Party support in a Lib–Lab pact.

The Claimants Union

The definitive story of the Claimants Unions (CUs) must be left to another writer. It is intended here simply to record what is relevant for the understanding of the events of 1969–1976 in South Shields.

Claimants Unions were first formed in the London area in the late 60s. Their membership was at first confined to those claiming state benefits (chiefly social security or unemployment benefits) i.e. the unemployed, pensioners, single parents, and later, students.

The CUs arose naturally from the culture of that period – they embraced grass-root direct action as an instrument of change; they confronted the establishment and its values; they were nominally apolitical; they represented an underclass in the face of what they saw as capitalist exploitation; they sought revolutionary change.

As the CUs grew they attracted the support of the sympathetic professional workers – teachers, lecturers, lawyers, doctors – as well as the politically motivated. However, while CUs attracted the usual political suspects, they successfully resisted all take-over attempts – possibly because of their lack of formal organisation structure. There was, in an organisational sense, nothing to take over. However, the leading activists were never members of any political group.

The CUs operated on an open, democratic basis, without officers or officials. Decisions on action were taken, not on a majority basis, but on a basis of discussion and debate until a unanimous decision was reached. They have been described, amongst other things, as anarcho-syndicalists and independent neo-Marxists.

One of the founders of the CU movement was a youthful Joseph

Slevin. In 1968 he returned from London to his home town, South Shields, where he founded the South Shields' Claimants Union (SSCU). In the fertile soil of high unemployment and social deprivation the SSCU took root. It is not surprising that it soon formed an alliance (some would call it 'unholy') with the newly independent South Shields Trades Union Council.

The weekly meetings of the CU were 'open' and attended by some 10-20 social security claimants seeking advice. They were encouraged to discuss their experiences openly in an attempt to destigmatise their status as claimants and it was from these meetings that issues were identified and campaigns developed.

In addition, social security claimants were offered representation at Department of Health and Social Security (DHSS) appeals tribunals. It was in this way that several important national precedents were established concerning the interpretation and implementation of social security regulations.

The other activities of the CU included proselytising visits to strikers, pensioners, students and other community groups, who were encouraged to set up their own claims groups to assist their colleagues.

At its peak the movement consisted of something like 120 CUs situated in the major industrial areas; independent bodies but loosely federated in the Claimants Union Federation. In the North East, South Shields was the most active CU, but others were established in Durham, Jarrow/Hebburn, Gateshead and Newcastle.

It is not known how many of these CUs (if any) survive but it is suspected that many metamorphosed into establishment 'rights' organisations.

The South Shields CU could claim a major role in three important achievements:

1. Establishing the right of unemployed students to claim social security benefit while attending college.

2. Establishing the right to heating allowances for pensioners.

3. Setting precedents for trade union, community, and student based, social security 'Claims Committees'.

At national level CUs succeeded in demystifying the bureaucracy of a major agent of social control–the Department of Health and Social Security–and exposed a government department operating with its own internal culture and rules (the notorious secret 'A' code), largely outside parliamentary accountability.

However, many CU members would claim that its most important achievement was to demonstrate the effectiveness of direct action at grass-root level by people commonly thought to be outside society's power structures.

The Claimants Unions expressed, perhaps more clearly than any other movement, the values, attitude and actions of the period. They were a natural product of that time, and the period cannot be fully understood without them. And yet, perhaps because of their principled rejection of organisation structures, and their rejection of the role of identifiable 'leaders', their story remains to be told.

A London demonstration by members of the Claimants Union in 1972.

the claimants union movement

FIGHTING CLAIMS TOGETHER

This is the bread and butter issue of every claimants union. At the weekly meetings we discuss our claims together in a group. There's no confidentiality or privacy. Claiming isn't something to be ashamed of. There's no need for 'experts' or 'specialists' since we each have something to contribute and can learn from other people's experience. Difficulties with claims have nothing to do with individual cases, but with the whole nature of means tested benefits and discretionary power.

We stress the unity of all types of claimants - single parents, pensioners, sick, strikers and unemployed. We back up every member unconditionally with no regard to so-called 'deservingness'. Ours is an offensive day to day battle for more money and against intimidation for young and old, male and female, black and white.

Initially people come to our meeting because they hear that we might be able to get them a few extra bob on their weekly money or an electric bill paid. And we agree to back them up at the social security, dole, and appeal tribunals. But we expect every member to get involved in the running of the union and taking his or her turn in supporting another claimant. Sharing knowledge and experience we get a broader perspective of life outside employment. We become aware of a whole range of sanctions which punish and discipline claimants. We can see the social security collaborating with employers and we learn quickly that the state is not on our side in the struggle for better living standards for 'ordinary' people.

We gain a lot of support and self-confidence through group activity. The claimants union movement is very much a friendship network for people who would otherwise be isolated by lack of money. Consequently we arrange holidays and outings for ourselves and playgroups for our kids.

SOCIAL CHANGE

We are a political organisation in so far as we are committed to changing the social security system and replacing means tested benefits by a Guaranteed Minimum Income for people in and out of employment. But we realise that our demand cannot be met in a capitalist society based on competition, and private profit.

As claimants we have traditionally been dismissed by the left as 'unorganisable' members of the working class - the lumpen proletariat. The 'labour' movement denies us access to trades councils and to other forms of trade union activity. But perhaps in consequence we are prepared to stand up and struggle against the wages system and capitalist exploitation of people in jobs. Similarly we raise questions which the left tend to brush under the carpet such as the uselessness of much of the work done by 'workers'.

As part of our struggle for a socialist society we produce literature, leaflet social security and dole offices, demonstrate, hold meetings and conferences, and provide speakers for a whole range of groups. We have continuously supported strikers and their families, and been actively involved in the struggle for financial and legal independence for women. We have argued publicly against the forceful right wing propaganda which labels claimants as scroungers and scapegoats claimants who happen to be black. We have to stand firm against any fascist exploitation of the unemployed, and the demands for work at any price.

THE NATIONAL FEDERATION OF CLAIMANTS UNIONS

We have no national executive or national headquarters. We are in daily conflict with a centralised state bureaucracy and we want a movement free from the controls implicit in this type of structure. Claimants Unions are localised and have no formal hierachical structure. Consequently we are all in touch with the harsh realities of claiming, and have no full-time paid officials set apart from the rest of us. The National Federation of Claimants Unions is a network of all those claimants unions who have affiliated together. To join the movement a claimants union must consist of claimants and ex-claimants, hold weekly meetings and support the 4 point charter. There are quarterly national conferences to which every union can send members, and there are also regional and other meetings arranged when necessary in order to communicate and cordinate activities between different claimants unions.

The philosophy of the Claimants Union as expressed in a 1972 issue of the national Claimants Newspaper.

The Claimants Union Movement

Claimants Unions are groups of people on social security who have got together to help each other and to fight collectively around the four demands known as the "CLAIMANTS CHARTER".
1. The right to an adequate income without means test for all people.
2. A socialist society in which all necessities are provided free and which is managed and controlled directly by the people.
3. No secrets and the right to full information.
4. No distinction between so-called "deserving" and "undeserving".

HEY, IT SAYS HERE THERE ARE 2½ MILLION O.A.P. CLAIMANTS!

HEY, DID YOU KNOW THERE ARE 2½ MILLION OF US?

THE NATIONAL FEDERATION OF CLAIMANTS UNIONS is merely a network of all those Claimants Unions which have affiliated together. To affiliate, a Claimants Union must be bona-fide; support the four points of the Charter; and hold weekly meetings which are open to all Claimants. The aim of the NFCU is to communicate and coordinate activities between Claimants Unions ; to facilitate this there are regional and national coordinating meetings , in addition to the Quarterly National Federation Meetings.

2½ MILLION REALLY IS A LOT

WE OUGHT TO GET TOGETHER!

HOW DO INDIVIDUAL CLAIMANTS UNIONS WORK ? Each Claimants Union is self governing and cannot be mandated outside the Charter. The essence of Claimants Unions is rank and file control which means that members make their own decisions at a local level at the weekly meetings of their Union. Consequently, Claimants Unions are not branches of a national organisation and they differ in character and tactics. In doing so they reflect their individual localities, their particular communities, and the personalities of their members. Different emphasis is placed from one Union to another on the political, social and fighting claims aspects of CU work.

This 1974 Claimants Union leaflet set out the philosophy more clearly.

WEEKLY MEETINGS: Here are major decisions are taken collectively by all the members present. Together we pool our knowledge, experience and ideas and decide on future action. New members, who join at these meetings, might be shocked initially by the lack of confidentiality and the friendly informality of the group. They might have come half expecting some sort of emergency social work organisation only interested in sorting their claim out. Instead we expect every member to get involved: no indispensable activists, no 'casework' by specialists, no permanent experts, etc.

LET'S TALK ABOUT OUR SITUATION

WE'RE ALL ANGRY ABOUT THE SAME THINGS!

THE NATIONAL STRUCTURE OF THE CLAIMANTS UNION MOVEMENT: We have no national executive or national headquarters. We are indaily conflict with an enormous, centralised state bureaucracy: the Social Security System. We want a movement which does not reflect this . An hierachical structure with a national headquarters would mean discipline and regulation from above with the strong possibility of state cooption or control.Local Unions would lose their spontaneity and militancy and power would be removed from the grassroots. "Officials" in secure, wellpaid posts would be far removed from the harsh realities of claiming, and would probably fall into the role of arbitrators, concilliators and mediators. (See later criticisms of the Poverty Industry and the Trade Union and Labour Party Bureaucracy.)

NOW THAT 2½ MILLION'S BEGINNING TO MEAN SOMETHING!

Old Age Pensioners are the largest group of claimants. Figures dated November '73, show that there are over 7½ million pensioners, compared to almost 3 million other people on Supplementary Benefit.
Although recent events show that pensioners are beginning to realise their previously unexplored political potential, we feel that it's important that they unite & fight with other claimants, as it is this group that they have the most in common with.

The Claimants Union national newspaper was published enthusiastically, but sporadically.

South Tyneside Claimants Union
Peoples Place,
Derby Ter.,
South Shields.
Wed. 12.30-1.30 Sat.11.0-12.00
Tel.65062.
Tyneside Claimants Union,
107 Elswick Road,
meets Weds at 7.30pm.
OpenMon- Fri. 1-3.00 pm.
Tel.36922

GET

HEATED

A CLAIMANTS UNION GUIDE TO SURVIVAL

Many of us will suffer hardship this winter through lack of
heating. There is no need for this. The 1966 Social Security
Act gives the Department of Health and SocialSecurity(DHSS)
the duty to provide an income <u>to meet our needs</u>. In spite of
this the DHSS admit that 1,500,000 families and 690,000
pensioners are not getting their correct benefits. You will
only get <u>your rights</u> if you learn what they are and thenINSIST
you get them. A heating allowance to meet your needs is one
of your rights.

who is entitled to a heating allowance

Any person on social security supplementary benefit is
entitled to a heating allowance if they need it. This means
most pensioners, unemployed, single parent families etc.
For some NOT on supplementary benefit because their
income is too high (unemployed on earnings related, pensioners
with an extra pension etc) a claim for a heating allowance
could put them into the supplementary benefit range so that as well
as getting a heating allowance they would   also become eligible
for other benefits such as diet, H.P. for essential items
laundry etc.

   IT IS MOST IMPORTANT THAT IF YOU ARE IN ANY
DOUBT ABOUT YOUR ENTITLEMENT YOU SHOULD APPLY.
If you have been refused once, read this leaflet and <u>apply again</u>

---

*The campaign for heating allowances (see 'Pensioners'). This set the
parameters (and the tone) of what was to be a lengthy campaign.*

FIDDLING ?

A CLAIMANTS UNION GUIDE TO SURVIVAL FOR

ALL CLAIMING SOCIAL SECURITY BENEFITS

Current preoccupation with 'social security fiddlers' has tended
to direct attention away from the more dubious practices of some
of those on the other side of the counter: the DHSS. These
people are quire often undertrained, ignorant of their own regulations and prejudiced against the claimaint especially in the
exercise of their ample discretionary powers.

These supposed servants of the public are prying, usually surly
and often impudent. Supplementary Benefits are means tested by
an army of civil servants and if traditional as well as current
prejudices don't deter you from insisting on your full entitlement
then the DHSS interview technique and a body of complex, ever-
changing rules well might.

So in dismissing the frenzied concern of the media with 'fiddlers'
as being irrelevant we are left with the real problems, problems
existing in fact rather than political fancy. Facts concerning
the low take-up of benefit (people not claiming what is rightfully
theirs), facts concerning the complexity of the Supplementary Benefits
system, facts concerning the anti-claimant attitude of some of the
DHSS staff and the resort to other deterrent ploys (like the
discontinuance of the appointment system at South Shields "Wouldhave
House" ensuring that people are made to wait ages before being dealt
with).   Much of what goes on is designed to humiliate and stigmatize
you so that while the real power wielders create more joblessness you
are called workshy, you are subject to propaganda designed to make you
feel rotten and inferior.   Don't believe it.   Get up and fight back!
This leaflet is designed to help you land your first blow.   .

ASK YOURSELF -- DO YOU KNOW YOUR RIGHTS AND HOW TO GET THEM?

*The introduction of a 1976 Claimants Union leaflet with its deliberately
provocative title.*

Shields Gazette, Thursday, November 18, 1976—7

Workless will get guide to benefits

JOBLESS people in South Tyneside dole queues will be told of their rights within the next few weeks. More than 1,000 leaflets called "Fiddling?" issued by the South Tyneside Claimants' Union, will be distributed to the dole queues.

The leaflets also attack their traditional opponents, the Department of Health and Social Security, whose workers, they claim "are quite often undertrained, ignorant of their own regulations and prejudiced against the claimant especially in the exercise of their ample discretionary powers."

"Current preoccupation with 'social security fiddlers' has tended to direct attention away from the more dubious practices of some of those on the other side of the counter: the DHSS," they say.

The leaflet sets out unemployment and supplementary benefit rights and also takes a swipe at the media for its "frenzied" concern with "fiddlers".

Mr Jack Grassby, of the Claimants' Union, said of the leaflets: "They are in response to the Tory attack on the new social security rates and in reply to the campaign being waged against so-called social security fiddlers.

The battle of words over the increased rates being waged in Parliament has been joined by the chairman of the Supplementary Benefits Commission, Professor David Donnison.

He has said that the rates paid to the unemployed have not improved over the last few years in relation to the earnings of workers. He says they have deteriorated slightly.

Prof. Donnison claims that only ten per cent of unemployed people now have an income from benefits which is equal or higher than their net income while working.

The local and national press quickly identified an issue of genuine interest and concern – for many at that time, 'workless' was synonymous with 'work shy' – it still is!

```
                                      SOUTH TYNESIDE CLAIMANTS UNION
                                      Peoples place,
                                      Derby Ter.,
J.O.Thompson,                         SOUTH SHIELDS
Regional Information                  Tyne & Wear.
          Officer,
DHSS,
Arden House,
Regent Farm Rd.,
NEWCASTLE UPON TYNE.                  29th Nov. 1976


Dear Mr. Thompson,
                Thank you for your letter dated 10th and 26th Nov.
The letter on our leaflet "Fiddlers." has been passed to the authors
who are themselves claimants.
      My own view is that the image you present of the DHSS, as its agent,
does not connect with the reality seen from the receiving end of the
service. Could I suggest that our view is likely to be the more objective.
Indeed we could not say the things we do were they not recognised as the
common experience of many claimants.
      The problem as we see it is not to justify our attacks on the
system but to find ways to change it. Any suggestions you can make here
would be welcome.
      Meanwhile it would perhaps be most fruitful if we concentrate on
these points we both agree to be factual and in this respect we thank
you for the information in your letters which has been most helpful.


                      SOUTH TYNESIDE CLAIMANTS UNION
```

The Claimants Union reply to the regional office of the Department of Health and Social Security who objected to the 'Fiddlers' leaflet and claimed that information was 'not being withheld'. The CU response was that 'if claimants guessed the right questions, the DHSS might give the right answers.'

FIDDLING AGAIN?

A Claimants Union Guide to Survival for the
Unemployed, Students, Strikers, Pensioners,
and all on Social Security Benefits.

If all 3 million claimants were to ask for everything they
might get, the service would simply collapse. To protect
itself from the real danger of chaos (already threatening
a few local offices). The service has to rely on rationing
procedures of some kind - on things like claimants ignorance
of their rights, and on delay, lost files, and the generally
forbidding character of the system."

These are not our words, they are the words of David Dennison,
Head of the Social Security System, Chairman of the Supplementary
Benefits Commission. (21st September, 1978). He had previously
said,

"The service (supplementary benefits) is in effect rationed by
ignorance, delay, squalor in the waiting rooms, hostility, stigma
(in the columns of the news of the world, and across the counter
of social security offices) and in many other ways." (Guardian,
14th September, 1978).

So there you have it. That's the view of the boss. The
Claimants Union has said it for a long time. Millions of claimants
know it by experience. Now it's official!

The complaints by some Tory MP's and the right wing press about
thousands of well-off layabouts fiddling social security is something
of a sick joke in the light of these f acts.

We know WHAT the situation is. The question is WHY is it like
that. One reason is that we are dominated by the needs of a
so-called 'free enterprise' capitalist system. Money and work goes
NOT where it is needed, but where it will make the most profit.
In this system you have to be made to feel guilty and inferior
when you are not working to make someone a profit. You have to be
kept poor to force you into any rotten job - even when the jobs
don't exist. The politicians have to put the squeeze on YOU so
that they can pay THEIR masters - the international bankers.

So you will have to expect the DHSS NOT to be helpful, NOT
to give you the information you need ..... and some of the information
you do get may be false!

To protect yourself, and your family, you will have to learn
what your rights are and how to fight to get them. You can do
this best if you learn from, and act with, other claimants. This
leaflet will help you to make a start.

1. UNEMPLOYMENT AND SICKNESS BENEFIT

This is due to you if you have paid the necessary national
insurance payments in the last contribution year (April 1978 -
April 1979) or if you have had these credited to you.

*The follow-up to the original 'Fiddlers' leaflet in the form of one of many
'Survival Guides'.*

SOCIAL SECURITY FOR STRIKERS

a claimants union guide

All strikers are entitled to claim Social Security benefits. But getting them is another matter. The Dept. of Health and Social Security isn't neutral in industrial disputes as the experience of many strikers has shown. Just like the newspapers and TV they're on the side of the bosses, and will support them by trying to starve you back to work. They will try to prevent you claiming by saying things like *"we dont pay single strikers"* ...or *"you'll have to wait three weeks before you can claim"* ...or *"we won't make a decision to pay you until the strike is made official"*. All these statements are nonsense. With strong organisation you can force them to pay up. Like ordinary claimants in the Claimants Union, you'll have to be as militant with the Social Security as you are with your employers.

FORM A STRIKE CLAIMS COMMITTEE

The Claimants Union movement has been working with strikers for several years now, and has found that the best way for strikers to organise is to form Strike Claims Committees. It's important from the start of the strike to act collectively. Form your own group to co-ordinate claims, call meetings, arrange mass visits to the DHSS office, print leaflets, etc. Everybody should be involved - strikers, wives/husbands, family, friends and neighbours. The better you organise the more effective your strike will be.

WHAT TO CLAIM

SINGLE STRIKERS

You will be refused Supplementary benefit unless you can prove that you are in "urgent need" ie. officially broke. Refer to the Supplementary Benefit Act 1976 part 1 para 4 :- "Nothing shall prevent the payment of benefit in an urgent case.". This includes "persons affected by trade disputes". Be persistant in your claim for you will be refused at first. Do not leave until they accept your claim. They will expect your income (eg. wages in hand + savings + tax rebates + strike pay etc) to last you at the rate of £13 per week (excluding rent). After this the DHSS will allow you up to £10 per week (plus rent). Any income you receive will be deducted from this.

Advice to stikers was an early, and innovative, project. Strikers 'Guides' were issued over several years–this is a 1976 version.

PICKETTING EXPENSES
ALTHOUGH ALL STRIKE PAY OVER £4 PER WEEK IS DEDUCTABLE FROM
BENEFIT,EXPENSES INCURRED DURING PICKET WORK ARE NOT DEDUCTABLE
RETURNING TO WORK
When you return to work you are entitled to claim Supplementary
Benefit for yourself and your dependants until you receive your
first pay packet. However, benefit is counted as being advanced
against wages and is recoverable on a weekly basis. Benefit
loaned to you is recovered over a minimum 10 week period. Make
sure you are not paying too much. The rates of benefit for :
> a couple are.........£23.55;
> a single householder..£14.50;

plus money for other dependants, rent etc. as on other table.
APPEALS
You have the right to appeal against any decision of the DHSS
which you disagree with. (Appeals can take up to 3 months to
be heard however).

CLAIMING TACTICS

1. Contact your local Claimants Union for help and advice in
   setting up a Strike Claims Committee.
2. Plan your claims carefully in your Strike Claims Committee.
3. Organise in groups from your Strike Claims Committee to go
   to each Social Security office.
4. Don't sign at the Labour Exchange. Go immediately to your
   local Supplementary Benefit office. NEVER GO ALONE.

At the Office:
5. Never go into your interview alone:take at least one of your
   group in with you.
6. Insist on making a written statement. Check that it is correct before you sign it.
7. In your statement demand :
   > a) a written decision on your claim;
   > b) an A124 assessment form, which shows exactly how
   >   your benefit is calculated.

   These will not be given to you automatically.
8. Remember, the DHSS will insist on seeing the following :
   your last wage slip, your partner's last wage slip, child
   benefit book, rent book, rate demand, mortgage statement,
   bank statement, etc.
9. If you have any difficulty in making your claim, demand to
   see a supervisor or the manager if you need to.
10. DHSS decisions are discretionary - they are not final.
    Challenge any decision you disagree with.
11. Finally, keep records of all communications and dealings
    you have with the DHSS.

```
EXAMPLE :- JACK AND JILL STRIKE CLAIMING
Jack  and Jill  have three   children  and own  a house.  Jack's
brother  lives with them.  Jill earns  £16 per week  part time.
With the  backing of the  Strike  Claims  Committee they argued
with the DHSS on several issues. They got statements from their
HP firms  on minimum  acceptable payments  on the cooker  and 3
piece suite. After the headteacher said they couldn't get  free
school meals  they pushed the  Education Dept.  to approve free
meals worth £2.50 per week.  Jill is pregnant and got a doctors
note to prove it thus  gaining an extra  milk token every week.
Jack's Union is not paying strike pay but Jack collects picket-
ting expenses of £1.50 daily.
```

JACK...............NIL	*"RENT":- Mortgage interest*..£12.00
JILL...............£11.60	*Rates*...............3.00
ANNA 4yr...........4.10	*Repairs,insurance*....2.00
TIM. 6yr...........4.95	£17.00
BUSTER 7yr.........4.95	*less*Brother's rent*.-1.45
"RENT"............15.55	..............................£15.55
HP................4.00	**The SS wanted £3.78 for the brother,*
CENTRAL HEATING....1.40	*but they appealed - he was only 17*
£46.55	*and on a low wage.*

DEDUCTIONS	*JILL' EARNINGS (NET)*........£16.00
	less nursery fees/fares......-6.00
	£10.00
Jill's	*less earnings disregard*......-4.00
income....£6.00..£6.00	
Child	*JACK'S INCOME Strike pay*......NIL
Benefit...£4.0C	*Tax rebate*.....£6.00
Jack's	*less income disregard*........-4.00
income....£2.00...£2.00	
£12.00..-12.00	
Take home Sup Ben£34.55	*Plus two milk tokens*

```
Jill's  expenses were only allowed after  an argument, particu-
larly the nursery fees.  Central  heating was "overlooked"  at
first because of the delay in sending a DHSS visitor.
ORGANISED  CLAIMING  AND CAREFUL PLANNING  BY THE STRIKE CLAIMS
COMMITTEE  HAS INCREASED THIS  FAMILY'S INCOME  BY AROUND £30pw
OVER WHAT THE DHSS WERE LIKELY TO HAVE AWARDED.
During your  period of struggle  you'll experience exactly what
it's like  for millions of  claimants  who have to  continually
fight the  system for the  pittance which they receive.  For us
it is a daily struggle - 52 weeks a year.
SUPPORT YOUR LOCAL CLAIMANTS UNION.
Issued by the NATIONAL FEDERATION OF CLAIMANTS UNIONS.
```

Benefit payment to strikers became a national issue.

```
R E Y R O L L E S   P R O V I S S I O N A L
    C L A I M S   C O M M I T T E E
```

Certain Social Security Benefits are available to men, women and their families engaged in in industrial disputes. These benefits are available as a right. Up to now many of us at Reyrolles have not obtained these rights.
The reason is :-

    a. The Officers of the Department of Health & Social Security only pay out what they are forced to give - and they often do not understand their own regulations anyway.

    b. We have not understood what our rights are.

    c. We have not acted unitedly as a group to demand these rights.

Some of our rights as set out in the 1966 Social Security Act are as follows :-

DEPENDANTS (wife, children etc.)

```
over 18 ...£5.20
16 - 17 ... 4.05
13 - 15 ... 3.40
11 - 12 ... 2.75
5 - 10 ... 2.25
under 5 ... 1.90
```

PLUS - Rent, rates, morgage interest, insurance, repairs.

PLUS - Free school meals, milk, vitamin tablets.

PLUS - Free prescriptions, dentistry, glasses, school bus-fares.

etc .... etc.

STRIKERS
We are claiming to be locked out and as such we should receive unemployment benefit. But even if this is refused (and we should still fight for it) men laid off and even strikers can obtain Emergency Payments under Section 13 of the Social Security Act. Single men have a particular right to claim under this section.

SPECIAL NEEDS
Extra payment should be received for any dependant needing special diet, extra heating etc.

EMERGENCY PAYMENTS
Further payments CAN be received if urgently required for rent, gas & electricity bills etc.

TO GET THESE RIGHTS, AND OTHERS, IT IS NECESSARY TO KNOW WHAT THEY ARE .... AND ORGANISE TO GET THEM.

It is prosed to set up a permenant "CLAIMS COMMITTEE " to handle this matter. The Miners in their strike last year showed that this is the only way to get full benefits.
This Claims Committee will not affect or invole the policy or course of our industrial action in any way. It is concerned only in getting full rights from Social Security.
To consider the formation of the Claims Committee and to give further information on rights to benefits a meeting will be held :-

7.00 p.m.

WED. 20TH. JUNE

JARROW LABOUR CLUB, Park Rd.

ALL MEN ON LOCK-OUT OR LAID OFF ARE INVITED TO ATTEND.

In the event of a settlement the meeting will still take place as claims will still have to be persued.

PLEASE PASS THIS LEAFLET TO A FELLOW WORKER .

Printed by the Provisional Claims Com. South Shields TUC
Jarr & Hebburn TUC.

Joint 'Claims Committees' were set up with all local groups of striking workers.

Photo: Claimants' Newspaper

Please address replies to
THE CHIEF CONSTABLE

DURHAM CONSTABULARY

CONSTABULARY HEADQUARTERS,
AYKLEY HEADS,
DURHAM.
DH1 5TT.

TELEPHONE : DURHAM 4929
TELEX : DURPOL 53530

YOUR REF   MY REF

27th November, 1972.

Dear Sir,

     With reference to your letter of 15th November,
1972 I have enquired into the incident on Friday,
10th November, 1972 at the Offices of the Department
of Health & Social Security, Wouldhave House, South
Shields and I am satisfied that the Police Officers
concerned acted properly with the propriety and
discretion required by the circumstances.

     The Police action was requested by the Department
and any improper advice given by the Department's
Personnel is not a Police matter.

            Yours faithfully,

Chief Constable.

Mr. J. Grassby,
Secretary,
South Shields Trades Union Council,
Ede House,
143 Westoe Road,
South Shields.

*An interesting view that a bureaucratic breach of the law is 'not a police
matter'. The police and the DHSS were later to admit they got it wrong.*

COPY

SOUTH TYNESIDE CLAIMANTS UNION
Peoples Place,
Derby Ter.,
SOUTH SHIELDS.

Barbara Castle, M.P.,
Social Security Secretary,
House of Commons,
LONDON   2 March 1974

Barbara Castle,
          In their recent election campaign the local Labour
Party candidate, Arthur Blenkinsop and Ernie Fernyheugh, made
public statements that "secret instructions" had been given to the
local and regional officials of the DHSS which had the effect of
clamping down on the payment of supplementary benefits to strikers
families and to single strikers claiming urgent need under Section
13 of the Social Security Act.

          Certainly benefits were refused which were paid during the
1972 strike and many miners and their families suffered hardship as
a consequence.

          We should be grateful if you would let us know :-

          a) where these "secret instructions" came from.
          b) What these instructions were.
          c) whether you will take immediate steps to withdraw them.

                              Reg Whitfield,
                    for South Tyneside Claimants Union.

---

*The 'secret instructions' (the 'A' codes) were only revealed when a copy was leaked
to a Claimants Union member. It is doubtful whether Barbara Castle, or other
parliamentarian, knew of their existence.*

Helping hands

Times have changed since the gilded youth of Oxbridge used to venture forth, full of piety and goodwill, into the slums of London and other cities, where they devoted themselves to the organisation of social services for the poor. The settlements in which they lived still remain, but with radically changed functions and attitudes. Voluntary work has been displaced by professionalism.

Just about everybody agrees – in debates like that in the Rouse of Lords on volunteers, on Wednesday – that volunteers are still needed, of course; but their role in the traditional social services has become more limited and less satisfying. So the volunteers, and especially the young volunteers, have turned to new ways of serving their less privileged neighbours. A major development of the fifties and sixties was the growth of voluntary work of the practical kind typified by Task Force.

Yet even this kind of practical do-gooding now seems slightly anachronistic, though it may remain valuable as far as it goes. The young people, who come together to decorate a pensioner's home, find themselves asking why pensioners not only can't afford to pay a professional decorator, but also can't even afford to keep warm in the winter. And they soon realise that these are political questions, involving the allocation of resources in a selfish society.

But the present trendy trend towards ''community action'' also poses problems for would-be volunteers. It takes rather more than goodwill to organise a tenants' association, a squatters' movement, or a claimants' union. Volunteers with organising skills may still have a part to play, but as outsiders, "looking in" on the problems of others, they may not be welcome. And, anyway, the militant style of the community activist may not appeal to the more conventional voluntary worker. As a result, volunteers are emerging from the underprivileged community itself. They are not, perhaps, voluntary workers in the traditional sense, so much as leaders or organisers. They are seen not as helpers but as trouble-makers. They are comparable to the people who first got trade unions going.

The "trouble-maker" reputation is not inevitable, as the squatters' associations have shown. A local authority which is prepared to accept squatting as a legitimate contribution to the easing of its housing problems has everything to gain. Squatters may bring their own problems; but these are as nothing compared with the difficulties in which a council which refuses to cooperate may find itself. But the squatters are in some ways a special case. Their aims are specific and limited; and their initial success in Lewisham provided an invaluable example to other local authorities.

With the social security claimants' unions it is another story. The Department of Health and Social Security has assumed from the outset that cooperation was, in general, not on. The aggressive tone of claimants' union literature is hardly calculated to elicit a friendly response from officials. Moreover, the demands of the claimants' unions go far beyond the discretionary powers of a local manager and, indeed, challenge the

New Society's article on the Claimants Union in 1972

very nature of the supplementary benefit system, with its emphasis on discretion, its secret rules, and its safeguards against "abuse."

The decision to meet aggression with hostility was, from the point of view of the DHSS, probably the wrong one. Cooperation might have introduced a much-needed element of consumerism into what is, at present, an extremely bureaucratic organisation. Even the cooperation with claimants' unions that some area social work teams are beginning, does not remove this reproach.

The strengths and weaknesses of grassroots social action are demonstrated to take one example that has come to our notice-by the South Shields Trades Union Council's campaign, in collaboration with the local claimants' union, to help pensioners to claim social security grants for special needs, especially fuel. The trades union council says that its enterprising information leaflet has led to 400 pensioners applying for extra allowances, one in five successfully.

Its weakness lies in the wording of the leaflet. This suggests, for example, that all pensioners are entitled to an extra 75p a week for extra fuel during the winter. In fact, extra fuel allowances, which are discretionary, are paid throughout the year, if at all: 75p is the maximum amount normally allowed, and it is only awarded in a small minority cases.

The Trades Union Council was, also, apparently unaware that the long-term addition of 50p paid to all supplementary pensioners is taken into account in deciding whether they are in need of an extra allowance for heating. As a result, old people have been encouraged by the council's leaflet to apply for such allowances-only to be told that it does not affect the amount of benefit payable to them.

None of this is intended to "pillory" the South Shields council. Indeed, one might say that, if the DHSS were more amiable, it would help people legitimately concerned with their rights to get their claims correct.

But it also indicates that there might be one step forward for organisations like claimants' unions, and one in which another kind of volunteer could reasonably help them. Mistakes of this kind could be avoided if claimants' unions and similar groups were serviced by a central information unit. which could use the services of old-style voluntary workers to produce reliable factual material on welfare rights and related topics. This is, at any rate, one role which the middle class volunteer, rightly concerned at social short-comings, can usefully fill, without direct involvement in the kind of organisation in which he is likely to feel both uncomfortable and unwelcome.

New Society 10 February 1972

New Society recognised a new style of campaigning 'comparable to the people who first got trade unions going'.

The People's Place

The People's Place was a converted Victorian church, bought by the Claimants Union in 1971, and used for many of the activities described in this book.

The disused Unitarian Church was bought by South Shields Claimants Union for £12,000 from the proceeds of the sale of property 4 Lawe Road, a large, three-storey, Victorian house, overlooking the Marine Park.

The house in Lawe Road had been bought at a knock-down price and rooms were rented out to students and young unemployed. Most were claiming DHSS benefits (which included rent and subsistence allowance) which covered running costs and mortgage payments.

The sale of 4 Lawe Road resulted in a hefty profit–at that time house prices were rising rapidly, but not the price of deserted churches which littered most Northern towns (and still do).

The SSCU intended that the People's Place be used as a base and an alternative community centre. They intended that the premises be owned by the community (the people) and were surprised to find that all things (and especially property) had to be 'owned' by named individuals or a registered company.

The SSCU sought to resolve this dilemma by registering a company name 'People' (the name is still registered) and by setting up a group of reluctant 'trustees' – a feat of organisational gymnastics as the CU operated without officers.

The People's Place consisted of a large upper hall and two lower semi-basement rooms and a kitchen. It survived for around ten years funded and run by the various user groups. These included: pensioners, students, trade union branches, strikers, the unemployed, youth groups, women's groups, jazz bands, dance groups (ballroom and formation – yes, really!) peripatetic theatrical groups, judo classes, rock groups (very heavy-metal), a food co-operative, various political groups (the Anti-Nazi League was notable), the Youth Theatre, the Blind Social Club and, from time to time, various homeless people. Its main function was however as a base for the Claimants Union.

The activities at the People's Place, and the work of the Claimants Union and the Trades Union Council soon attracted national publicity. This drew the attention of many social and political bodies including international revolutionary groups. A visit by the then student revolutionary Tariq Ali (now writer and TV producer) was memorable chiefly for the post-meeting fish 'n' chips supper. Members of the Redgrave family (of the Workers Revolutionary Party) paid a visit with a revolutionary theatrical production – and played to a somewhat bemused audience. It says something for the organisational structure (or lack of it) that all the various usually warring groups worked together in harmony while, no doubt, following their own agenda.

The building was handed over to the South Tyneside Blind Social Club in 1982.

The People's Place in Derby Terrace, South Shields, in 1971.

Photo: Lee Foster

The People's Place in 1999. Now the home of MHIST (Mental Health In South Tyneside)

Campaign Against Youth Unemployment

PUBLIC MEETING

YOUTH ON THE DOLE!

Speakers

David Clark MP

John Creaby

7.30

Wednesday 25th July

Peoples Place Derby Terrace South Shields

4 Lawe Road, South Shields–bought (unwittingly) by the DHSS for the Claimants Union.

Photo: Lee Foster

REGISTRATION OF BUSINESS NAMES ACT, 1916

as amended by the Companies Act, 1947

CERTIFICATE OF REGISTRATION

I hereby certify that a statement of particulars furnished by

PEOPLE

pursuant to sections 3 and 4 of the above-mentioned Act was this day registered in London.

Dated the **6th February 1973**

(R. W. WESTLEY)

Regn. No. **1730561**   *Registrar of Business Names*

This certificate is required by the Act to be exhibited in a conspicuous position at the principal place of business. Notification of changes in particulars or cessation of the business should be sent to the Registrar, Companies House, 55-71 City Road, London, EC1Y 1BB

R.B.N. Cert. 2.

PATTERSON, GLENTON & STRACEY
DONALD HARVEY & CO.

PARTNERS

DONALD HARVEY
E. C. GLENTON M.A .LL.B.
PETER STRACEY
A. G. BROWN
K. S. LOCKERBIE
W. N. DODDS
D W J ERRINGTON. LL.B

OUR REF   AGB/JAC

YOUR REF

SOLICITORS
NOTARIES
AND
COMMISSIONERS FOR OATHS

PLEASE ASK FOR

M r. Brown.

LAW COURT CHAMBERS
WATERLOO SQUARE
SOUTH SHIELDS NE33 1AW

TELEPHONE   SOUTH SHIELDS 60781
(4 LINES)

ALSO AT
JARROW
NEWCASTLE UPON TYNE
GOSFORTH

15th May, 1973.

Re: Unitarian Church

        At long last I have received the Grant of Planning
Permission issued by the Council and enclose the original
herewith for your papers.

        You will see that Permission is granted for general
use as a "Meeting Hall" and the only condition imposed is that
relating to car parking. No time limit has been imposed.

        The condition provides that use as a Meeting Hall
will not commence until the proposed car park on the adjoining
land is available for use. I have written to the Council
immediately saying that we are ready to complete an agreement
with them for the car parking facilities and the ball is therefore
firmly in their Court to make progress.

                Yours sincerely,

*Planning permission for the People's Place was finally received in 1973.
With hindsight the local authority might have had second thoughts.*

PEOPLE'S PLACE
_____

THIS BUILDING HAS BEEN LIBERATED ....
    It has been freed from the capitalist system of exploitation of property for private profit and personal gain(- in this world or the next!)
    The Peoples place is run on a non-profit making basis by voluntary labour.
    On the other hand there is no individual or group responsible for subsidising the place. It is entirely self supporting with regards to finance and labour.
    The peoples place is open to use by any individual or group for any purpose consistent with the nature of the place.
    To meet running costs those using the place are asked to contribute according to their means. Organisations unable to pay can use the place free. Organisations able to afford it are asked to pay the economic cost to cover rates, repairs and maintenance.
    The economic costs are thought to work out as follows :-

            Upper hall .... £1.00 per hour
            Large downstairs room ..... £0.50   ..   ..
            Other   ..   rooms .... £0.25   ..   ..
    These costs include lighting but NOT heating.

    All work is carried by voluntary labour. Organisations using the place are asked to leave it clean and tidy. There is no one to clean up after you!'
    Voluntary workers are also needed for

            Cleaning
            Painting & decorating
            Electrical wiring
            Bricklaying   etc.

    The organisation of the peoples place will be unofficial, informal, non-beaurocratic and self regulating. Ultimately the running of the place will be entirely in the hands of those using it. Meanwhile any enquiry concerning its use, or offers of help, can be made to :

The original People's Place notice to community, trade union, and political groups. The absence of a formal administrative structure did seem to work.

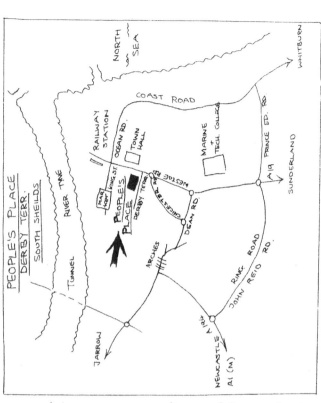

Once upon a time, just 5 years ago, there lived a Poor person. Well a relatively poor person because he had obtained, by means never disclosed, a Large Sum of Money of magnitude One Hundred and Fifty Pounds.

Now this person lived in that part of the country called variously the North East, or Geordie Land, or Depressed Area, and it was inhabited by an ubiquitous tribe called the Unemployed. The young members of this tribe were very wild and they had long hair. They said Rude Things to the authorities and had been known not to Move Along Quietly There. And their elders did not understand them and some of them had no where to live.

So our poor person took his money to a Housing Agent and said I will give you all the One Hundred and Fifty Pounds if you will give me a Big House.

So the housing agent said Yes I have a lot of big empty houses but you will first of all have to get a Mor-

The story of the People's Place as reported in Muther Grumble.

POWER TO THE PEOPLE

tgage for One Thousand and Five Hundred Pounds from a Building Society. And the Housing Agent then put on another hat and said I am a Building Society what do you want and our person said a Mortgage.

Are you of the Unemployed Tribe said the Building Society. No said our person and the Building Society said if you pay me sixteen pounds every month you can have a Mortgage for Twenty Years.

Ooh thanks said our person.

So the House was bought and it was filled with members of the Unemployed Tribe who were financed by a group on kind philanphropists called the Department of Health & Social Security who paid their rent which paid the Mortgage.

And they had many Adventures.

Now the Leader of the Country at this time was a politician one of whose names was Edward Heath although he was called other things such as Harold Wilson. And one day the Leader made a magic spell called an Election Pledge. Now this is a special sort of spell which means that whatever you say the Opposite is sure to happen. So the Leader said at the Stroke of my Magic Wand I will Reduce Prices. And our person was very pleased because he knew all about election pledges.

And 5 years later the house was sold for Six Thousand and Five Hundred Pounds. And this is called a Profit.

So our person took the profit and bought another two houses and a Church Hall. And he said in Thanksgiving to our Leader for his election pledge I will give this hall to the people and the Law said No. The Law said this Hall is Property and people cannot own Property only a private person or a company.

So our person said I will make people a Company and he did and called it People and got a Certificate from a Man called a Registrar who lives in London so it must be true.

And to this day People live in the Hall which is called the Peoples Place in Derby Tce in South Shields. And many activities are carried out there including the Claimants' Union and the Tennants Associations and political actions of Various Kinds.

And if you call there you will be made very welcome especially if you are of the Unemployed Tribe and People will tell you all about their Adventures and how to use the Magic Election Spell and how to deal with other spells that even now the Politicians are brewing.

And they will show how you too can become People.

The Peoples Place consists of a large hall (up to 250 people), a smaller meeting room (up to 100 people) and smaller rooms suitable for office purposes. It is self supporting and run by voluntary labour. It is available for use by any group or organisation whose aims are consistent with People.

A charge is made to cover costs according to means. Organisations without means can use the place free of charge.

SOUTH SHIELDS ANTI NAZI LEAGUE

public meeting to SMASH the

NATIONAL FRONT

Thurs.

21st SEPT

7·30pm

AT THE

PEOPLES PLACE

(DERBY ST.)

SPEAKERS:

BOB BAGNALL

n'c'le a.n.l. sec.

ABDUL HAMED

n.a.t.f.e.

MICK PEEL

s'land anti-fascist c'm'tee

One of the many organisations to use the People's Place – The Anti-Nazi League.

Students & School Leavers
The School Leavers' Guide To Survival

A major prolonged campaign by the South Shields Trades Union Council was its fight for the right of claimants of social security and unemployment benefits to attend college. Or put in the reverse, more controversial manner, the right of students to social security and unemployment benefit. This campaign was in line with the mission the council set itself to engage in direct action and to challenge establishment tradition. The campaign had a permanent effect on the national school and further education system and on the national social security system.

The rationale for the campaign was argued as follows:

The conventional manner by which the working class have fought unemployment has been under the banner 'The Right To Work'. The 1936 Jarrow March is archetypal. The Trades Union Council sought to identify genuine constructive alternatives to unemployment and campaigned under the slogan 'The Right Not To Work'.

It was this inversion of the argument, striking directly at the traditional work ethic, which caught national attention and brought the most bitter response from the establishment. The Trades Union Council had identified a central problem which dogged free-market economics. It still does.

A capitalist economy has never been able to answer the question 'why should a person who chooses to be unemployed be forced to work – if this means that someone who wants to work loses the chance of a job?'

The Trades Union Council posed another question, 'why should benefits ('hand-outs' if you like) be paid to the unemployed if they choose to live in idleness but are refused to them if they attend college and, ironically, improve their employment prospects?'

Until this time attending college had never been seen as an option for the unemployed. The Trades Union Council discovered that, surprisingly, the then current legislation did not prohibit such attendance. (Based on the 1966 Social Security Act which allowed for the payment of benefit to any person 'over 16 who registered, and was available for work').

'Availability for work' was the crux of the argument; but in times of high unemployment availability cannot be tested by the offer of a job. Initially the 'availability' of students was disputed by the Department of Health and Social Security (DHSS). However, following several appeals to DHSS tribunals, precedents were established and 'availability' was accepted if a student declared they were prepared to give up their college course if a suitable job was offered. Their declaration was rarely tested.

Around 1969, under pressure from mounting claims, the DHSS tried to exclude 'O' and 'A' level GCE courses. Soon, following a national row, this token resistance collapsed. The effect was quite dramatic. Colleges started to advertise courses for the unemployed and throughout the country many hundreds, possibly thousands, of unemployed young people started to attend college courses, particularly unemployed school leavers.

In something like desperation, the DHSS referred to the Social Security Act which denied benefit rights to a person 'attending school or receiving full-time instruction of a kind given in schools'. The SSTUC argued that college 'vocational' courses and 'part-time' courses were not of a kind available in schools. The DHSS appeals tribunals accepted the SSTUC argument.

With some dismay the Department of Education (DES) discovered that there was no official definition of 'part-time'and an arbitrary definition of a maximum 21 hours attendance week was hastily introduced.

This in turn created its own problems: there was no accepted definition of 'attendance' (did it include private study?), and the resulting chaos resulted in an unusual reversal of tradition whereby students asked tutors that their attendance *not* be recorded.

At one stage a delightful bureaucracy muddle resulted in the DHSS accepting that a course was 'part-time' and eligible for supplementary benefits, while the DES recognised it as 'full-time' and thus eligible for 'family allowance'. As a result some 16-18 year old students were in receipt of both family allowance and supplementary benefit, a total of around £15 a week–a significant amount for many poorer families at the time.

A further effect was that school 6th formers soon realised that they could get paid while taking 'O' and 'A' level studies by leaving school and attending 'part-time' at a college. A desperate attempt by secondary schools heads to stem the leakage by offering 'part-time' school courses was frustrated when the DES found them to be illegal. The leak of the 6th formers to the colleges threatened to become a flood. The then Secretary of State of the DES, Margaret Thatcher, initiated an investigation. It was inconclusive–and ineffective.

Another different campaign was directed at university students. These were encouraged to register for work during the Christmas, Easter, and Summer vacations and to claim benefits. In many cases the benefit claim included rent, heating etc. – and long arguments ensued as to what exactly their education grants were supposed to cover. Students Unions were encouraged and assisted to set up 'Claims Committees' to advise students on these issues.

Around 1975 permissible college attendance under the '21 hour rule' was reduced to 19 hours as the DHSS sought to close off what they considered to be an embarrassing loop-hole. The arguments between colleges, schools, the DES and the DHSS continued fitfully for the next 10 years. Finally, under the premiership of Margaret Thatcher (perhaps recalling her experience at the DES) all 16–18 year olds were disqualified from social security benefit.

(The Trades Union Council might have lost one battle but the force of their arguments won the war. The 1997 Labour Government reintroduced the right for young unemployed people to attend college under the 'New Deal').

The SSTUC campaign for students and school leavers was promoted by the publication of a leaflet – 'The School Leavers' Guide to Survival'. The primary purpose of this leaflet was to encourage young unemployed people to take action themselves to find constructive alternatives to unemployment.

A second objective was expose the incompetence and contradictions of the social security system, the indifference of the further education establishment, and the callousness of the unregulated capitalist free-market.

A further objective was to generate a national campaign to confront the government on the issue of youth unemployment and to force national action to deal with it.

The SSTUC can claim some success in all their objectives.

HANSARD

1455   *Unemployment Benefit*   30 MARCH 1971   *(Part-time Students)*   1456

UNEMPLOYMENT BENEFIT (PART-TIME STUDENTS)

Mr. Arthur Blenkinsop (South Shields): I am grateful for the opportunity so relatively early in the evening of raising a matter which is of considerable importance to my constituency. I hope that we shall be able to clear up the difficulties and confusion that have arisen about the payment of unemployment benefit to young people who are out of work and are also attending part-time courses at the Marine and Technical College in my constituency. The same problem arises elsewhere in the country. This is no new problem but the present heavy unemployment in South Shields is highlighting it.

I wrote to the Secretary of State for Employment in January about this matter and the papers were passed to the Secretary of State for Social Services. The matter affects both Departments and possibly also the Department of Education and Science. I do not mind which of the three Departments provides a satisfactory solution.

South Shields is suffering particularly heavy unemployment which affects also Tyneside and Wearside. Although a large proportion of the unemployed are older people, unhappily, a considerable number of young people are also out of work. In my constituency 10 per cent. of the men are unemployed. There are about 140 boys on the register and some hundreds of adolescents up to the age of 20, the great majority of whom are not skilled. We should be doing everything we can to encourage them to improve their educational background, but the absurd position is that if these young lads sit on their bottoms at home and make no effort to get extra training, they will be entitled to unemployment benefit and, sometimes, to supplementary benefit. Yet those who show a keeness and desire to take a course at the Marine and Technical College to improve their general educational standards towards G.C.E. or on a part-time, training basis receive unemployment benefit only after an interminable struggle. It is intolerable that this should happen.

Many facts have been elicited by the South Shields Trades Council, which has taken a particular interest in this subject. and they bring to light an extraordinary situation. For example, when

24 H 40

a young lad who is taking a part-time day release course becomes redundant and goes to the employment exchange, he is likely to be told that if he loses his job he will also have to give up the course. Why should he have to do so? Some of these young workers should be entitled to receive unemployment benefit provided that the courses are part-time ; they could still sign the register as being available for work, as indeed they are.

After a good deal of discussion and argument, we have managed to enable some of these young people to receive benefit, but in other cases our arguments have not been accepted. Some young people have not a full contribution record because their period in work has been too short and have to apply for supplementary allowance. I have with me a form issued by the Department of Health and Social Security in which supplementary allowance is disallowed for one man on the grounds that he is alleged to be undergoing, which is a curious word to use, full-time education. I do not understand why they regard that course as full-time since the Ministry of Education and Science consider it to be a part-time course and so classify it.

There are endless disputes of this kind in my constituency about individual cases. However, in spite of these difficulties, the man in question is carrying on with the course and is being helped by his family, which is not particularly well off. We hear many stories about people who try to get benefit when they are not entitled to it. I wish that more attention were paid to enabling those keen enough to want to continue courses to do so and to improve their situation in life. It appears that the powers-that-be are against them and are trying to prevent them continuing courses of study. If this is the attitude, it is wrong. If a young man becomes unemployed when in mid-course, why should we not encourage him to continue? Should we not make it quite clear that they are entitled to their unemployment benefit or to the supplementary allowance?

While we have had very satisfactory discussions with the manager of the local employment exchange who has been extremely helpful in trying to work out those courses which could be accepted as clearly part-time, when cases are referred to the Department of Health and

The first expression of parliamentary concern–and confusion.

1457   *Unemployment Benefit*   30 MARCH 1971   *(Part-time Students)*   1458

Social Security, matters are not so easy. There appears to be no common line of agreement about them between the two Departments. Furthermore, there is no common line between one employment exchange and another. Young people living in nearby areas who seek to attend courses at the South Shields Marine Technical College find that their local employment exchanges disallow benefit which is allowed by the South Shields exchange. That is even true of exchanges as near as Jarrow. Applications for benefit have been rejected in Jarrow when, if they had come to us in Shields, they would have been allowed under the arrangements which have now been reached. Clearly there is complete confusion between the two Ministries and, to put it mildly, the situation is most unsatisfactory.

We are determined to see that the matter is put right. I would not mind if it were said that unemployment benefit is not the right term to use and that a special grant should be provided to people who want to do this work. However, I do not see why they should be put to this kind of trouble just because they want to do some extra training, realising that there are deficiencies to make up and that they want a better chance. Surely we should encourage them.

I appeal to the Minister to say that he will try to clear up the confusion. I know of cases of people who have had to give up courses and sit at home, which is just foolish. I know of other cases of people who are carrying on with a good deal of hardship to their families. In one case, the father is out of work, but the family is trying to help the son carry on.

We must try to make it clear that these facilities are available. Most counter staffs in employment exchanges do not appear to know and are not able to offer much in the way of advice. Their general reaction is simply to tell people that if they are taking a course at the Marine Technical College they are automatically excluded from unemployment benefit. We know that that is not necessarily the position, but that is the impression.

I hope to hear from the Minister that there will be a real attempt to publicise the facilities that are available. In

24 H 41

addition, I hope that steps will be taken to sort out individual cases. The Committee of Inquiry into Abuses of the Social Services is currently looking into the misuse of funds. In my opinion, its terms of reference should be extended to the investigation of cases where people do not get that to which they are entitled.

The Minister has a special responsibility under the Ministry of Social Security Act, 1966. Section 9(2) sets out his responsibility to define these courses and says:

" The Minister may by regulations specify the circumstances in which a person is or is not to be treated for the purposes of this section as attending a school or receiving full-time instruction of a kind given in schools ".

I invite him to use the powers given to him in that Section to make clear what are the courses available to young people which would still permit them to be entitled to receive unemployment benefit, accepting that their availability for work and their contribution record are also factors to be taken into account.

Many of us would be willing to help the Minister draw up a list of that kind. We have already done so locally in South Shields where it has been found possible to agree a list with local officers of the Department of Employment who understand and accept the position. We find it much more difficult to get the same acceptance from the hon. Gentleman's own local officers, although in my experience those officers in other matters have been as friendly and as helpful as officers in the Department of Employment.

I should be delighted if the Minister were able to say at once that he was prepared to give the necessary instructions to clear up all these difficulties, settling the matter on the spot. That would be the best of all. However, I should accept with rather less satisfaction his statement that the case had been made out, that clarification was needed, that the position should be made clear to young people. I hope that he will be able to make at least that statement and within a short time issue the necessary instructions to local branches of his Department so that people will not be put into the difficulties which now appear to exist.

Hansard 30 March 1971

The Unfinished Revolution

from 233 Wingrove Road,
Newcastle upon Tyne NE4 9DD

30th December '71

HOUSE OF COMMONS
LONDON, SW1

<u>Unemployment and Supplementary Benefits</u>

Dear Jack,

I just want to confirm that I saw Paul Dean, the Junior Minister at the Department of Health and Social Security together with officials before I left London. The main points that emerged were –

1. Anyone on a block release course at the time he was made redundant should be able to complete his course and receive benefit or allowance. The Minister promised to follow up any case I cared to submit where this was not happening.

2. The Supplementary Benefits Commission were however not able to grant allowances to fresh applicants who were receiving 'fulltime' instruction whether at school or elsewhere. They were left to interpret ' full time ' and had recently issued instructions to their staff to regard over three days a week as 'full time' . They felt they were falling over backwards in their generosity in this interpretation. They did not have to rely upon the Social Security Act of '66 (S 9(2))though they did not accept our interpretation of it.
   The Minister would be glad to follow up any examples of allowances granted to those taking A Levels or other Higher Education qualifications as against those taking commercial or industrial courses.

3. The Minister said his discussions with the Department of Education were designed to review that Department's responsibilities in the whole of this field. He expressed his personal view that local education authorities might at least be asked to look at this area to see whether they could help.

   I said that I would come back with the further examples he asked for

Can you help?

Yours,

Shields youth beats ban on student benefits

Ian Imrie, promised benefit 'backpay' after a social security test case.

— Shields Gazette 11 September 1971

A 16-YEAR-OLD unemployed South Shields youth has won a two-month battle with the Department of Social Security over supplementary benefits payments.

Ian Imrie, of Masefield Drive, Biddick Hall, was one of 70 youths who claimed supplementary benefits while they were taking an induction course at South Shields Marine and Technical College in June. They were refused benefit under a regulation which says money will not be paid to school-leavers until the end of the term in which they leave school, except in special cases.

After two appeals against this decision, a Social Security Tribunal has decided the case in Ian's favour. He was notified by post.

One of the first students to publically claim the right to social security benefits while attending college. The Times Educational Supplement was quick to recognise the importance and implications.

The Unfinished Revolution

2   LEADERS/LETTERS

EDUCATIONAL SUPPLEMENT
Printing House Square London EC4P 4DE Telephone 01-236 2000

No incentive to idleness

The Government have made an important concession to the needs of unemployed young people. For eight months, South Shields Trades Union Council have been fighting to get the Department of Health and Social Security to establish more firmly unemployed young people's right to attend college while drawing unemployment and social security benefit. This week the council announced a qualified victory, brandishing a letter from the chairman of the Supplementary Benefits Commission to Mr Arthur Blenkinsop (South Shields's Labour MP), which promised that more would be done to make young people on supplementary benefit aware of the possibility of attending part-time college courses. The Department of Health and Social Security have now laid down the types of course which can be undertaken without losing social security entitlement, and under what conditions, and—a big advance—they have decided to put up notices in local offices telling claimants of this.

"Availability" for work is the crucial criterion used by local social security officers when deciding who shall get benefit. The signs are that this rule may now be more sympathetically applied in this context, provided that both the student and his college agree that he can abandon his course for a job at any time. As things stand, much hinges on the interpretation put upon "part-time". The 1966 Social Security Act allows a person drawing supplementary benefit to attend college providing— among other things— that the course is not "full-time instruction of a kind given in schools". The DES regard block release courses as part-time: the DHSS—so far—do not. Part-time courses are defined by the DHSS as those lasting for not more than three days a week.

In South Shields, much of the argument has been directed to persuading the DHSS to accept that block release courses should not disqualify for benefit. Now it looks as though a breakthrough could be established if colleges would put on special three-day-a-week courses which could provide valuable skill training without entailing any loss in unemployment pay. There is clearly no point in paying young people *not* to go to college.

It is impossible to tell at present how the numbers of students whom this could affect may grow. South Shields, with a high rate of unemployment, had 40 unemployed young people attending the local technical college last term, many of whom were on what were technically block release courses. But as unemployment remains high and the schools continue to pour out large numbers of people with no qualifications at all, no regulations should be allowed to function in such a way as positively to deter the unemployed young from trying to improve their own chances of a job.

The Times Educational Supplement 31 December 1971

Jobless leavers winning benefits

by Michael Church

The battle over unemployed school leavers' rights to draw supplementary benefits while attending further education courses, which South Shields Trades Union Council have been waging for many months, has now resulted in what the Council regard as " something of a victory ".

Lord Collison, chairman of the Supplementary Benefits Commission, has written to the Council telling them that after high level discussions it has been decided that " more can be done " for young people in this category.

The Commission have in fact for the first time officially set out the types of college courses which do not disqualify students from getting benefit. The Commission had hitherto limited itself to saying that each case would be considered on its own merits.

The new regulations say that benefit may be available for those on part-time courses (not more than three days a week), provided that their college principal agrees that they may abandon the course at any time, that the students continue to register for employment, and that they should not have given up work or abandoned a full-time course in order to take a part-time one.

Mr Jack Grassby, secretary of the Trades Union Council, emphasizes

that he is now going to carry on the fight to reverse the Department of Health and Social Security's decision to interpret block-release courses as full-time—although the DES regards them as part-time.

" We shall challenge the decision on the grounds that it contradicts the findings of the independent Appeals Tribunals, that it is against the letter and intention of the 1966 Act, and that it creates an anomaly between academic GCE students (for whom part-time courses are readily available) and non-academic technical workers and apprentices for whom City and Guilds courses are often only available on a block release basis ", he says.

The Times Educational Supplement 31 December 1971

10—Shields Gazette, Wednesday, June 21, 1972

New courses will mean State extras for students

By Our Education Reporter

THE SOUTH SHIELDS Marine and Technical College and the town's Trades Union Council have together blasted a hole in a Government ruling, which has prevented many jobless youngsters from claiming supplementary benefits. The Government had ruled that students taking block release courses at colleges up and down the country could not claim benefit because the courses are classified as "full-time".

But now the Marine and Technical College has agreed to proposals put forward by the Trades Union Council, and from September will run three-day-week block-release courses.

Six half-days

Because the students taking these courses will have to attend college for only six half-days a week, they are classed as "part-time students" and therefore qualify for benefits.

In a statement issued today the Trades Union Council says: "The college has agreed to proposals from the Trades Union Council for special three-day-week courses to enable unemployed young people to qualify for social security benefits while attending college.

"This will be of particular importance to this year's school-leavers for whom the unemployment situation will be particularly serious.

"This is the first time that such courses have been offered, and it could well be that this will form a national pattern in all areas of high unemployment.

A leaflet

"South Shields Trades Union Council is now seeking maximum publicity for these courses and has proposed that a special leaflet be produced and distributed to schools, youth employment and social security offices."

The college registrar, Mr Gordon Teasdale, said today that there would be three courses starting in September, all of which were approved at the last meeting of the college's Academic Board.

One course will be in general engineering, one in general education, which will include commercial, arts and science GCE courses, and one in general building which will cover building and shipbuilding trades.

The courses will be advertised, and the college is planning to produce a leaflet giving further information.

Term-to-term

"We will have to see what response we get to the advertisements before we can start allocating staff and materials to the courses, and produce a timetable," said Mr Teasdale.

The engineering courses will last for 24 weeks, the building course for 16 weeks, and the education course on a term-to-term basis.

The decision culminates a year-long campaign by the Trades Union Council and the South Shields MP, Mr Arthur Blenkinsop.

A 16 or 17-year-old student will get £3.60 a week from 18 to 20, £4.05 a week, plus a rent allowance, bringing it up to £4.70.

THE HARDE

MARTIN SPENCE IS SEVENTEEN AND HE W WORK BUT THERE IS NO HOPE FOR HIM

WHEN all the years of educating are over, when all the Ministers and examiners and teachers have had their pounds of prime cut, when all is said and done— they open the trapdoor under your feet.

When Martin Spence picked himself up and dusted himself off, he began to wonder why any of them had bothered.

Martin's world is South Shields, Co. Durham, and he served his time at St. Cuthbert's Roman Catholic Secondary School.

He enrolled at the local Marine and Technical College to take O-level maths, English language and literature, geography and physics. He made it only in maths—but at least by then he knew what he wanted to do. He would try to become an electronics engineer.

MARTIN SPENCE (centre): through the educational trapd

The 2-page Daily Mirror article was based on the South Shields Trades Councils' campaign.

DAILY MIRROR, Monday, May 22, 1972   PAGE 17

ST LESSON
/ANTS TO
SHOCK REPORT

...or into a vast unemployment queue.

Shields Gazette

and Shipping Telegraph

HOME

No. 33269 (Established 1849)   Wednesday, April 26, 1972   3p.

BENEFITS BATTLE

Unions in bid to help students

THE first shots in a battle to blast a hole in a Government ruling, which prevents many jobless youngsters from claiming supplementary benefits, were fired today by South Shields Trades Union Council.

The ruling being challenged means that students who are attending block release courses at colleges up and down the country, can not claim benefit because the courses are full-time.

And South Shields TUC's answer is for colleges to change their timetables so that the youngsters concerned will have to attend college for only three days each week.

Not 'the first shots' – and certainly not the last shots.

A SCHOOL LEAVER'S GUIDE TO SURVIVAL.

A GUIDE TO SURVIVAL FOR SCHOOL-LEAVERS, STUDENTS, AND
UNEMPLOYED YOUNG PEOPLE, PRODUCED BY TYNESIDE CLAIMANTS
UNIONS AND LOCAL TRADE UNIONISTS WITH THE HELP OF UNEMPLOYED
YOUNG PEOPLE.

This leaflet gives information on your rights and
practical advice on how to get them. This is necessary
because we live in what is called a Capitalist society whose
main concern is making money. You will have to learn how to
deal with this system. (You can also help those who want to
change it!)

Remember that as a person who has left school you have
certain rights. This leaflet is designed to help you fight
to get them.

School Leaver's

School leavers   If you leave school at 16 you will be
entitled to Supplementary Benefits immediately.

If you say you intend to return to the 6th Form or
College, benefits might be refused. This is NOT the law –
simply a self-made DHSS rule.

If you think you might go back to school or college it
is better to keep this to yourself! If you decide to go
back to school any threat that you will have to repay
benefits is not true.

*An early 1972 copy of the School Leavers Guide – there were several,
versions including the notorious Muther Grumble version.*

Any other income you might have over £2.00 per week will be deducted from your Supplementary Benefits. This includes earnings from a part-time job.

How To Claim Benefits

You have to "register" for employment at an Employment Exchange and "sign on" as available for work. In some cases school leavers have to go first to the Careers Office.

BEFORE LEAVING THE EMPLOYMENT EXCHANGE MAKE SURE YOU ASK FOR AND FILL IN A B1 FORM. If you don't do this you cannot get Supplementary Benefits.

Getting Your Rights

Do not expect to get your rights simply by asking for them You will first have to learn what they are and then be prepared to fight for them.

You must be prepared for officials NOT being helpful, NOT giving you the facts, and even giving you FALSE information. Some will try to make you feel guilty about not having a job.

You will be kept hanging about. DON'T BE PUT OFF! This is part of the system to discourage people from claiming their rights. And if it's tough for you - think what it is like for an elderly or sick person - or a woman with kids.

Remember also that the DHSS make up their own rules. They are NOT the law and can be challenged. If you are not satisfied with your treatment - COMPLAIN TO THE MANAGER. If you are not satisfied with your benefits - ASK FOR WRITTEN ASSESSMENT. You have a legal right to this. If you are still not satisfied - DEMAND an APPEAL FORM

The School Leavers Guide to Survival.

Part-time students i.e. students attending college up to three days a week or six half days or the equivalent) can claim benefits during term time – as well as during holidays. You must say that you are prepared to give up the course if suitable work is found. Get further advice on this from the Claimants Union.

Full-time students are deemed to be not available for work during term time and therefore not qualified for benefits. They CAN obtain benefits during holidays and in the period between leaving school and starting college i.e. whenever they are "available for work".

Refusing a Job. You do NOT have to take any lousy job offered to you – although they might try to pretend you do. Sometimes they try to get young people to do rotten jobs no one else will touch. You don't have to do it. If the job is not "suitable" refuse it. If you take a job and find it is unsuitable – leave it. Get further advice on this from the Claimants Union.

The Armed Forces. As a young person you are subjected to government pressure to join the Armed Forces. If you live in the North East or other areas of high unemployment you will have to face special recruitment campaigns designed to exploit the pressure on you to get a training and find a job.

The areas of high unemployment are used to provide the cannon-fodder for the forces.

And don't be conned by Army propaganda about "Training for a trade". Ask at the Employment Exchange how many vacancies they have for Field Gun Mechanics or Chieftain Tank Drivers!

The School Leavers Guide to Survival.

If you are still not satisfied contact the Claimants Union.

STRENGTH FROM UNITED ACTION

Whether you are employed or unemployed, you need the strength of collective action to defend yourself and get your rights.

The Trade Unions provide this strength when you are working and the claimants union provide this strength for all those claiming benefits.

The Claimants Union is a national organisation with groups in South Shields and Gateshead. They will help you organise and fight back.

FOR MOST YOUNG PEOPLE THESE FACTS WILL COME AS A SURPRISE. WE HOPE THEY HELP YOU. YOU CAN GET FURTHER HELP FROM US AT THE ADDRESS BELOW AND IF YOU PASS YOUR OWN EXPERIENCE ON TO US IT WILL HELP US TO HELP OTHERS.

TYNESIDE CLAIMANTS UNIONS:

SOUTH SHIELDS	GATESHEAD
Peoples Place,	Gateshead
Derby Terrace,	Tyne & Wear Resource Centre,
South Shields 65062	13 Swinburne Street
Wed. 12.30 - 1.30 p.m.	Sat. 10-11 a.m.
Sat. 11.30 - 12.30.	Tues.10-11 a.m.

The School Leavers Guide to Survival.

ED551

DEPARTMENT OF
EMPLOYMENT XXXXXXXXXXXXXXXXXX
EMPLOYMENT XXXXXXXX OFFICE
NORSE HOUSE, 22 OCEAN ROAD, SOUTH SHIELDS
NE33 2HZ

Your reference:
Our reference: EM/JG/EFD   *Telephone:* 64513 Ext 42

25 October 1971

Mr J Grassby
Secretary
South Shields Trades Union Council
Ede House
143 Westoe Road
SOUTH SHIELDS

Dear Mr Grassby

Your letters of 14 and 17 May were submitted to the Local
Employment Committee which met on 13 October 1971.

The Committee considered that there was an area of
uncertainty about the effect of attendance at educational
courses on eligibility for unemployment benefit or
supplementary allowance, and members were, in general, in
favour of some action on the lines of your suggestions.

As these suggestions have not a strictly local application,
and affect another Department, I have referred your letters
and the Committee's thoughts to the Northern Regional Office
for consideration as to the possibility of general
application.

I will keep you informed of developments.

Yours sincerely

J GILLESPIE
Manager

*The letter which confirmed the 'uncertainty' at the DHSS which was to be
creatively exploited by the SSTUC and the CU.*

SCHOOL-LEAVERS TOLD TO 'FIGHT'

By Our Education Reporter

ABOUT 2,000 leaflets have been distributed to students and school-leavers in South Shields by the town's Trades Union Council and the Claimants' Union explaining their rights and the opportunities available to them.

Entitled A School Leavers' Guide to Survival, the four-page leaflet tells school leavers to "remember that as a person who has left school you have certain rights. This leaflet is designed to help you fight to get them."

Explaining the need for the leaflet, which follows a similar one published by the Trades Union Council on pensioners' rights, a spokesman for the Shields TUC said today: "Information is being deliberately withheld from young people concerning their rights at 16.

POSSIBILITIES

"The intention of this leaflet is to enable them to make an informed choice at 16 concerning the possibilities open to them on leaving school, going to college, starting work — if they can find a job — or standing on the street corners."

He added: "The policy of the South Shields Trades Union Council is for every person to remain in education for as long as possible, but this should be a free and informed choice not one based on ignorance or deceit or affected by the force of economic circumstances."

The leaflet tells school leavers, students and unemployed young people that "it is intended to help you survive in a society based on greed, personal gain, force and exploitation."

It contains sections explaining young people's rights to leave school, their entitlements to supplemetary benefits, unemployment benefits, how to claim them and how to appeal if their claims are turned down.

It concludes: "Don't expect to get your rights without a struggle. In some cases, you will have to put up a real fight to get them.

READY TO FIGHT

"The Claimants' Union and the Trades Union Council are prepared to help you get your rights — if you are prepared to fight."

● About 1,000 pupils at schools in South Shields are leaving school at the end of this term.

● About 400 of them are 15-years-old, and there are also about 300 boys and 250 girls aged 16-18.

A spokesman for South Shields Youth Employment Office said that of these 16-18 year-olds about a quarter of the boys and a third of the girls have so far been fixed up with jobs.

The spokesman added: "The situation this year is no better and no worse than it was last year."

Shields Gazette 3 July 1972

The early press reports were objective (even friendly) – helped by sympathetic reporters.

Storm over school leaflets

By Journal Reporters

HEADMASTERS have been told to destroy "undesirable and inflammatory" leaflets which have been handed to last-year pupils in a North-East school.

Newcastle Journal 8 July 1972

The education establishment responded to the leaflet in a manner guaranteed to ensure its circulation amongst school leavers – they banned it!

CLAMP ON SCHOOL 'GUIDE'

SOUTH SHIELDS head teachers have been told not to allow a "school-leaver's guide" leaflet to be distributed on school premises. The leaflet, produced by the town's Trades Union Council and the Claimants' Union, is aimed at explaining to school leavers their rights. But Coun. Jim Doneghan, chairman of the Education Committee, said today that the leaflet gave "stupid and irresponsible" encouragement to pupils to leave school early.

This was one reason for his instruction that it should not be distributed in schools. He said that, contrary to one report, he had not given any instructions for leaflets to be destroyed. Coun. Doneghan said that the leaflet, entitled A School-leaver's Guide to Survival, contained an "unwarranted attack" on careers masters and the Youth employment services in that it suggested they were not interested in finding young people suitable jobs.

Shields Gazette 8 July 1972

COUN. DONEGHAN
'Unwarranted attack'

The Unfinished Revolution

NEWCASTLE UPON TYNE
CITY LIBRARIES
CITY LIBRARIAN: A. WALLACE, F.L.A.

Telephone: Newcastle 610691 **CENTRAL LIBRARY**   NEWCASTLE UPON TYNE NE99 1MC
Telex 53 373 (Library N/Tyne)

Our Ref. Cr/B5   5 October 1972   Your Ref.

Dear Sir,

    I should be grateful if you would supply two copies of the leaflet "A School Leaver's Guide to Survival".

    These would be valuable additions to our Local History Collection where they would be preserved for future use.

    Please mark them for the attention of Mrs. Goodwin, Local History Collection.

                    Yours faithfully,

                    (Miss) J.W. Thompson
                    Local History Librarian

                        COUNTESTHORPE COMMUNITY COLLEGE
                        Winchester Road
                        Countesthorpe
                        Leicester.

                        14 september 1976

Dear Sirs ,

    I am a tutor at the above college, I read about your leaflet ' A school leaver's guide to survival ' - such information would be very useful to many of our students and ex students.   Could you spare us some copies ?   If the demand is great I will attempt to get some printed by the school.

              Thanks in anticipation,

              Adam Newman Turner

The demand for the leaflet was widespread.

COMMUNITY SERVICE VOLUNTEERS

TOYNBEE HALL
28 COMMERCIAL STREET
LONDON E1 6BR
Telephone: 01-247 8113

EH/EBF

10th June, 1971

The Secretary,
South Shields Trade Union Council,
Ede House,
Westoe Road,
South Shields,
Co. Durham.

Dear Sir,

We have read with interest the report in this week's Peace News about the creative use of unemployment. This is a matter of great concern to Community Service Volunteers and we should very much like to learn more about the scheme you have established, in order that we could discuss with various groups the possibility of applying it elsewhere. I enclose a large stamped, addressed envelope and should very much appreciate any more information you may be able to let us have.

Yours fraternally,

Elisabeth Hoodless

Elisabeth Hoodless (Mrs.)

Enc.
<u>Executive Director</u>

Thames
Television

Thames Television Limited
Thames Television House
306 Euston Road
London NW1 3BB
01-387 9494

4th October '71

Dear Mr Grassby,

Thank you for coming down to our programme and for being so good.

We received this pathetic letter which we thought you might be interested to see. Please don't bother to return it, but if you can do anything to help the boy, we would be so happy.

Yours sincerely,
Susan Kyle

Grams Thamestel London NW1
Telex 22816

Thames Television Limited

Directors:
Lord Shawcross PC QC (Chairman)
Howard Thomas CBE (Managing Director)
George A. Cooper
John T. Davey FCA

D. R. W. Dicks
H. S. L. Dundas DSO DFC
Bernard R. Greenhead OBE
Clive May FCA
Brian Tesler MA
Humphrey Tilling
Colin S. Wills MA ACA

National television used the South Shields' campaign for several special features and reports. The public response confirmed the validity of the SSTUC claims.

<u>Unemployed ?</u>

There may be a course for you at South Shields Marine and Technical College, Westoe, South Shields.

If you are unemployed have you considered enrolling on a course at the South Shields Marine and Technical College?

You may enrol on courses involving attendance of up to three days a week - most courses involve attendance for only one day per week. Unemployed students may apply for remission of tuition fees.

Some of the courses listed below may improve your general education or be related to your field of work. Successful attendance on a further education course may improve your job prospects.

Courses which may be of interest particularly to those who have just left school are listed below.

Carpentry and Joinery	Business Studies
Domestic Plumbing	Catering
Painting & Decorating	Dressmaking & Ladies' Tailoring
General Engineering	Creative Studies
Electrical Craft Studies	Art
Office Studies	Photography
Retail Distribution	G.C.E. 'O' levels in many subjects

If you are interested in studying any of these subjects, many of which have a large practical content, visit the College during our enrolment period - Tuesday, 6th September to Thursday, 8th September, 1977.

Many other courses are available - for further details see our prospectus or enquire at the College.

If you wish to study, please consult the College to see if we can help you.

* 1 to 3 days with NO LOSS of benefit.
* Fees refunded
* Improve your education and JOB PROSPECTS.

Ring: South Shields 560403 or call at College
     "   "   569217 "   "   " Careers Office.

Colleges of further education were soon to appreciate the mutual benefits of offering free courses on benefits for the unemployed. Some local Careers Officers were pleased to co-operate.

A SCHOOL LEAVERS
GUIDE TO SURVIVAL

A GUIDE TO SURVIVAL FOR SCHOOL-LEAVERS, STUDENTS, AND UNEMPLOYED YOUNG PEOPLE, PRODUCED BY GLASGOW CLAIMANTS UNION AND SOUTH SHIELDS CLAIMANTS UNION WITH THE HELP OF UNEMPLOYED YOUNG PEOPLE.

This leaflet gives information on your rights and practical advice on how to get them. This is necessary because we live in what is called a Capitalist Society, whose main course is making money. You will have to learn how to deal with this system. (You can also help those who want to change it!)

Remember that as a person who has left school you have certain rights. This leaflet is designed to help you fight to get them.

SCHOOL LEAVERS

School Leavers. If you leave school at 16, you will be entitled to Supplementary Benefits immediately.

If you say you intend to return to the 6th Form or College, benefits may be refused. This is NOT the law – simply a self-made DHSS rule.

If you think you might go back to school or college, it is better to keep this to yourself! If you decide to go back to school any threat that you will have to repay benefits is not true.

Any other income you might have over £2.00 per week will be deducted from your Supplementary Benefits. This includes earnings from a part-time job.

Another version of the SSTUC leaflet which the Daily Telegraph reported under a head-line 'Full Marx'.

POISONING YOUNG MINDS

JUST who are the nameless, mind twisted rabble - rousers who have produced the tatty, dubious School - leavers' Guide to Survival which is being handed out to youngsters as they leave the school gates for the last time on South Tyneside?

It is produced in the name of the Tyneside Claimants' Union which has offices in South Shields and Gateshead.

The guide is a disgrace. Our advice to South Tyneside school - leavers, students and young unemployed is — tear it up and if you have an unemployment problem go to your local office of the Department of Health and Social Security where you will find ordinary decent people ready to advise you and help you.

The Claimants' guide purports to set out for school - leavers and others how they should go about claiming benefits; some of its advice is sound; a great deal of it, however, is nothing more than an exercise in anarchial mind - bending.

We report on page 9 the sweeping accusations which this poisonous pamphlet makes against the local offices of the DHSS — accusations which, as the spokesman says, make the staff out to be ogres.

Every headmaster on South Tyneside should read this gruesome guide. — and advise his school - leavers to ignore much of it.

South Tyneside Education Committee should read the guide — and then seriously consider for the future inviting DHSS spokesmen to talk to school - leavers about benefits and their rights.

Parents of school - leavers should read the guide — and warn their teenage sons and daughters about its insidious implications.

Editorial, Shields Gazette 13 July 1976

While press reporters were generally sympathetic, some editors soon reverted to a reactionary stance – this editorial was a classic (of invective, if not of balance). Successive 'Guides' continued to generate controversy.

Benefit rules explained

School leavers' guide attacked as 'subversive'

WIDE-RANGING allegations that local dole offices are being unhelpful — and in some cases not giving school leavers benefit money they are entitled to — are made in a pamphlet being circulated through South Tyneside. The pamphlet, which has already been labelled "subversive", is being distributed by South Tyneside Claimants' Union outside schools and on dole queues.

It alleges that officials have not given school leavers the facts about how to claim benefit.

It warns: "You will be kept hanging about. This is part of the system to discourage people from claiming their rights."

It advises school leavers to keep quiet if they think they may go back to school so they can claim benefit money during the summer holidays.

And it says: "Don't be conned by Army propaganda about training for a trade —

you will have to face special recruitment campaigns designed to exploit the pressure on you to get a training and find a job."

The pamphlet, entitled School Leaver's Guide to Survival, sets out in simple terms how to claim benefit money.

It says. "This is necessary because we live in what is called a Capitalist society whose main concern is making money.

"You will have to learn how to deal with this system. (You can also help those who want to change it)."

Mr Jack Grassby, spokesman for the Claimants'

Union, said: "One of our main aims in this pamphlet is to educate school leavers about attitudes.

"This year looks certain to be a record year for school leavers going straight on to the dole. Few have been adequately prepared for this experience, which can be humiliating and frustrating."

He said the union had case histories of a number of school leavers who had not been given benefit they were entitled to, but refused to release any names or examples.

A spokesman for the Department of Health and Social Security admitted that mistakes might have happened.

"We deal with millions of people, and we can't guarantee that everyone has always been given 100 per cent accurate information. The procedures are simple enough, and if followed correctly there should be no problem.

"What is worrying about this kind of pamphlet is the effect it can have on the staff, who work very hard trying to ensure everyone gets money they are entitled to.

"Also, this kind of propaganda may put some people off coming to see us to claim money because they think they have a right to, because of the DHSS as ogres.' Pigott of the Maurice condemned Coun. Shields) as subversive: (Prog. pamphlet believe that civil the 'I do not out to deceive servants are about their young people the rights — in fact, I think this converse is true," he said. "The trouble with this ccun'ry is that we try to find ways of giving better and bigger handouts. "I do not know what these people are trying to achieve by making these allegations — the Social Security was set up to help people.

Shields Gazette 13 July 1976

DAILY MIRROR, Thursday, September 2, 1976   PAGE 9

DOLE HINTS FOR THE KIDS STORM

ADVICE to jobless teen-agers on how to handle life on the dole has angered social security officials.

For a ten-page pamphlet warns the youngsters to be prepared for officials in social security offices not being helpful—"or even giving false information."

The dole queue kids are also warned that they will be kept hanging about—"part of the system to discourage people."

Advice

The advice comes in a pamphlet entitled "A School Leaver's Guide to Survival."

Five thousand copies have been distributed outside schools and job centres.

The 10-page pamphlet is published by the Claimants' Union on South Tyneside, a social security rights organisation.

It says its aim is to

By JOHN GILBERT

make school - leavers aware of their rights and how to get them.

The pamphlet tells teenagers: "Don't be conned by Army propaganda — you'll have special recruitment campaigns designed to exploit the pressure on you to find a job.

"Areas of high unemployment are used to provide cannon fodder."

Yesterday a spokesman for the Department of Health and Social Security said: "We deplore this publication.

"It is likely to create a confrontation between the youngsters and our staff from the word go.

"This pamphlet is provocative and only serves to destroy any relationship which may be built up between our staff and the youngster seeking a job."

In London a Defence Ministry spokesman denied any "special recruitment campaigns" in high unemployment areas.

One of the organisers of the Claimants' Union, technical college teacher Jack Grassby, said yesterday:

"We think the youngsters are being exploited and cheated of their rights."

The national press took a generally neutral stance while exploiting the news value of the story.

The Unfinished Revolution

LETTERS

Claimants' reply to Gazette leader

Your editorial attacking our leaflet A School Leaver's Guide to Survival displays the very characteristics we warn against — officiousness, prejudice and inaccuracy.

Your blanket defence of the establishment and the bureaucrats contradicts the experience of thousands of claimants and hundreds of school leavers.

Our leaflet was written out of the experience of local young people and produced with their help. Every point in it has been verified and can be substantiated — often by people not connected with the Claimants' Union. Here are some facts that led to its production:

a) This Easter young people claiming benefits were kept waiting more than two hours. Then they were not given the necessary forms and lost benefit as a consequence. A counter clerk (not in South Shields) has made a statement that he has been instructed not to give the necessary forms unless asked.

b) School leavers have been persuaded to say they might go back to school if they don't find work and have been refused benefits as a consequence. Some have been told that if they return to school they will have to repay any benefits received.

c) Students have been wrongly refused benefits during holidays because their course was "non-advanced" — an abuse of Section 9 of the Social Security Act.

d) Students are having a "vocational element" of £3.18 of their grant deducted from their benefits — even those who receive no grant.

We could go on. We have repeatedly called on the DHSS to make a clear public statement on benefit rights for school leavers. Their refusal confirms our point and justifies our leaflet.

GRAHAM PERKS
for South Tyneside
Claimants' Union.

(If the Claimants Union had confined its leaflet to genuine advice to youngsters the Gazette leader would not have been necessary; since it was made an excuse to peddle political poison, the Gazette felt it right to warn parents. We do not believe there are hundreds of school leavers on South Tyneside who are being deliberately misled and robbed of their rightful benefits by the local DHSS. If Mr Perks has scores of examples during the next few weeks when more school leavers will be seeking jobs, we shall be only too pleased to take them up with the DHSS.

Your explosion of editorial wrath against the authors of the School-leavers' Guide to Survival suggests a visceral rather than a rational response.

As one who takes his Bible seriously, I have no desire for a neo-Marxist utopia. I fear that whatever system replaces capitalism will be no less subject to the ravages of original sin. Like most groups of heretics however, the Claimants' Union has highlighted an area sadly neglected by the orthodox.

Four times in the past year, on a purely personal basis, I have helped students win appeals against decisions of the Supplementary Benefits Commission. On each occasion, a parent has come to the hearing, and in every case, respectable taxpayers all, they have been incensed by the wall of bureaucratic obstruction which confronted their children.

Without totally condemning the system, I contend that there are serious defects in the operation of the D.H.S.S., whose task is not made easier by the ambivalent attitude of Ministers, by manpower cuts, and by deplorable working conditions for the lower echelons.

E. B. ROWSON
214 Ashley Road,
South Shields.

(The D.H.S.S. has admitted that sometimes mistakes can occur in dealing with thousands of applications. But this does not mean that there is a deliberate intent to deny people their benefit rights which is the sweeping accusation of the Claimants' Union — Editor).

With regard to your criticisms of the School Leavers' Guide to Survival, I should like to point out that had I had the benefit of such literature last year when I left school, it would have made the hours of fruitless waiting at the DHSS offices a lot easier to understand.

No doubt the writer of the editorial has long forgotten what it means to be a penniless school-leaver bewildered and intimidated by DHSS beauracracy.

GAIL BRADY
99 Temple Park Road,
South Shields.

Shields Gazette 16 July 1976

The Shields Gazette did allow the other side of the story to be told. Meanwhile the DHSS admitted '...mistakes can occur.' Clearly they missed the point.

TEENAGERS' BENEFITS

YOUR readers may have seen a report (Gazette June 9), describing our new leaflet for students and school leavers — "Claiming Benefits — a young person's guide to the Social Security System."

They may also have heard on Radio Newcastle, an attack on the leaflet by the regional PRO of the Department of Health and Social Security on the grounds that we say they, the DHSS, make up some of their own rules. Many who have claimed benefits from our local DHSS offices will have experienced some instant rulemaking, first hand. Some will have challenged the 'rules' and had them revoked.

A recent example of the way DHSS rules affect school leavers is the refusal to pay benefits to those leaving school after exams until the end of the official (and sometimes mythical) "end of school term''. Meanwhile, identical students taking 'A' levels, for example, at a college, are not subject to this rule.

Another example is the refusal to pay to those over 16 during the holidays if they say they intend to return to the 6th form.

A further example is the refusal to allow parents on supplementary benefits to claim for their children as dependants if they are over 19 and taking full time education at school or college on courses up to 'A' level.

All these are examples of the DHSS' own rules. They can be overruled by the Appeals Tribunal.

Because of the discretion allowed to the DHSS in making their own rules it is important that young people facing unemployment and claiming benefits for the first time should know how the system operates. Our leaflet explains these facts. It is available, free, from the People's Place.

REG WHITFIELD.
TYNESIDE CLAIMANTS UNION
People's Place
Derby Terrace,
South Shields.

Shields Gazette 17 June 1975

The Claimants Union continued to expose the contradictions and anomalies of the DHSS regulations. Several important precedents were established at Appeals Tribunals which effectively changed the law regarding benefit entitlement.

16　THE GUARDIAN Monday June 23 1975

Doleful outlook for young

South Tyneside Council has been astonished by a decision of the local branch of the Claimants' Union to urge unemployed teenagers to " milk the State dry."

To ram the message home, the branch produced 1,000 copies of a three-page stencilled leaflet—" Claiming Benefits : A Young Person's Guide to the Social Security System " —and asked the local education department to distribute them among school-leavers.

The council, which is concerned about the tone of the leaflet, has yet to reply. But Mr Jack Grassby, the union's South Tyneside organiser, says they made their point, and most of the leaflets have now been circulated through other channels." Mr Grassby said : " So many deputations have gone from this place with the begging bowl, asking the Government ' Please give us some jobs ' that we need a different line of attack. We want to make it as expensive as possible to keep youngsters on the dole. Maybe then the

By PETER HETHERINGTON

Government will take action when they see how much in extra benefit they are dishing out here."

The council prefers a more restrained approach, but nevertheless concedes that youth unemployment in the district, which incorporates the towns of South Shields, Jarrow, Hebburn, and Boldon, is a grave problem.

It is now estimated that 15 unemployed teenagers are chasing every vacant job on South Tyneside. This is partly because the local factories and shipyards are cutting their apprentice intake this year— Swan Hunter by about one fifth alone. The council's careers officer estimates that youth unemployment could soon be double last year's level.

Mr Ray Hurst, chief careers officer of Cleveland County and secretary of the 2,000-strong Institute of Careers Officers, estimates that in his area the number of vacancies has

dropped by about three quarters this year—and Cleveland, with its chemical works, steel plants, and oil-related industries, is reckoned to be a growth area.

Although the North-east of England presents the gloomiest picture, the position in some of the other old industrial areas is not much better. In Liverpool, for instance, where another 6,000 school-leavers will soon be looking for work, 1,660 teenagers have still not found regular employment.

In Fife the regional council is considering engaging school-leavers temporarily to under-take " community improvement projects." The council, which estimates about 1,250 young people will be unemployed by August, would pay a nominal wage for the work. The plan is similar to the national Community and Industry Scheme, under which teams of 10 do work of " social importance." Any unemployed teenagers over 18 can apply for this

scheme, but there are only 1,600 places at present in the whole country.

While some careers officers favour an extension of the scheme, they believe it is far more important for the Government to maintain and extend apprentice training so that there will be an ample supply of skilled labour to serve industry when the economy improves. In addition, they favour a scheme similar to that recently introduced in France, where the Government is offering employers the equivalent of £50 a month for each youngster taken on.

Traditionally, unemployment among school-leavers is artificially high during the summer for a short period when teenagers register as unemployed before starting work.

By August, unemployment could reach a million, partly because thousands of school-leavers will be unable to find work. And, unlike previous years, the figures will no longer be artificially high.

The serious national press took up the issue on several occasions.

Department of Health and Social Security
Northern Region
Arden House Regent Farm Road Gosforth
Newcastle upon Tyne NE3 3JN

Telex 53107 Telephone 0632 (Gosforth) 850111 ext

Mr J Grassby
South Tyneside Claimants Union
Peoples Place
Derby Terrace
South Shields

Please reply to The Regional Controller
Your reference

Our reference

H/RINFO/22
Date
7 July 1976

Dear Sir

Thank you for your letter of 3 July 1976. We, too, regard it as a very serious matter that young school leavers should be deterred from claiming benefit to which they are entitled because they have been misinformed about their rights. When it first came to our knowledge that some young people were not claiming supplementary benefit because they had been told that it would have to be repaid if they returned to full-time education, we asked local office managers in South Tyneside (there have been no complaints from anywhere else) to check with their staff on the advice school leavers were being given. After their investigations, the managers were confident that no member of the public had been wrongly informed on the subject. This does not, of course rule out the possibility of a school leaver misunderstanding what he has been told and because of this possibility a statement denying requirement to repay benefit legitimately claimed was published in the Newcastle Journal and the Shields Gazette on 26 June. Radio Metro broadcast a similar statement as a news item at 5 pm and 7 pm on 6 July and the Evening Chronicle are to print something on the subject as well. I think you will agree that we have done all we can reasonably do to clear up the misunderstanding.

You say in your letter that you have 'quite independent evidence which shows that the error and its effect are widespread'. We would be grateful if you would give us (with their permission, of course) the names and addresses of one or two of the young people who claim to have been misinformed by Department of Health and Social Security staff. If these names and addresses are forthcoming we will investigate the matter further, otherwise we must accept that our staff have not given wrong advice and the misinformation must stem from elsewhere.

Yours faithfully

for Regional Controller

The DHSS made sporadic attempts to justify their position often claiming a claimants 'misunderstanding' of the information they had been given.

12—Shields Gazette, Thursday, January 25, 1973

SIXTH FORMS 'WAGE' CALL BY SHIELDS UNION MEN

SOUTH SHIELDS Trades Union Council is calling for a "wage" for all school sixth formers. School pupils and college students should be no worse off than friends who leave school at 16 and draw unemployment benefit, the council says in proposals to the town's Education Committee.

It suggests maintenance grants of £1.20 to £4.60 a week for students over 16 who are still in full-time education.

The "wage" for senior pupils is the most radical of a number of proposals for changes in the system of local education grants, course fees and examination fees.

Criticised

Mr Jack Grassby, trades council secretary, said today: "This scheme can be described as providing a practical basis for a 'wage' for sixth formers. It is designed to ensure that they will be no worse off financially than their mates who leave school at 16 and go on the dole.

"Last summer, the education committee criticised the trades council's School Leavers Guide to Survival for enticing young people away from school.

"The committee made great play of their desire to keep young people in full-time education for as long as possible. Their reaction to this proposal will demonstrate the sincerity of their public statements at that time."

Mr Grassby said the money was less important than the feeling of independence that the grant would give to sixth formers.

Arbitrary

"They would feel that they were contributing to the family income, in the same way as friends who had left school," he said.

The trades council says that present maintenance allowances are "fixed on a basis which is arbitrary, anomalous, and at an unacceptable low level. In some cases families on Social Security are above the income to qualify for benefits."

The scheme would mean that no student would have a financial inducement to leave school or college the council says.

It estimates that the new system would cost the education authority about £1,500 a week. Students would be paid each week by Giro.

A call for 6ᵗʰ Form wages was viewed as 'revolutionary' – but proved to be prescient.

2A, Brookside Rd.,
Gatley, Cheadle,
<u>Cheshire.</u>

Mr. J. Grassby.   Jan. 28th. 1973.

Sir,
          What sort of unrealistic man are you.
               <u>"Wages for Sixth formers"</u>
Don't we spend enough on educating young people who do not
want to stay on at school without setting them up with
money? If a Boy doesn't intend to learn after the age
of I5 or I6, no amount of bribery will make him.
I have seen young Girls of about II or I2 years of age
leaving School and a dozen or more stopping to light
cigarettes. Imagine what pleasure they will get at the
age of sixteen to be handed some cash from the poor
exploited Public.
          I suggest that you make this a voluntary
scheme, with <u>YOU MAKING THE FIRST CONTRIBUTION.</u>

                                    Yours Truly,

Mr. J. Grassby,
     Secretary to the Trades Council,
          South Shields,
               Co. Durham.

The campaign for 'Wages for 6th Formers' ('grants' would have been less provocative) received national attention and a generally unsympathetic response.

Plans to pay the 'stay-on scholars.

By Our Education Reporter

A REVOLUTIONARY scheme entitling pupils who stay on at school after 16 to a weekly wage from their education authority, is being considered by South Shields Trades Union Council.

The scheme, which would cost the local education authority about £1,500 a week, has been worked out by the Trades Union Council's education committee, and will be presented to this month's meeting of the full council.

It would mean the payment each week of a sum varying from £1.20 to £3.70 for 16-year-olds, to £2.10 to £4.60 for 18-year-olds.

DRAW BENEFIT

The scheme would replace the present local education maintenance allowances, which are described by the local TUC's education committee as "arbitrary, anomalous and at an unacceptably low level."

The new scheme, says the committee's report, would be "based on the principle that every student over school-leaving age would receive a weekly payment or 'wage' and that no student would have a financial inducement to leave school without a job."

It proposes that "the scheme would be based on that amount which the student would obtain were he to leave school, or college, and stand in idleness drawing Social Security supplementary benefits."

PAID WEEKLY

"The scheme would take account of the family allowance and tax allowance that parents may be able to claim for a child in full-time education."

Payment would be made automatically to each student each week by Giro, if the Trades Union Council's scheme was implemented.

Shields Gazette 3 July 1972

Sixth form howler ?

DOES Mr Jack Grassby, of the South Tyneside Claimanys Union, really wish to be taken seriously when he says his union is campaigning for wages for sixth form students?

Doesn't he know there is an inflation on? That money is scarce? That Government spending has got to be drastically axed? That regional and local councils are now having to slash their budgets as never before?

Where on earth does he suggest hundreds of thousands of pounds would come from for the luxury of paying up to a million sixth formers a weekly wage?

We know where most people, asked to list priorities for cash handouts, would put sixth form wages. Underneath the last item.

And that's too high.

Editorial, Shields Gazette January 1973

Youth dole advice sparks row

A YOUNG persons' guide to the dole office was today slammed as "dangerous" by a careers committee councillor.

Coun. Maurice Piggot said leaflets aimed at school leavers on South Tyneside stirred up trouble.

About 1,000 leaflets—entitled "A young persons' guide to the Social Security system" have been printed by South Tyneside Claimants' Union —an organisation formed to help people with benefits problems.

The leaflets criticise the Department of Health and Social Security for their attitude towards young people seeking work.

More than 15 youngsters are chasing every job available in the South Tyneside area and this summer it is expected about 1,000 young people will be out of work.

The Claimants' Union claim that the school leavers will find signing on at the dole office a confusing and humiliating experience not helped by the attitude of DHSS officials.

The pamphlets read: "Do not expect to get your rights simply by asking for them. You will first have to learn what they are and then be prepared to fight for them.

"You must be prepared for officials not being helpful, not giving you the facts and even giving you false information.

"Some will try to make you feel guilty about not having a job."

Youngsters are warned not to be put off by being kept hanging about.

"This is part of the system to discourage people from claiming their rights," the leaflet says.

"Remember these benefits are yours as a right. They are not a charity."

The leaflets also accuse the DHSS of making its own rules and urges youngsters to challenge them by complaining and appealing.

And youngsters are told, when going to claim benefits, it is better to act with others in a group.

The pamphlet reads: "Trade unionists form a claims committee during a strike to study benefits and help each other.

"You should get together with your friends to do the same. The Claimants' Union will help you to do this."

The pamphlet gives youngsters detailed information about what they can claim, what offices they should go to and what forms they need.

Coun. Piggot of the South Tyneside careers service sub-committee said: "These people are stirring up trouble, where it need not be.

"This is dangerous. It is totally wrong for young people to go to a Government department for the first time with the preconceived idea that officials are against them.

"We have heard complaints about officialdom from time to time and I do agree that people should know their rights.

"But I am absolutely certain there is no conscious attempt by the Department to confuse anyone who has a rightful claim."

Members of the union are distributing pamphlets to school leavers and have written to the director of education, Mr. Kenneth Stringer, offering to provide free copies to youngsters.

A spokesman from the Department of Health and Social Security said today: "The manner in which this leaflet is presented is regrettable.

"The way in which the supplementary benefit commission deals with school leavers follows the law exactly and school leavers have the right to claim after they have reached the official school leaving age."

Education committee chairman Coun. Septimus Robinson said he had just received a copy of the leaflet and had not studied it depth.

"But you see there are certain derogatory comments in it and a great deal of thought would have to go into the question of it going to schools," he said.

He pointed out that the council had a good careers service department which could deal with school leavers' problems.

Newcastle Chronicle 12 June 1975

PAYING SCHOLARS

The idea that a grant of £10 a week might be paid to pupils over the age of 16 to encourage them to stay on at school might look worthwhile at a time of rising unemployment.

A quite substantial section of the population might be shifted from the job-quest to the classroom.

On the other hand, is there much point in damming up the tide for two years, at considerable expense, if there is still going to be a shortage of jobs at 18-plus?

There is a diverse element to the proposal in that, like student grants, it will be subject to a parental means test. Also, how is the £10 to be paid? To the children, or to their parents?

The proposal, ventilated by the Education Secretary, Mrs Shirley Williams, is full of idealism. But the social implications need to be thought through fully.

Editorial, Shields Gazette 15 May 1978

An interesting Gazette comment considering their view in January 1973 was– 'can they be serious?'

HOUSE OF COMMONS
LONDON SWIA OAA

18 May 1976

Dear Jack,

I have your further letter on the whole question
of supplementary benefits as they apply to students and
school leavers.   I did in fact have a long discussion with
David Donnison, the new Chairman of the Supplementary Benefits
Commission, and some of his staff.   I think they all agree
that this is a very difficult area where it is extremely
difficult to define where the responsibility of the
Supplementary Benefits Commission ends and the responsibility
of the Department of Education, and indeed of the Training
Services Agency, begins.

They regard the ruling that we helped to get
established some years ago, so far as part time courses were
concerned, as the absolute maximum that they could concede
and still retain their function as a body concerned with
the relief of hardship and distress.   They particularly
stress the danger that they would be up against in coming
into conflict with young people carrying on in full-time
secondary education courses, although I am fully aware
that you have your own answer for that!   I made clear my
own view that there was a need for a clarification of
responsibilities between the three different agencies mainly
concerned and I have agreed to have discussions with the
Training Services Agency to see how far they are prepared to
go in helping the young school leaver, who is possibly taking
the kind of short course you mention.

I am, of course, willing to put up a case for the
short vocational course on the terms you mention again to
the Supplementary Benefits Commission but after our
conversation have not got very much hope of getting much
further.   I shall let you know as soon as I get any further
word.

ARTHUR BLENKINSOP

*The arguments on students' right to benefits continued to rage for
several years.*

South Tyneside Claimants Union
Peoples Place,
Derby Ter.,
SOUTH SHIELDS,
Tyne & Wear.

The Editor,
Shields Gazette,
Barrington St.,
South Shields   25th Jan. 1973

Dear Sir,

Your editorial of the 23rd Jan. asks "does the South
Tyneside Claimants Union realy believe in wages for 6th formers ?"
The answer is that the Claimants Union has campaigned for over 3 years
for an income for all over 16, at school or college, equal to what
they would receive kicking their heels in the dole queue. This
policy is based on social justice, common sence, and simple
economics.

At the moment young people are paid social security supplementary
benefits for standing idly on the street corner on the dole. If they
return to school or full-time college to improve their job prospects
their benefits are stopped. As my colleague Jim Rowson has remarked
"this puts a premium on ignorance".

Next it should be remembered that 6th formers work to develop
their academic skills for their own benefits and the future benefit
of society in the same way that an apprentice develops his practical
skills. Work in a 6th form is no less socially valuable than
training as a plumber. It should be rewarded accoordingly.

Finally, and this should appeal to your editorial writer,
a 6th form wage can save the state cash. The current rate of
supplementary benefits for an unemployed person of 16 to 18 is
£7.70 a week. The average benefits for an unemployed adult is £30.
With our present level of unemployment young people and adults are
often in competition in the job market. And with the government's
£5 a week grant to employers taking on young people many employers
give them preference. To coin a phrase " one boys job is another
man's dole ticket ".

In this situation in every young person who is persuaded to
return to full-time education rather than compete for jobs could
save the state an average of £22.30 a week. in paid out benefits.
And if we take account of tax and family allowance etc the saving
to the state will be around £25 a week. It will be seen that if
a payment at supplementary benefit level is paid to all 6th formers
then an increase of 20% in those staying on at school would mean
that the 6th form wage would pay for itself. Other long term
benefits would accrue, social and economic, not to mention the
effect on our unemployment figures.

Your editorial writer places 6th formers at the bottom of
his hierarchy of the socially deserving . And then he says, " that's
too high". I would have thought the Gazette has reserved this
category for our vandals and muggers. The attitudes expressed in
your editorial which put an economic premium on idleness and
ignorance will ensure that these continue to flourish.

                              Yours faithfully,

              for South Tyneside Claimants Union.

The Claimants Union spells out its argument – again!

PUPILS' WAGE IDEA HAILED

TRADE unionists on South Tyneside are claiming a victory in their campaign to get wages for sixth-formers.

Education Minister Mrs Shirley W liliams announced at the weekend that the Government had decided in principle to give grants to youngsters staying on at schools and colleges after 16.

The Government is now planning talks with local authority associations to work how large the grants should be and how they would be means - tested.

South Shields Trades Union Council today hailed the news as a victory. It has been campaigning for the past five years for this type of grant because it believes that youngsters staying on at school could miss out financially in comparison to other youngsters who are on the dole.

The campaign has since gained the support of South Tyneside Council, South Shields MP, Mr Arthur Blenkinsop, and became national Trades Union Congress policy last year.

"We are pleased it has now become official Government policy, but we could decide to oppose the proposal that the payments are to be means - tested," said the Trades Council's joint assistant secretary, Mr Jack Grassby.

"The South Shields Trades Council can take credit for generating a major policy of social reform which could have a prominent effect on youth unemployment.

Shields Gazette 13 May 1978

In 1978, grants for 6th Formers was accepted as policy by the Labour government. Its implementation was sporadic – and ended by Margaret Thatcher.

South Shields Trades Union Council

A YTS GUIDE

TO SURVIVAL

The South Shields Trades Union Council does not believe that the new Youth Training Initiative is a long term solution to Youth Unemployment, and is opposed to the programme being used for the purpose of replacing existing labour or the existing system of apprenticeships.

It will be up to <u>YOU</u>, the participants in such schemes, to make Trade Unions aware of any abuse being practised.

This leaflet will tell you what your rights are and how to get them.

The SSTUC published several 'Guides' including this one for the then new Youth Training Scheme (YTS) trainees.

Seats 'on the board' for students and staff

South Shields Education Committee

TWO MEMBERS of staff and two students will sit on the various governing bodies of South Shields Marine and Technical College. The staff members will sit on the Board of Governors — the major decision-making body at the college — and the students will sit on the Academic Board, which is largely an advisory body.

And three representatives from South Shields Trades Union Council will sit on the Board of Governors. This was agreed at last night's meeting of the Education Committee, but it is subject to confirmation by the Town Council and the Department of Education and Science.

One of the two staff members of the board will be appointed by the Academic Board, and the other will be directly elected by the teaching staff, but he will have to be a lecturer grade II or of higher rank. About half the staff would be eligible for appointment under this rule.

Shields Gazette 22 December 1970

The Trades Union Council loses one representative under the new arrangements. Initially, under the draft final document circulated two months ago, the unionists were to have lost all their representation, but the college's Board of Governors recommended three of them should be retained, and this was agreed by the committee.

The new governing rules will come into effect in May, provided the D.E.S. does not hold up the South Shields proposals. The full board of governors will comprise: 14 members from the local authority, the college principal, the vicar of St. Hilda's Church, 12 members representing education, commerce and industry, and the two staff members. The 12 representing commerce and industry will include the three trades union council nominations.

Coun. Robert Hunter (Prog.), committee chairman, last night criticised the letter written by the Trades Union Council for "jumping the gun." Their secretary, Mr Jack Grassby, had written earlier to protest about the exclusion of the trades union council representation on the board of governors, and suggested this might not be allowed under the terms of the Winterbottom Trust, by which the local authority took control of the college in 1951.

"This letter written by Mr Grassby is so devoid of fact and so abusive that one is greatly tempted to treat it with the contempt it deserves," said Coun. Hunter. He said the unionists had four representatives on the governors, and should have waited until the governors meeting when their representatives would have been given an opportunity of making their point of view known.

He also criticised the fact that the unionist "went to the Press" with their complaints. "It is quite deplorable that they should have written in this manner, and equally deplorable that they should go to the Press."

Mr Grassby said today: "I suppose that any belated recognition of the justice of our claim is to be welcomed, even though it is only partial. But I hope it is not expected that the trades union council will fall over backwards with gratitude for having its representation chopped by 25 per cent."

The Trades Union Council was an early campaigner for staff and student representation on the Boards of Governors of colleges – now common-place in South Tyneside and most colleges and universities.

A GUIDE FOR STUDENTS ON MANDATORY AWARDS

(all College of Education Students (Certificate, B.Ed. etc.))

Last Christmas the DHSS issued secret instructions to their staff ordering them to "actively discourage" students from claiming.

As a consequence, we can expect little assistance in exercising our legal right to claim.

Supplementary Benefits are non-contributory benefits, you do not need to have worked or paid National Insurance Contributions to qualify.

It is NOT A CHARITY. You will pay into the system for the rest of your working life. It is yours AS A RIGHT. You have the right to use it now when you need it.

Students can still get Social Security payments during all vacations. Get to know the system.................... AND KEEP ON CLAIMING.

LOOK!! MY GIRO'S ARRIVED
* * * * * * * * * * * * *

THIS LEAFLET WAS PRODUCED BY THE TYNE & WEAR AREA COMMITTEE OF THE N.U.S. AND SOUTH TYNESIDE CLAIMAINTS UNION

The Claimants Union extended its campaign to university students–with the co-operation of the NUS.

Major clash near over student benefit

By JOHN EZARD and HUGH HEBERT

The Government is expected to face a head-on clash with the students over its plans to cut supplementary benefit.

The National Union of Students said last night that it had unimpeachable evidence that the Government is about to table a Bill withdrawing the right of students to claim benefit in the Christmas and Easter vacations—saving about £10 millions. Although this was officially unconfirmed there were certain strong pointers that the claim is correct.

Last year 143,000 students took advantage of this right at Christmas and 176,000 at Easter. Sue Slipman, NUS secretary, said that its withdrawal would be the first step towards a broader "erosion of the welfare state."'

According to detailed information which the NUS says has been leaked o it but which it cannot produce in detail to protect its informant, the cuts are for yesterday

due to be made as part of the Social Services (Miscellaneous Provisions) Bill.

As already foreshadowed, this will reduce the benefit rights of occupational pensioners who have retired early on pensions of more than £25 and are unemployed.

According to the NUS's leak the Bill was expected by the Department of Health and Social Security to be included in yesterday's schedule of legislation after the Queen's Speech. It referred to the move on occupational pensioners but did not mention students. It said the Bill to be introduced would "adjust the national insurance scheme in certain other respects."

As a form of words this is not conclusive since supplementary benefits are not strictly part of national insurance. But the NUS is satisfied that a Bill covering students was originally on the Labour Whips' agenda for yesterday

This would come only a week after the Government's own survey revealing to the surprise of even the NUS, that 73 per cent of parents do not pay the full assessed contribution towards grants. For many students shortfall is £100 a year or more. This tends to make nonsense of the notional £11.35 included by councils in most grant assessments for Christmas and Easter.

Mis Slipman said that the Bill would mean hundreds would have to drop out of the courses unless parents could fully maintain them in vacs. There was also the fear that students in very severe hardship would no longer be able to present their cases to benefit commissions. All students on less than maximum grants would be hit

The rules were changed earlier this year to cencentrate the grant payments for holidays in the two short vacations and the supplemtary benefit support in the long summer break,

The Guardian 1975

The government took fright and sought to withdraw the right of students to social security benefit in the vacation periods. The argument was to continue for several years and was the focus of many joint Students Union ~ Claimants Union campaigns.

THE GUARDIAN

6

A new model subsidised sixth former

Yesterday's decision to give all sixth formers means-tested mandatory grants could in the end do more to increase equal opportunity in Britain than any other education policy of this Government. Few countries in Western Europe waste as much talent as the English school system manages. Fewer than one out of every three children aged between 16 and 18 is in full-time education. (Only Ireland and Portugal are as bad). Predictably, it is the children or poor families who suffer worst. They have been leaving school in their droves. The last survey carried out by the Department of Education found only 20 per cent of children in social classes C and D staying on at school, compared to 74 per cent of children in AB homes.

Of course some of the waste is created by social and cultural factors. Many working class families do not even consider keeping their children in school. But finance, too, plays its part. Maintenance grants are few and far between and those lucky enough to get them receive far less than is needed to sustain an energetic teenager. (The average allowance, in the last survey, was £2.50, which was awarded to less than 3 per cent of the age group.) Yet two new moves by the Government to help unemployed teenagers have rarely threatened to make the already serious school-drop-out situation worse. Under the new Youth Opportunities Programme, teenagers who have left school and been unemployed for at least six weeks can receive £19.50-a-week for attending courses at a further education college. Similarly, children who are available for work, can go back to school and claim £11.10 supplementary benefit as long as they restrict their education to three days a week. Why spend five days in school for £2.50 at the most when both the Manpower Services

Commission and the Supplementary Benefits Commission are ready to pay part-time students so much more?

To introduce a £19.50 grant to all students in fulltime education between the ages of 16 and 18 would cost £1,000 millions. Clearly no government could afford to take such a large slice out of its education budget. To apply the £11.50 supplementary benefits concession, without means tests, to all students could cost well over £350 millions. (The exact figure would depend on how many extra students were attracted.) Mrs Williams has said that this, too, would be too costly. So instead she is going to introduce some form of mandatory means-tested grant, which she hopes will be in operation by September, 1979. (It will require legislation.) This leaves her with a tricky political decision. There are two options: she can give a modest sum to a relatively large number of children or, alternatively, give a much bigger grant to a smaller group of students. The first option, obviously, would please more people but the second, which would mean restricting the grants to the poorest families, would be more radical—as well as more sensible.

Mrs Williams raised one other controversial issue in her announcement. She is prepared — although not yet committed — to use the grants discriminatingly with the aim of luring students on to courses which will either lead to a job or to a higher academic course. The local education authorities will not like this. It will smell, to them, of reviled central direction. Yet the idea should not be dismissed out of hand. The purpose of the new grants is to persuade students with potential to stay on. The last thing they should be used for is to encourage pupils to pursue futile courses purely for the cash.

The Guardian 13 May 1978

There was, nationally, a belated acceptance of the SSTUC argument to pay 6th formers.

Drop-outs to be paid to go to college

TEENAGE DROP-OUTS are to be paid to go back into education under a Government scheme to be announced this week.

David Blunkett, the Secretary of State for Education and Employment, is to announce a pilot programme for 16 and 17-year-olds who have left school and have no jobs. They will be given a Government allowance if they decide to go back to college to gain GCSEs or another equivalent qualification.

The move is part of a new Government initiative targeting the 100,000 16 or 17-year-olds who are unemployed or in dead-end jobs. Because of changes made by the former Conservative government, young people in this age group do not qualify for Income Support.

In a speech to the Confederation of British Industry on Tuesday, the Education Secretary also will announce the creation of a National Traineeship Scheme to replace the Conservatives' Youth Training Scheme. The system of apprenticeships will offer employers financial incentives to train young people on the job.

Labour is keen to avoid comparisons with the last government's programme which was criticised for using young people as cheap labour with no prospects at the end of their traineeship. The Labour scheme will offer "paper" qualifications at the end of the programme.

Youth campaigners are likely to insist that the new qualifications have

BY MARIE WOOLF
Political Correspondent

a value that will improve young people's career prospects. They will be critical if the traineeships do not offer rewarding employment which can lead to the advancement of young people.

"There will be a gateway approach, a targeted approach," an aide to the Education Secretary said. "These are young people who don't get benefits, who are not in education and training. The overall programme is to help achieve national targets to help young people into training and work."

At the moment the parents of 16 or 17-year-olds at college qualify for extra benefits if they are on Income Support. But in the pilot scheme the Government intends to reroute benefits to the students themselves to give them greater independence and an incentive to study.

The Government is concerned that many young people have opted for dead-end jobs with no prospects for the future, such as road sweeping or waitressing in a greasy-spoon cafe. It intends to introduce measures to allow youths to retrain and will take steps to allow young people to take off one day a week to attend a further education college to acquire more skills.

The Government is to target companies without in-built training programmes. It will place notices in JobCentres and launch a national advertising campaign.

The Independent 1 November 1998

1998 Final Victory? In 1998 The Labour Government paid 16–17 year olds to go to college.

70

NEW SOCIETY   9 JULY 1970

THE TRADE-UNIONISATION
OF THE STUDENT SEVENTIES

American campus protest has won some victories, despite all the counter-reaction. The next move may be into a more traditional, quasi-proletarian approach.

**Irving Louis
Horowitz**

Consider, first, this press report, datelined Madison, Wisconsin:

"A wholly new chapter in the annals of American university politics was formally inscribed here . . . After a year of negotiations and a 24-day strike, the University of Wisconsin's Madison campus signed a labour contract with the Teaching Assistants' Association (TAA), a local labour union of graduate students who are paid for part-time teaching and research assistance at the university. The contract not only covered various bread-and-butter issues traditional in labour-management bargaining but also granted, in a fuzzy fashion, the right of students and teaching assistants to participate in planning the educational courses in which they are involved.

"The Wisconsin strike was fundamentally different from other student manifestations of recent years. The organisers, as teaching assistants, were not only students but workers as well, with an economic weapon. By staying out of the classroom they were able to prevent instruction in many courses. As workers, they availed themselves of the traditional collective bargaining process to present their demands to the university. But their demands went beyond the traditional economic aims of American trade unionism to embrace policy and power issues that have motivated other student strikes across the country. The strike leaders claimed, in effect, the right to speak for undergraduate students as well as for their own constituency in bargaining on such issues.

New Society recognised student direct action in class-war terms which it described as moving towards a "quasi-proletarian approach".

The co-operation in direct action between students, workers and the unemployed was an objective of the SSTUC–and a reality in many instances, notable the 1974 miners strike – but the phenomenon was international.

Muther Grumble

Muther Grumble was a monthly community magazine edited and published (mostly) by a group of graduates and undergraduates (mainly) from Durham University. Their editorial office was at 13 Silver Street, Durham City.

In addition to reviews of theatre, films, festivals etc., it carried reports of the many community actions and events common at that time. Its nearest current magazine equivalent is Private Eye.

Muther Grumble had a natural affinity with the South Shields Trades Union Council, and the Claimants Union, and it generously reported their activities.

It also had a hard non-party political edge and it famously was the first (in 1971) to expose the corruption of the Andrew Cunningham dynasty (of the T. Dan Smith, John Poulson gang), by listing the various public bodies (including chair of the Police Authority), on which he, or his family, sat.

In 1973, Muther Grumble published an extended version of the South Shields Trades Union Council leaflet 'A School Leavers' Guide To Survival' in a 'Schools Out' edition. This outraged the local authority and some establishment-minded trade unions, and the local education authorities banned it from schools and colleges.

Not surprisingly the publicity given to this enterprise quickly resulted in the national media taking up the story. Oddly enough it was reported sympathetically (on the whole).

However, the News of the World, scenting a political scandal of '"lefties" corruption of youth' sent reporters to dig the dirt. They failed and their newspaper published the story largely without prejudicial comment.

The Survival Guide had many successors in many fields and, with classic survival tactics, the establishment has itself produced many more respectful versions. Nowadays there are 'survival guides' for almost every activity and human condition – many of whose authors would be reluctant (or unable) to acknowledge the original.

The Guide attracted international as well as national attention and has been the subject of research by American and German, as well as British universities. A copy is held in the British Library.

Muther Grumble started publication in 1971 and was sold in the pubs and clubs and on the streets of Tyneside and Wearside. It stopped publication around 1975. It was a real child of the 60s and the cultural/political climate has never again (at least not yet) been fertile enough for a re-birth.

The following extracts, reproduced from 1972 and 1973 issues, give something of its flavour.

Muther Grumble was one of a network of several alternative community organisations operating in the region. The Tyne & Wear Resource Centre at Gateshead was another important example.

The Resource Centres were central government funded and aimed to assist alternative community action. In retrospect these were a surprising and brave development from the beleaguered Labour Government, showing quite a revolutionary perspective – although it is not certain that the government had this concept when they authorised the funding.

Thatcher soon put a stop to all this nonsense!

Page 2

Contents

Muther Grumble would like to
thank Tim and Marlene for their
fantastic gift, which put new
life into us all.
Also, we'd like to thank Ahimsa,
Mike and his turntable, Andy and
the Wobblies, Les Cofton and everyone
who came to the benefit. Woops
nearly forgot the Durham Mobile
Theatre, see ya in Silver St.

We also send best wishes to
Ian and Pam who went off and did
it. Good luck to ya mate.
We mustn't forget George who has
gone to L.A. to get away from us
no doubt.

This issue was produced? or is
it reproduced? by the following
band of gypsies,

Don, Bill, Pat, Sue, Mike, Janis,
Geoff, Malcolm, Ted, Marion, Chris,
Viv, Andy, Nora, Paul, Sian. That's
not many is it?

Published by Parrot
Publications, 13 Silver St,
Durham City. Tele. 61242.

Printed by Moss-side Press,
Manchester.

Morden Tower

Since 1964 the Morden Tower has played host to many great poets, who bothered to make the journey northwards (or as in the case of McDiarmid and other great Scottish masters, south) for a small fee and relativly small audience, poets have come from America and Canada and may other points of the world. Whatever it had, it made it worth the journey. Allen Ginsberg came in 1965 before his performance at the legendary Albert Hall reading, and imparted what wisdom he had weaned from the east and breathed the winds of change, which influenced the then young regular audience to zoom off eastwards and seek a broader vision than the confines of our own northern English city gave us.The building was used in the early days as a focus for spotty,beautiful struggling youth to get stoned,make a platform other than the industrial commercial educational establishments of the city acknowledged. People stumbled along the unlit lane in winter,huddled in the half light, round an inefective fire and made their own warmth from proximity of one to another. Many attempts were made throughout its history to sabotage the building. Police were not infrequent visitors, the council's freaked out, and the then North Eastern association for the arts tried to starve it out when we applied for grants.

Allan Ginsberg said he'd learnt more in the Morden Tower than he had in a hundred universities. Poets felt at home there. After the demorilisation of the means of lighting and heating being ripped out, Connie got another mate to install electricity again and the corporation to put in new windows (the old ones were falling out). After eight years they finally got the message and realised it was worth the effort. They had the structure repaired and she planned the first reading for the new season to take place on 12th May

"I learned more reading at Morden Tower than I had at a hundred universities." Allen Ginsberg.

with Ted Berrigan. We had both despaired at the thought of opening it again, but the Northern Arts in the persons of Phillip Comford and Sid Chaplin had encouraged us enormously to get the place on its' feet again. The audience had begun to miss their place and its' function had not been adequetly replaced.The night before the re-opening some arsehole set fire to the building and gutted it. Ten years work gone up in smoke. Connie managed at the last moment to find a suitable alternative. The Miners Institute, between the Lit and Phil and the Royal Station Hotel. An incredible building at the best of times, but still not our own place. Never mind. Undaunted she continues, with one of the best seasons on record. Two of America's greatest poets, Robert Duncan (23rd May) and George Oppen (date unfixed,though within the next few weeks)are coming McDiarmid in September.Eric Moytramm on 1st June.Hope to see you there. Any queries to Morden Tower Bookshop (formerly McKenna's) 38 Handysides Arcade, Percy Street, Newcastle, NE1 4PZ. (Phone 29460).There is a mailing list if you want to be on it.

Tom Pickard.

In June of this year the South Shields Trades Union Council made a decision to oppose the Housing Finance Bill. This decision was acted upon using techniques which have proved to be effective over a range of issues and for which the S.S. Trades Union Council has developed something of a reputation as in its campaigns for students, pensioners, and during the miners and dockers strikes.

An analysis of action to date brings out 5 basic principles upon which effective grass root campaigns depend :-

1. The campaign must involve a specific issue genuinely affecting those it is intended to involve in the campaign. Direct action must be possible by these individuals acting as a group. There must therefore be a realistic appreciation of the practical objectives of the campaign and an assessment of what particular action is expected from individuals.

(The South Shields campaign started with the specific intention of defeating the Rent Bill in the South Shields area by involving tenants in a rent strike. No time was wasted on petitions or appeals to local or national goverment)

2. A thorough campaign of agitation and education must be mounted to ensure emotional and intellectual involvement in the issue.

(In South Shields over 30,000 leaflets were distributed explaining various aspects of the Housing Bill. Several Trades Council members became experts in interpreting the Bill and explaining the issues at tenants meetings.)

3. Organisations must be created at grass root level. All existing organisations are likely to be too rigid or too conservative to be effective. Existing leaders are likely to be suspect and new leaders must be allowed to rise.

(In South Shields 10 tenants' associations were established electing their own leaders most of whom were new to the political scene. The associations were united under a Federation.)

4. Political parties should NOT be involved or included in the organisations as such. Party members should be involved only on a non-party basis. One of the most characteristic features of public meetings of tenants has been the insistence of "keeping political parties out" - even when expressing such obviously political views as opposition to the Industrial Relations Act or the Rent Act. Thus while politically motivated individuals are necessary for sustained efforts to promote action they must be capable of sinking their long term philosophy in the short term interests of a narrow objective.

(In South Shields, political parties were specifically excluded from the Tenants Associations, and an attempt to set up a "Council of Action" to include political parties was resisted. Nevertheless, L.P., C.P., I.S., and S.L.L. members all co-operated in the forming of the tenants associations.)

5. Trades union involvment should be sought at all levels. This should include union branches and trades councils, and, if national indications can be developed, the TUC Involvment should include financial, and organisational support, and ultimately, the threat of supporting industrial action.

(In South Shields, a strike liaison committee was set up similiar to those set up during the miners and dockers strike. The committee consisted of strikers, and trade union council representatives, with the control of the committee firmly in the hands of the strikers. The experience of active trade unionists, was thus available to the tenants and several donations

of £50 were made by local trade union branches).

Due to the temporary resistance to the Rent Act by the South Shields Town Council rent increases have not yet been imposed on council houses. However, despite a demonstration by about 400 tenants outside the Town Hall, the Council recently decided on a free vote to implement the Act. This means that in about six weeks time council tenants on nine estates will join the 130 tenants on NorthEast Housing Association estates who are not paying the increase in their rent.

A Muther Grumble report on the South Shields Rent Strike.

The Bigger They Are .....

Power has taken a turn for the worse in the north-east over the past few months, with the much honoured and admired Alderman Andrew Cunningham falling off the pedestral from which he's ruled much of what has gone on in the area for so long.

In December 1971, Muther Grumble No. 1 carried an article about the man. He was at the height of his power then, being, among other things, a member of the National Executive of the Labour Party, the Chairman of both the Chester-le-Street and the Northern Region Executive of the Labour Party, the head of the Northern region of the General and Municipal Workers Union (the biggest union in the north-east), an Alderman of the County Council and a member of the Chester le-Street council, Chairman of the Durham Police Authority, Chairman of the Newcastle Airport Consultative Committee, a member of the Northumbrian River Authority, the Peterlee New Town Development Corporation, and the planning and education committees of Durham County Council. Last, but not least, he was also Chairman of the Tyneside Passenger Transport Authority. Quite a bundle of positions.

His position as GMWU boss gave him power in some of the local Parliamentary Constituences over who was to be the Labour candidates (and in this area that means MP's) for the elections. So this, together with his influence in the national Labour Party gave him many powerful friends in Parliament. This influence pervaded local politics as well, where many Labour politicians saw him as the guiding light firmly controlling the entrance to the ladder of national and power based politics.

So, a year ago, Godfather Cunningham was a force to be reckoned with. But now his empire has crumbled due to some illegal, or (to be safe) at least highly sensitive dealings he had with a certain architect - Mr. John Poulson - a few years back which have only recently come to light. Any intripid reader of Private Eye or of the more informative press will know all about Cunningham and Poulson, and Andy's wife, Freda, and his buddy Dan Smith, who, until the Poulson hearing began was Chairman of the Northern Economic Development Council, and another north-east strong (arm) man of how Poulson paid Smith who paid Freda; of how Poulson sent the Cunningham family for free holidays; of how all this was done in the hope that our friends Dan and Andy might be able to push some contracts Poulsons way. This they did. Smith put pressure on members of local councils to accept Poulson as consultant architect for various developments, while Cunningham used his position to get tenders for Poulson to design houses, offices for the Tyne River Authority, (which subsequently weren't built but Poulson got paid for), blocks.

(Continued)

Andy Cunningham

Muther Grumble was first to report N.E. power corruption.

The Bigger They Are ..... continued

of flats and a police station. In some instances, the contracts were not even put out to tender – Cunningham just pursuaded the council or committee in question to accept Poulson's offer without consider- ing any others.

But alas, all came to an end, Poulson started going bankrupt and cut the money available to Dan Smith who had to release Freda Cunningham (a teacher by trade)

from her obligation to him as an Interior Design Consultant. Finally, Poulson did go bankrupt and in the resulting court hearings the much started to soil the respectability of the power elite, among them Smith and Cunningham. Smith disappeared immediately from public life but Cunningham, who made a strong stand, is finally beginning to be overwhelmed. Both will come under investigation by the police to see if they've done anything wrong (sic).

This is an account of Cunningham's downfall. Soon he'll

almost certainly loose his seat on the National Executive of the Labour Party; he'll also almost certainly loose his chairmanship of the Northern Region Executive and already has on the Chester-le- Street one. In April, he failed to secure nomination as Chester-le- Street candidate for both the County Council and the local dist- rict council; this means that he'll loose all his positions on these councils. Soon he'll be replaced as Chairman of the Police Authority, and he's to be asked to leave his post as Chairman of the Tyneside Passenger Transport Auth- ority, the Transport Minister says he would prefer a chairman who was a member of the Tyne-Wear Metropol- itan council which takes over res- ponsibility for the TTA next April, and the Metropolitan Council, bel- ieve it or not, is one of the few institutions that Cunningham is NOT a member of. Funny how this didn't seem so important last year.

Muther Grumble recorded the downfall of the Andy Cunningham gang – first exposed by Muther Grumble in 1971.

Resisting

The Social Security is a part of the Welfare State. Whose welfare? They have used many and varied euphemisms in the past also, but always to the same purpose:- the prevention of riot and revolution amongst the dispossessed.

People in work are kept under control by the threat of dole queues, immigrants, women, who will seize their jobs if they misbehave themselves. Their pay is sufficient to keep up a demand for production – and thus profits for the bosses.

People non-employed must also be kept in check; so they are given welfare benefits which ensure that they stay alive (in case capitalism should need them in the future) and have just enough spending power to keep the economy (profits) in motion. Controls are applied by propaganda, which attempts to make the claimant feel demoralized for not having the 'right to work' (right to be exploited), and by the general sadistic humiliation techniques employed by the agents of the State administering the benefits. Claimants have greatest value to the ruling class in that they are a visible

deterrent (a means to depress wages) to those in work who might otherwise agitate too fiercely for the State's equilibrium.

Despite differences in the faces of the agents of oppression, then, employed and non employed are being used to the same ends. The apparent divisions are fostered by the capitalist machine in order to avoid a united working class.

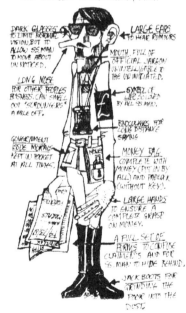

THE COMPLETE SOCIAL SECURITY MAN.

Muther Grumble's version of the Claimants Union story.

By destroying the controls the State has on claimants, the Claimants' Unions are simultaneously weakening the bosses' hold on those in work.

The Claimants' Unions are out to gain as many reforms in the treatment of claimants as possible – like any Trade Union would, though the methods and motivation are different; but this is merely as a practice in the resistance techniques of mutual aid, self management, the making of collective demands (NUT bargaining!), grass roots direct action, and so on.

Ultimately the C.U.'s are a revolutionary movement. Claimants who hope to win control over their own lives by piecemeal attacks on the S.S.'s worst excesses soon see that it's not the Social Security that oppresses, but the ruling class that creates and nurtures such a system. And they have only to look at their neighbours in work to see that their oppression stems from the same source. At work, the bosses and the profits can be seen more directly.

Direct confrontation with the State in its S.S. guise is only going to smash it when there are simultaneous

attacks on all its other fronts.

The Claimants' Unions are collectives of militant people seeking to chip away at the system until such time as the working class as a whole realises its power to destroy the whole edifice. They go on the offensive to escalate the conflict rather than shielding people from it: welfare workers and such like, act as a barrier between the people and the struggle, thus obscuring the issues and preventing people from gaining practice in the control of their own lives. The C.U.'s are totally opposed to the welfare approach. They are not advice centres:

anyone wanting advice on 'rights' under the National Insurance or S.S. Acts can go to the local Citizens Advice Bureaux where they will find staff prepared to devote a considerable amount of time and effort unraveling tile intracies of legal entitlements.

Muther Grumble June 1972

The Unfinished Revolution

Muther Grumble.

HELP, ADVICE, INFO

CLAIMANTS UNIONS
Durham
13 Silver St. Durham
City, Tel.61242
Newcastle
258 Westgate Rd., N/cle 1
Weekly meetings Tues.
afternoons at 2.
S. Shields
Claimants Union is
temporarily of no
fixed abode - watch this
space.

CYRENIANS
N/cle C/o The
Chaplaincy, The
University, Durham. C/o
David Constantine, 6
Kepier Terrace.

SAMARITANS
Newcastle 27272
Durham 63737
Sunderland 77177
Middlesbrough 56777
Hartlepool 2020

WEST END TENANTS
At Elswick Action Centre
Elswick Road, Phone
39767

OFF THE RECORD
Provide Info and help
Mon-Fri 7-9pm at 5
Charlotte Square,
Newcastle, Phone
N/cle23588.

Want to talk to someone?
We will try to help you
in any way we can or
with any problems. Call
at Muther Grumble, 13
Silver Street, Durham
City or phone Durham
61242.

Stockton Help
20 Laurence St. Stockton
on Tees, Tel Stockton
66667 for 24 hr. service.

N.C.C.L.
Helps people defend
their rights and
investigates violations
of those rights. Also
produce some excellent
pamphlets. 152 Camden
High St., N.W.1.
(01-603-8654)

RELEASE
Elgin Ave. London W9
01-603-8654)

BIT
24 hour free info & help
service for young people
and those trying to
create an alternative to
present society. We are
interested in what's
happening in your area -
so let us know. BIT have
changed their address -
now at 132 Great Western
Road, London W11.
Phone 01-229-8219

**FAMILY PLANNING
ASSOCIATION**
Northumbrian Branch 'A'
floor, Milburn House,
Dean St., Newcastle,
27090

CAG
3 Blackwellgate,
Darlington. Advice and
information etc.

RENT TRIBUNAL
If you're in a furnished
flat and having landlord
problems, the rent
tribunal can give you
security.
Warwick House, Grantham
Rd., Newcastle 2. Tel
N/cle 610372

Please help us keep
this and the whats on
up to date.

GROUPS

GAY LIBERATION FRONT
Newcastle GLF meet 8pm
every Wednesday at 38
Westgate Rd., N/cle.
Sunderland Acting Sec.
Howard Llewellyn,
Students Union, S/land
Polytechnic.

New address for Tyneside
GLF
Chairman:- David
Mitchell, 65 St.
Anselm Rd, Billy Mill,
North Shields.
Nth Shields 76454
Teesside Contact Frank
Smith 57 Belmont Ave,
Billingham, Teesside.

PROP
(Preservation of the
Rights of Prisoners) At
96 Victoria Avenue, Hull.
Produce PROP magazine
available from them.

FRIENDS OF THE EARTH
Now hold regular
meetings in private in
the Percy Arms Haymarket
Newcastle at 7.30 every
other Monday. For details
contact Colin Cleves,
C/o Fullbeck Grange,
Northgate, Morpeth.

SOC'EM
Save our City from
environmental Mess. For
information contact 79
Roseberry Crescent, N/cle
7.

**TYNESIDE ENVIRONMENTAL
CONCERN** Contact Colin
Marsh, 63 Beatty Ave.,
Jesmond. Tel N/cle
856714.

DIVINE LIGHT MISSION
15, Holly Ave, Jesmond,
Newcastle.

SHELTER GROUP
Contact K. Murray,
3 Monks Crescent,
Gilesgate, Durham
Tel 62007.

COMMITMENT
(Radical Environmental
Action Group) 26
Gresvenor Road, St.
Albans, Herts.

WHITE PANTHERS
10 Fairview Ave.,
South Shields.

CLEVELAND COMMUNITIES
Related to the Dwarfs
non-violent revolution
through communes, craft
workshops etc.
John Hodgson, 25 Newcomen
Terrace, Redcar, Yorks.

RADICAL EDUCATION
Anyone interested contact
Jon & Marcia Taylor, 5
Astral House, S/land
SR1 3DX.

TRADES COUNCILS
Durham D.O.Ellison,
11, Attlee Crescent,
Haswell Plough,
Durham.
Newcastle Gordon
Steele, 26 Garth
Twelve, Killingworth.
Sunderland H.Mitchell,
23, Springdon Rd.,
Springwell Estate.
South Shields 4, Weston
Village, South Shields
Chester-le-Street C.M.
Warner, 26 Weldon
Terrace.
**Federation of Trades
Councils** (Teesside)
F.Munroe, 7, Lumley St.,
Middlesborough.

Spectro Arts Workshop
10, Station Rd., Whitley
Bay. Tel W.B. 22336.

YOUNG VOLUNTEER FORCE
c/o College of Further
Education, Bath Lane,
Newcastle. Tel 21171

CHILD POVERTY ACTION GROUP
Contact the local secretary
at 79, Woburn Square,
Whitley Bay.

If you are interested in
learning yoga, I would
like to help you. Please
phone Gordon at Newcastle
811876, or come round and
see me at 51 Larkspur
Terrace. We've already
started an improvisation
session and a yoga session
once a week (Tue. & Thur)
but anyone is still
welcome to join. Please
get in touch with me
Gordon, 51 Larkspur Tce.,
Jesmond. Tel. N/cle
811876

Wanted one or two
community activists to
live and work with
community action project
in Handsworth, non-
sectarian socialist group,
housing and claimants
action, and full time
advice centre. No salary,
some expenses otherwise
support self. Write for
full project report to
The Action Centre, 40
Hall Rd, Handsworth,
Birmingham B20 7BQ or
ring 021-527-6891

BIT INFORMATION SERVICE
produces the only travel
guide to all Africa.
'Overland Through Africa'
goes to BIT and Operation
Omega for the liberation
of Namibia)

SMALLS

**NEWCASTLE FREE INFO
SERVICE:-** We can be
contacted at the follow-
ing places and times:-
Monday-Friday. Ultima
Thule Bookshop, 22
Arcadia, Percy St, N/cle
Nights & weekends...82
Cardigan Tce, Heaton,
Newcastle 6

DISQUE:- all folk, blues
heavy contemporary
music. Branches at N/cle
Chester-le-Street,
Wallsend, Jarrow, &
Whitley Bay.

**DURHAM BOOK CENTRE WANTS
BOOKS.**
WE WANT BOOKS
BOOKS BOUGHT FOR CASH
DURHAM BOOK CENTRE,
Vine Place, Sunderland.

GAY DANCE
Come and dance with your
Gay brothers and sisters
at the G.L.F. Dance - The
SALLYPORT TOWERS N/CLE.
SATURDAY JUNE 9TH. Starts
8pm or there abouts

IRON - 15p, No.1 Spring
1973. Ginsberg in N/cle,
Pickard in America
Available from Tom,
McKenna Bookshop &
Ultima Thule, & 92

Anybody interested in
street theatre? Contact
MICK, 2 Sunderland Bridge
Village, Croxdale.

Good Homes wanted for 3
kittens. Contact Tony
Jackson through Ultima
Thule, Arcadia, N/cle

RISING FREE - without
knowledge, without under-
standing there can be no
revolution. Rising free
distributes material from
revolutionary groups &
publishers.

Antistudent, 15p; Isling-
ton Gutter Press, 3p; Sex-
pol, Reich 40p; Freedom -
The Wolfe Tone Way, 70p;
Up Against the Law, 15p;
Street Research Bulletin,
15p; Community Action,15p;
Imperialism, a definition
12p; Floodgates of Anarchy
Stuart Christie, 35p

50p- The Complete Book of
IRA Jailbreaks; Send S.A.E.
for full literature
lists. Add postage 15%
to:- Rising Free, 197
King's Cross Rd., London
WC1 Tel. 01-837-0182

At BYZANTINE on Saturday
in Durham covered market.
Gold & frankincense &
myrrh, pure oil, essences,
hand made jewellery,
candles, herb incense, gum
benzoin, ligneoloes, henna,
& kohl etc.etc.

Stuart & Eileens Stall.
Bigg Market N/cle.
Candles, incense, Indian
perfumes, leather goods
& big skins.

Books antiquarian & other-
wise, large stock. The
Bookstall, left hand side
Durham New Market.

KARD BAR has largest range of posters in the world
KARD BAR has full range of KRSNA incense sticks/oils
KARD BAR has mod. cards without greetings
KARD BAR has Peanuts pennants, books, nitees, sheets,
pillowcases and trays
KARD BAR is open 10-5.30 six days
KARD BAR is in Arcadia, Percy Street. Newcastle

Back issues of Yoga &
Health wanted:- Vol 1
nos 1,11 & 12, Vol 2 Nos
1,2,3, & 7. Write to J.
Jobus, 5 Porchester St.,
South Shields

Art Classes start May 7th
• Mondays - 7.30 - 9.30pm
Wednesdays   "   "
Thursdays   "   "
Behind the Dun Cow

Ultima Thle Bookshop
is in Arcadia Percy St.
N/cle and sells many
nice books and mags.

*Muther Grumble listed some of the many alternative activities and
organisations of that time.*

The Muther Grumble's extended version of the SSTUC leaflet –
'A School Leavers' Guide to Survival'.

The ideas expressed in this article are revolutionary – that is, they are not aimed at improving or reforming the existing system but at undermining and destroying it and replacing it with something better.

Because these ideas are revolutionary, they threaten the established order and the people who run it. They will therefore be resisted by them. Parents will try to stop you reading this, schools will ban it employers will condemn it. In some countries these ideas are being resisted with bombs and bullets. People have died for them. The authors of this article want to create the revolution by peaceful means. What happens, in fact, will depend upon the wisdom and skill of those who seek the revolution, and the methods used by those who seek to resist it. The revolution will happen, the only question is when and how. What you do (or do not do) will count.

This article then, is aimed at changing the system – that is, at changing what things are done by individuals and society, the way they are done, and the reason for doing them.

The System

For over 10 years you have been subjected to a process called "education". This has been designed to make you fit into "The System". You have been brainwashed to conform, to think and do as you are told, to respect "authority", to get a job, to "get on" etc. This has been done to you so that someone can make money out of you – out of the things you buy, and the work you have to do to get them. You will get work, and food and clothes, and a house only if someone can make money out of it – only if you agree to be exploited.

You have been brainwashed to want to want to own things – a stereo, a coloured telly, a bike – not because you need to own them – and so that you will have to work (and make

someone else a profit) to pay for them. This is the vicious circle of the Capitalist Consumer System.

You have been brainwashed to want to marry, and have a family of 2 so that you will form a stable social unit of the economic machine that keeps the system going. All of your life is dominated by the need for someone to make a profit out of you.

Education is given, work is provided, law is enforced, only because they are needed by the Capitalist system of profit, private gain, and private ownership. 95% of the wealth of this country is in the hands of 5% of the people. And this 5% controls the way you have to live, the things you will be brainwashed to want, and the way you will have to work to get them.

If you get a job your boss will demand a large chunk of your life so that he can make money out of you. He will listen to your demands and your needs only when to resist would threaten his profit. He will be nice to you only because be needs you to make money. He will sack you when he does not make enough.

The main political parties – Labour, Conservative, Liberal – are simply trying to get the system to work better. They cannot see, or do · not want to see, that it is the system itself which is wrong. They pretend to be democratic but in effect allow a handful of people in business, or

The Muther Grumble version of the The School Leavers' Guide.

parliament or the local council to use their power to control us. They have a vested interest in keeping the system going as it is.

Your parents will blackmail you with their "love" to get you to do what they want. The system needs a stable family unit to keep production and profit going, and uses your parents to see that they produce one.

The press, the telly, and all advertising is designed to make you want more so that you will have to make more, and so that someone will make more profit.

Why do adults fall for this? There are many reasons. Your parents and your teachers have taught you to conform to this system because they were brainwashed to conform themselves – and because most of them are too selfish, or too scared to do anything else. They have learned to do as they are told.

Many adults see the young as a threat to their authority, their jobs, and their security. They will use all the powers of the system, its rules and its regulations to beat you. In some cases their resentment will be based on their sexual frustration and your sexuality – they think you live on drugs and orgies. They would like to join you but they are afraid and feel guilty. They will try to punish you for their guilt. It some cases they will want to love you – but fear and convention will make them seek self defense in hate.

But the basic reason why adults fear and mistreat the young is because they are all victims of a system based on selfishness and greed. All authority, parliament and the law, all rules and regulations, schools and colleges, the churches, the political parties, the family – all of these are distorted to keep the Capitalist system of private property and profit going.

And the schools teach us to want to be exploited in this way, to want a lousy job, to want to "get on", to want their stupid qualifications and high positions, to want to buy the

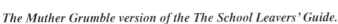

The Muther Grumble version of the The School Leavers' Guide.

The Unfinished Revolution

unnecessary, unimportant goods that the system forces us to produce.

The alternative to this capitalist system is a society where "work" is carried out by those who can do it for those who need it. A person will be "paid" according to his needs. They will give what they can and want to do in the way they want to do it. Some people call this system Socialism, some call it Communism, or Maoism, some call it Anarchism. No-one has created this society completely yet but many are trying. It will be difficult to achieve but the alternative is the continuation of the system where we are slaves, being forced to work for someone else's profit – even if we become willing slaves.

Those people who want to change the basis of the existing capitalist system into a system of the kind described above are called revolutionaries – and the Capitalist system is trying to crush them.

Meanwhile the Capitalists system is kept going by the education process, by the Officials, the bosses, the police and those in authority. They do it by brainwashing, by not telling the facts, by lies, by making you do a rotten job – and finally, if necessary, by force.

We cannot do much about the brainwashing – you have had ten years of it and will have to fight it yourself. We can do something about

telling you the facts that have been kept from you – and hope you will draw from your own conclusions.

The Things They Did Not Tell you

There are many elementary facts which affect your life and your future which have been kept from you because they might cause you to question and to challenge the existing system. For example: –

You have not been told the truth about drugs. Pot is probably less harmful than lemonade and it might even do you good. Certainly it is not addictive, not as harmful as tobacco, and can give you a great amount of pleasure. Alcohol is the greatest drug threat in this country. There are more alcoholics than all the other drug addicts combined. But alcohol is acceptable because some people are making a fat profit out of it – and most adults use it!

You have not been told how to get cheap or free contraceptives. Some of you have not even been told what they are.

You have not been told how to apply for an abortion – or what to do if your doctor refuses – and he probably will if he is Catholic. Is he?

You have not been told what trade unions to join, how to join, or how to use it.

The Muther Grumble version of the The School Leavers' Guide.

You have not been told about your rights when faced with arrest. You don't have to "go along quietly". You don't have to give your name and address unless you have been specifically charged with a specific offence, unless the offence you are being connected with is a driving offence. Nor do you have to submit to questioning without being officially charged with a specific offence, nor can they finger-print you without either your consent or a magistrates order.

You have not been told how to get legal aid.

You are told that "true love" means owning one person, of the opposite sex, for life (in some cases a real "life sentence"). You are not told that love can involve more than two people, of the same or different sex, for a short or long period.

You have not been told about the Gay Liberation Front organisation for homosexuals.

You have not been told about the revolutionary political parties – International Socialists, Socialist Labour League, International Marxists Group. Some of you have not been even told about the Communist party.

You have not been told anything that would reduce the pressure on you to find a job, almost any job, at any price, or anything that might cause you to question the existing system of authority, power and wealth.

Some of the facts you have not been told are given in this article.

BUT MOST IMPORTANT OF ALL YOU HAVE NOT BEEN TOLD THAT YOU BELONG ONLY TO YOURSELF AND THAT YOU HAVE A RIGHT TO FREEDOM AND INDEPENDENCE TO LIVE YOUR OWN LIFE IN YOUR OWN WAY.

The insistence on this right lies at the heart of possible revolutionary action by young people. It poses a direct challenge to the existing system which seeks to force you to have to work in their work, to meet their needs.

To resist their system and to fight for survival as a free person in this capitalist system it is necessary to understand the possible alternative ways of life open to everyone over 16. It is a revolutionary attitude to demand the right to do the things you want to do in your way and to demand the right to the means of existing while you do so.

This principle is embodied (confused and accidental though it may be) in the 1966 Social Security Act which sets out you rights to claim benefits. Section 14 of the act states:- "Every person in Great Britain over

The Muther Grumble version of the The School Leavers' Guide.

the age of 16 years or over whose resources are insufficient to meet his requirements shall be entitled, subject to the provisions of the Act, to (Social Security) benefits."

This could mean that every person over 16 has the right to cash to meet their basic needs for clothes, food, and accommodation etc., independent of their parents, and whether they are working or not. It can be made to mean that and it is revolutionary action to set out to make it mean that.

Living on Social Security is one way for a person to survive free of the work situation, whatever other problems there might be in this society. This article is designed to help you do this and to explain other choices open to you at 16. This choice is another of the things that no one will have told you about.

The Choice At 16

Every person reaching the age of 16 has a choice as to how they intend to live. You can: –

1) Stay on at school. You can claim a local authority education grant if your family income is very low. These grants can be claimed if your family income falls below these levels:

15 years old–£705 net (annual)
16 years old–£780 net (annual)
17 years old–£855 net (annual)

The net amount is calculated by taking the gross family income and deducting tax, amounts for dependents living off that income etc. A form giving all the details and explaining how the net family income is worked out is available at the local education office.

Alternatively if your family income is above these amounts your parents can claim about £1.60p a week tax allowance, and if there is another child at school £0.90p family allowance. Free school meals can also be claimed and free travel if you live a certain distance from the school (usually 3 miles or more).

All of this is not much – but it does show that you are not entirely a drain on the family income and that you have your own rights in the family group - even as a school student.

2) You can go to college. Any person over 16 can attend college on a GCE, technical, commercial or arts course. IF THE COURSE IS OF 3 DAYS A WEEK OR LESS (OR SIX HALF DAYS) YOU CAN CLAIM SOCIAL SECURITY BENEFITS OF £3.60p A WEEK (AGED 16-17) OR £4. 5Op 4 WEEK (AGED 18-20) PLUS THE RENT OF A FLAT IF YOU DO NOT LIVE AT HOME (OR BOARD AND LODGINGS PLUS £1.85p).

If the course is "full time" of a

The Muther Grumble version of the The School Leavers' Guide.

kind not available in school you are entitled to claim Social Security benefits - but you will have to fight to get them.

If you are entitled to Unemployment Benefit i.e. if you have the necessary employment stamps, you can take any college course full time or part-time and draw benefits.

3) You can live on Social Security. Not only is the Capitalist system immoral, it is also inefficient. It cannot organise work for you even if you want to do it. So anyone over 16 can register for a job without much fear of getting one and can claim Social Security Benefits. A householder gets £5.80p plus rent, a person living in another persons household gets £3.60p (16-17), £4.05p (18-20), £4.60p (21 or over). Plus 65p rent addition.

4) If you are a woman you can get married and start a life of work for no money.

5) You can drop out altogether. You can sponge off your friends and your family and tell them to stuff their system – but it's a shame to waste the Social Security benefits you could be claiming. If you drop out of work it is important to use this free time to develop your own life style and your own values and ideas. Use the public facilities that are available for free – public libraries, exhibitions, lectures etc. Many university and college facilities are also available and there is no real check as to who is a genuine student. Cheap meals are available in college canteens and refectories. Other possibilities are youth or street theaters, arts labs, film societies etc.

6) You could go to university, polytech, or teacher training college. Entry to teacher training college is a minimum of 4 'O' levels. Entry to university or polytech. is two suitable 'A' levels – and remember that you can take 'O' and 'A' levels at a technical college and draw weekly Social Security benefits providing you do not attend for more than 3 days a week (or 6 half days).

Entry to a university or polytech. is also possible with an 'Ordinary National Certificate' (O.N.C.). These courses can also be taken at a technical college on Social Security benefits - provided you do not attend on more than 3 days (or 6 half days) a week.

Alternatively if you can get a job with an apprenticeship or official training then it should be possible for you to attend an O.N.C. course on a 'day release' or 'block-release' course – and get paid while attending college. In this case you just leave your job when you get the necessary qualifications (this should take 2

The Muther Grumble version of the The School Leavers' Guide.

years) – but it is not advisable to tell your employer that you intend to leave unless he is prepared to sponsor you (i.e. pay you) while at university.

(Once you have worked for 26 weeks you can take any course at a college full-time or part-time and it would then be possible to take a normal 5 day a week block release course and continue to draw your full unemployment benefit.)

Entry to a university or polytech can be financial in another way. Your grant is based upon your family income - the higher the income the less the grant.

If however, you have worked for over 3 years with a minimum average wage of £7.50p a week then you will be classed as an "independent student" and will qualify for the maximum grant, regardless of your family income. Similar conditions apply to grants received while at teacher training college.

Remember also that any student can register for work during any college holiday – and if suitable work is not offered they can claim weekly Social Security Benefits.

Universities, Polytechs and Training Colleges are also part of "the system". But usually they are so confused as to what they are trying to do that you can get away with your own thing more easily there than at most other places – that is if you're

not prepared to let your work interfere with your education.

7) You could get a job – that is, if you are lucky enough to find someone prepared to exploit you.

If you do get a job remember that you have certain rights, even under a capitalist system. Once you enter the rat race you will have to learn to fight as hard as your employer. You will have to learn how to exploit your rights to the maximum advantage. Your employer will be exploiting his position (and you) and don't be deceived by the fact that he has learned to smile while he does it.

Your first protection should be to join a trade union. Most work places have a single union to cover a given type of worker. Find out which union it is. Contact the shop-steward if there is one, or the Branch Secretary. Don't expect to be welcomed by the union with open arms. The unions are in the rat race too. Many of the paid union officials are more concerned with their job than with yours and you will have to learn how to demand your rights from the Officials paid to protect you.

If you have difficulty in finding a union contact at your works – get in touch with the local Trades Council (or Trades Union Council). Addresses of local ones are given at the end of the article.

If you stay at home, remember

The Muther Grumble version of the The School Leavers' Guide.

The Unfinished Revolution

that you will come under pressure from the rest of the family to conform to their values and their way of life. It is exceptional for parents to be able to allow their children to adopt their own life style without a fight. They have been brainwashed by the system for longer than you and they will try to force you to give in to them with arguments, fights and fits of sulking. Worst of all, they will try to bribe you by using their love and their money, and your affection.

If the pressure gets too great, you should think of leaving home and setting up in your own flat or digs.

Conclusions

You will have to be prepared to fight if you want to survive as a free independent person in this capitalist consumer society. The system will try to force you to conform, to make you sell yourself in a job, so that they can make money out of you.

You have a duty to yourself to fight to save yourself for yourself. If you fight to change the system you are a revolutionary. We can all make the revolution in our own way. You can do it by fighting for your rights as a human being and an individual whose rights are more important than someone else's profit. You can do this in your home, your school, your college or work-place, or in the dole queues and Social Security offices.

You can do it by yourself.

Sometimes you have to! But you can do it better with others. Join up with other people with similar interests and ideas in existing organisations – but if there is no suitable organisation, form one.

Further information can be obtained from the following centres:- Trades Councils, Claimants' Unions, Muther Grumble.

Claimants' Unions addresses can be found on the Graffitti Page (page 20).

Some trades council addresses are:
Durham
11, Attlee Crescent,
Haswell Plough, Durham

Newcastle
26, Garth Twelve,
Killingsworth, N/cle 682204

Sunderland
23, Swindon Road,
Springwell Estate, Sunderland

South Shields
143, Westoe Road, S. Shields
(Saturday mornings only.
tel. 60762).

Red House, 4 Westoe Village,
South Shields (evenings) 60816

Chester le Street
6, Weldon Terrace, Chester.

Federation of Trade Councils
(Teesside),
Lumley Street, Middlesbrough.

The Muther Grumble version of the The School Leavers' Guide.

The above article is an expanded version of a leaflet that was handed out to school leavers in South Shields. The reaction to the leaflet by the authorities was remarkable.

School students had these leaflets confiscated by teachers, and were threatened by the withdrawal of their school leaving testimonials if they continued to distribute it. This was reported to be on the instructions of the Education Office.

Apart from the dubious legality of teachers confiscating private property, and apart from the blackmail implicit in the threatened stopping of testimonials, this raises fundamental questions concerning the nature of the educational process and the quality of its administration.

It would seem that the Labour Chairman of the Education Committee has made a unilateral decision to try to prevent 16 year old school students from being made aware of the facts concerning their educational future.

Unless education is based on respect for the truth and the freedom of individuals to choose then we move into a system which is at best paternalistic and at worst fascist and dictatorial.

It seems to be the determination of the Chairman of the South Shields Education Committee to promote an educational system based on concealment and deceit.

The implications of this decision go far beyond the effect on school leavers and draws into question the whole nature of our educational process and the so called democratic political structure which supports it.

Muther Grumble

If the reaction to the SSTUC 'School Leavers' Guide' had been one of outrage, the reaction to this Muther Grumble version verged on the hysterical: Education Authorities and head teachers sought to have it banned from schools and colleges; it was debated at a special meeting of the Governors of South Tyneside College; The national press sent reporters to investigate.

Academia received the Guide more kindly.

Pensioners
The Campaign For Social Security Rights

This campaign was started primarily to increase pensioners' take-up of Department of Health & Social Security (DHSS) benefits. It had three strands:

1. To involve pensioners in action regarding their right to social security benefits.
2. To expose the anomalies, contradictions and failings of the Social Security system.
3. To confront the state and achieve changes in government policy by the force of grass-root action.

The efforts to obtain heating allowances were an important element of the campaign. The 1966 Social Security Act allowed for discretionary payments where a house was 'damp or otherwise difficult to keep adequately warm.' The SSTUC and the CU argued successfully at appeals tribunals that most houses in the North East were damp and/or difficult to heat. A precedent was established for weekly payments of 50p–75p to be made (a considerable amount at that time) only to have this 'offset against long-term additions' so that usually no extra payment was actually received.

This anomaly regarding the heating allowance was raised at local and national level involving the DHSS, the TUC, and parliament. Several thousand leaflets were distributed in the region. In a notorious incident one leaflet addressed 'To All Senior Citizens' was distributed by Post Offices in the belief that it was an 'official' document.

Success was achieved when Keith Joseph, Secretary of State for Social Security, announced in Parliament that, as from the 1st October 1973, extra heating allowances would be paid on top of supplementary benefits and that, for the first time, recipients would be entitled to the full amount of heating allowance awarded. It was estimated that over 400,000 pensioners benefited at an annual cost (then) of around £6 million

The campaign for heating allowances was used to spearhead other campaigns for increased benefits. Several important changes in social security benefit policy were achieved and, equally important, a change of attitude by pensioners to claiming benefit rights.

The campaign can also be seen as contributing to an awareness by local authorities to the importance to local economies of maximising the take-up of benefits. Rights 'advice-agencies' were established in many areas. In such ways the state absorbed and deflected popular protest and revolt while, at the same time, economic interests were served in the guise of philanthropic intent.

EVENING CHRONICLE

No. 29,468. Newcastle. FRIDAY, JANUARY 28, 1972 3p

Unions' council chief accuses Ministry

OLD FOLK 'DENIED FUEL ALLOWANCE'

THE Department of Health and Social Security was lashed today by a group of Tyneside trade unionists for its alleged "scandalous treatment" of old folk living on the breadline.

South Shields Trades Union Council launched a massive campaign recently to encourage pensioners in the region to claim extra allowances from the Department for clothes, rent and fuel.

The secretary, Mr. Jack Grassby, said old people who did not realise they could claim a fuel allowance of up to 75p a week, were living in freezing conditions and sometimes dying of the cold.

The notorious 'official' leaflet; *3,000 copies of which were distributed in the Tyneside area in November 1971. The leaflet was designed to look like an official document to encourage pensioners to apply for benefits. In this it was so successful that Post Offices took part in their distribution.*

Many hundreds of pensioners applied and received an increase in benefits – but the action revealed an anomaly in the benefit system whereby a claimant could be awarded an increase in heating benefits but receive nothing.

Further, and perhaps more seriously, the action revealed that the DHSS were operating a so called discretionary system of benefits, based upon a secret code of practice (the 'A' codes). Access to this code was denied even to establishment individuals and organisations (like the TUC).

The issue was resolved only when a DHSS worker broke the secrecy code and distributed copies to Claimant Unions. The question of parliamentary accountability remained unanswered.

To all Senior Citizens

PENSIONERS,

Welcome to the **Welfare State !**

The days of the Poor Law and charity are gone. . . .

Since 1966 the Social Security Act has given you the RIGHT to certain benefits :—

When you come on to the Old Age Pension, if you have no other income, it is **your right** to have your rent paid by the Social Security.

Similarly, it is **your right** to claim the NEW price of essential household goods and clothing that you lack or that need replacing.

Some examples are given below; all these examples are taken from the official publication "The Supplementary Benefits Handbook" 1971 edition.

1. CLOTHING : Overcoat, jacket, trousers, jumpers, skirts, flameproof nightwear, all underclothes, etc.

2. FOOTWEAR : Warm waterproof shoes.

3. BEDDING : Beds, mattresses, blankets, sheets.

4. HOUSEHOLD EQUIPMENT : Heating appliances, tables, chairs, curtains, lino, etc.

5. REMOVAL EXPENSES may be claimed when accommodation has to be changed.

6. RE-DECORATIONS : Essential re-decoration costs may be claimed.

The following special expenses should also be claimed :—

7. "FARES TO VISIT RELATIVES IN HOSPITAL."

8. "THE COST of renting the SAFETY GAS COOKER available for use by old or infirm people."

9. "HIRE PURCHASE INSTALMENTS to which the claimant is committed for articles of household equipment or furniture which are absolutely essential."

10. WINTER FUEL ALLOWANCE
Your health depends on keeping yourself and your home warm and dry this winter. The Social Security Act allows you a winter allowance of 75p per week to cover additional fuel costs incurred during the cold, damp, winter months. This allowance **must** be claimed as the Social Security **refuse** to increase benefits automatically. **CLAIM NOW BY FILLING IN AND SENDING OFF THE FORM BELOW !**
(Claims for essential items of **household equipment**, clothing, etc., should be made by writing or calling at the Social Security Office, Wouldhave House : claims can also be made when the Social Security Visiting Officer calls to discuss your Winter Fuel Allowance.)

- -

The Manager,

Dept. of Health and Social Security,

Wouldhave House,

Market Place,

South Shields.

Address of Claimant

....

....

....

....

Dear Sir,

The Supplementary Benefits Handbook 1971, Section 63, states : "It is RECOGNISED that EXTRA FUEL may be required, particularly in the case of a recipient of supplementary benefit or a dependant whose mobility is seriously restricted by chronic ill-health, or through general frailty or advanced age, or the accommodation is damp or otherwise difficult to keep adequately warm."

As an Old Age Pensioner, I consider that I fall into the above category by reason of advanced age alone. ALSO ....
(ADD HERE ANY SPECIAL CONDITIONS SUCH AS ILL-HEALTH OR DAMP HOUSING, ETC.)

I therefore claim a winter allowance of **at least 75p per week** to help pay for the EXTRA FUEL that I shall need this winter.

Yours faithfully,

....
Signature

Published by South Shields Trades Council, Ede House, and South Shields Claimants Union, 4 Laygate Road.

HEXHAM & DISTRICT TRADES COUNCIL

(Registered with the Trade Union Congress).

Treasurer :
L. FIEDOROWICZ,
21, Priestclose Road,
Prudhoe,
Northumberland.

15th November 1971

Secretary :
GEOFF. EGGLESTONE,
88, Wanless Close,
Hexham,
Northumberland.

Dear Jack,

I do not think you will know who I am but I got your name from Maurice Ridley of Consett T.C.

We are interested in your campaign on pensions, as you may have seen from the "Sunday Sun" of Sunday 14th NOV., and are planning to hold a public meeting on Pensions on either December 11th or the 18th.

I have written to the TUC (Mr Woodbridge) Newcastle for likely speakers, and I wondered if you would be interested in speaking at any such meeting.

I understand Maurice Ridley will be contacting you re an informal meeting of Hexham T.C., Consett, and your own T.C.

If I do not see you before the I hope to see you at the next federation meeting

Yours Sincerely

Geoff Egglestone

Sec.

The campaign swiftly gained support from other Trades Councils.

<u>WALKER WARD LABOUR PARTY</u>

5 Southfield Terr.,
Walker
Newcastle-upon-TyneNE6 3EL

<u>Leaflets re Benefits for Pensioners</u>

Dear Colleague,

The members of Walker Ward Labour Party, wishing to support your campaign on behalf of O·A.P. would be very grateful if you could let us have a number of your leaflets for use by the party in a door to door campaign.

The ward would like to express it's gratitude to people like yourself in sponsoring such a campaign

Yours sincerly,

A.D.Train.

The campaign spread to constituency Labour Parties.

Business Studies Dept.,
The Technical College,
Consett

Telephone 2906 ex., 30

15th November

Mr. J. Glassby.

Dear Jack,

Further to my request for you to open the discussion at a get together of Crook, Consett and Hexham Trades Council members in Newcastle on December 4th (Saturday) at approx., 1 p.m. Please confirm this is O.K. before I contact the lads.

The main topics to be Trades Councils and the O.A.Pen. Trades Councils and Government in relation to the new rent regulations.

Please ring acceptance as quickly as possible. If more convenient after five my phone number is Ebchester 569.

Best wishes,

Maurice Ridley

P.S That was a shoddy compromise on Saturday to suit Sandra and one or two others. However an across the board claim is the line of march.

NATIONAL FEDERATION of

OLD AGE PENSIONS ASSOCIATIONS

68 Collingwood Street

SOUTH SHIELDS BRANCH

South Shields

Co. Durham

NON-PARTY POLITICAL

UNSECTARIAN

NE33 4JY

Mr J. Grusby.

Thurs. Nov. 25th 1971

Dear Sir,

I regret to inform you that after much discussion, the members of the above organization, decided by vote that they do not wish to be connected with any other organization. We do thank you for all you have tried to do, but the members state that if they should require anything from Social Security they can call on the Federation Officers at any time to help them. Wishing you success in all you do.

Yours Truly

Mrs E. Bunn

Hon. Secretary

The Pensioners Association early got cold feet. As happened in other campaigns the SSTUC soon found itself up against the establishment structures.

SOUTH SHIELDS TRADES UNION COUNCIL

EDE HOUSE, 143 WESTOE ROAD, SOUTH SHIELDS,
CO. DURHAM.

Tel : South Shields 60762
South Shields 60816

Mr. R. Thompson,
Manager, Dept. of Health & Soc. Security,
Wouldhave House,
Market Place,
SOUTH SHIELDS

3rd. Jan 1972

Dear Mr. Thompson,
We have received reports that your visiting officers are informing pensioners that they will not qualify for a winter fuel allowance unless they are bed-ridden.
You will know that this is not in fact the case and that it is simply necessary to prove restricted mobility through " chronic ill-health or through general fraility or advanced age , or (that) the accommodation is damp or otherwise difficult to keep adequately warm". (Supplementary Benefits Handbook 1971)
Further, your X'mas message to pensioners implied that additional allowances for winter fuel, special diets clothing, hire-purchase etc would only be available by the amount that the total of expenses for these items exceeded XXXXX the 50p. which is already added to long term cases such as pensioners.
We would remind you that this 50p is added to all long term cases "to provide a margin over and above the basic requirements for extra expense of the kind which may be expected to arise in the generality of long term cases". The 50p is therefore made available to cover many contingencies and while it is required to be "taken into account" in considering the need for extra allowances the total amount of 50p cannot fairly be placed against any single item such as fuel.
Your press statement and the advice of your officers has already deterred many pensioners from claiming extra allowances. We deplore the fact that again the attitude of your department seems to be motivated by a desire to disallow benefits - rather than to seek the means of helping people some of whom are in desperate need. We would remind you that between 60,000 and 90,000 old people die unecessarily each year through hypethermia.
We are making this letter available to the press in the hope of correcting misunderstanding. We hope that you will find some way of publicising pensioners rights in this respect and of encouraging them to claim extra allowances.

Yours sincerely

Jack Grassby, Secretary

The campaign takes direction. The anomaly was exposed whereby a heating allowance could be awarded, and then payment disallowed. This proved a useful focus for the campaign.

118

Ministry of Social Security

(MSS)

Reference
013O 67200

.................13/1/196.72.

Dear Sir or Madam,

Ministry of Social Security Act 1966
Supplementary Pension—Notice of Determination

The Supplementary Benefits Commission have decided that you are entitled to a supplementary pension of an amount which when added to your retirement pension *(including the increase of retirement pension paid to you in respect of your wife), will equal the amount shown on the orders in the enclosed order-book. † The order-book therefore covers the combined amount of retirement pension and supplementary pension payable. *It has been decided to allow you 50p per week towards extra heating duty as you are already in receipt of 50p special addition there will be no change in amount payable.*

The weekly amount of retirement pension *(and increase of retirement pension) included in each order is shown on the coloured notice inside the front cover of the order-book.

If you would like a full explanation of the way in which your supplementary pension has been worked out I shall be glad to send you one—you can ask for this on the enclosed blue form.

You have the right of appeal to the local Appeal Tribunal against the decision of the Commission. If you wish to appeal you should let me know within twenty-one days of the date of this letter.

† *Please note that the first order includes arrears of*...........................

S.P.3/1C   ° *Delete if inappropriate*   (P.T.O.)

A typical decision by the DHSS which awarded an increase in benefits with one hand – and took it away with the other.

Clarify rules on heating aid for old, urges MP

IN VIEW of some obscurities about the basis on which the Supplementary Benefits Commission pays heating allowances to elderly people who are also in receipt of the special long-term allowance, Mr Arthur Blenkinsop, MP for South Shields, has asked for a clarification of the rules.

MR PAUL DEAN

He has sent Mr Paul Dean, Joint Parliamentary Secretary, Health and Social Security, details of an application by a South Shields pensioner who was allowed the 50p - a - week special heating allowance, but was told on the same form that it was cancelled out by the fact that a 50p long-term allowance had already been granted.

"I have asked Mr Dean to look into the position in South Shields because the idea has grown up that it is no good asking for a special heating allowance if one is in receipt of a special long-term allowance."

Damp walls

Mr Blenkinsop is puzzled by one of Mr Dean's statements in the Commons. This was that "in some cases having more money available for heating merely means heating the street or damp walls. We must tackle bad housing as well."

Mr Blenkinsop agrees that bad housing must be dealt with. "But," he commented yesterday, "that takes some time. In the meantime people who live in such conditions are the very people who need proper attention."

Shields Gazette January 1972

Local M.P., Arthur Blenkinsop, was an early supporter of the campaign.

Rulebook robs pensioners of extra benefit

By ROSALIND MORRIS

A campaign to encourage pensioners to claim extra social security allowances for heating, clothing, household equipment, and redecoration has shown that many old people are prevented by regulations from receiving these benefits, Mr Jack Grassby, secretary of South Shields Trades Council, said yesterday.

The council has distributed 3,000 leaflets to old people in South Shields during the last two months and more than 400 pensioners have made claims for special allowances.

Mr Grassby said the campaign had shown "serious anomalies" in the awarding of extra benefits to old people and he claimed that many had not been given correct information about their eligibility to apply.

"Our campaign has shown that the Department of Health automatically subtracts this long-term allowance from any extra allowance granted. This procedure is laid down in the official Supplementary Benefits Handbook and it means that no extra payment is made even when special need has been proved.

"For instance, a pensioner awarded an extra 50p a week for fuel will not receive any change in benefit because the 50p long-term allowance will be automatically subtracted from the award.

"We are hoping the Department of Health will change the rule. It is illogical and unjust to remove an allowance just when extra need has been proved."

Mr Reginald Thompson, manager of the social security offices at South Shields said yesterday that he rejected Mr Grassby's allegation about information being given to pensioners.

He went on: "We have had 419 claims from pensioners in the last two months, of which 386 have been cleared. In 101 of these cases, extra payments ranging from 5p to 80p a week have been made." Some of the other claims dealt with had already been covered by the long-term allowance and therefore no extra benefit had been paid.

The Guardian 10 February 1972

The issue was taken up by the national press.

THE LABOUR PARTY

TRANSPORT HOUSE SMITH SQUARE LONDON SW1P 3JA
TELEPHONE: 01-834 9434
TELEGRAMS: LABREPCOM SOWEST LONDON

GENERAL SECRETARY: H. R. NICHOLAS OBE
HON. TREASURER: Rt Hon L. J. CALLAGHAN MP
ASSISTANT GENERAL SECRETARY: J. G. MORGAN
NATIONAL AGENT: R. G. HAYWARD

TJP/AB/EP

24th January 1972

Mr. Arthur Blenkinsop, M.P.,
House of Commons,
London, S.W.1.

Dear Mr. Blenkinsop,

With regard to your enquiry about the Senior Citizens Benefits handout prepared by the South Shields Trades Council and the South Shields Claimants Union, the following points are of importance.

These are quotes from the Supplementary Benefits Handbook 1971 edition, para. 77, 78 and 79 page 23.

Paragraph 77 "The Commission has power to award to people entitled to Supplementary Benefit a single payment of benefit to meet an exceptional need, where it appears to them reasonable in all the circumstances to do so. Such payments are for exceptional needs arising on single occasions as opposed to continuing special expenses which are provided for in the weekly payment of benefit".

Paragraph 78 "In deciding whether to award an exceptional needs payment, the Commission may take account of any resources which would otherwise be disregarded, including any capital a person may have. The Commission, however, normally ignores capital of up to £100 in considering an exceptional need. And only if there were a savings of more than this amount which are available and sufficient to meet the need will a payment normally be refused on these grounds."

Paragraph 79 "Claimants for help with exceptional needs arise in a variety of circumstances which might justify a payment. Each claim is considered in a light of individual and local circumstances, but the main factors governing the award of lump sum payments are whether the need is a normal requirement i.e. whether it is covered by the basic scale rate or whether it is essential; and whether the person is already in a position to meet the need from disregard sources (on the basis explained in para. 78)".

As you will see from the above, the main point to be taken from this handbook is that these extra payments are discretionary and it is up to the Commission whether or not the claimant is entitled to them. Seen in these terms this document is misleading insofar as it states that, and I quote, "It is your right to claim the new price of essential household goods etc." To cite a few specific examples from the pamphlet the reference made to clothing allowances refers to paragraph 80 of the Benefits Handbook. This paragraph specifically states that this allowance for clothing and indeed for footwear, the second example used in the pamphlet, can be obtained only under exceptional circumstances or under exceptional conditions. Similarly, examples 3 and 4 which refer to bedding and household equipment it is made quite clear in the handbook that they are payable under exceptional circumstances or, if repair of the bedding and household equipment is impossible or if they are being bought for the first time. With regard to removal expenses, example 5 in the leaflet, the handbook again says that these are payable only if the removal is for a good reason, and in most cases the local authority would be more likely to be liable for the expenses incurred not the Supplementary Benefits Commission.

The main point of this pamphlet is the so called Winter Fuel Allowance. It correctly quotes the relevant section of the handbook, but like most of the other benefits cited, this is again a discretionary payment and is hedged in the same way as all the others, that is by paragraph 79 quoted above. Presumably, therefore, what the local D.H.S.S. office have done is to investigate the claims lodged with them and have found that a number of them, perhaps the majority, are not entitled to an extra fuel allowance or indeed any other kind of allowance because of the conditions laid down in this document. There is of course a right of appeal against refusal to grant supplementary benefit or payments over and above supplementary benefit: If it was felt that in the case of South Shields, discretion had been unfairly excercised, then it might be worthwhile considering whether an appeal should be lodged on behalf of one of the claimants whose claim was turned down.

I hope this information satisfactorily answers the questions by the department's refusal to grant these additional allowances.

If we can be of any further assistance, please let me know.

Yours sincerely,

Terry J. Pitt
<u>Research Secretary</u>

The national Labour Party made a bureaucratic contribution.

HOUSE OF COMMONS
OFFICIAL REPORT
(HANSARD)

Heating Allowances

20. **Mr. Blenkinsop** asked the Secretary of State for Social Services how many extra heating allowances had been paid by the Supplementary Benefits Commission at the latest available date ; and in how many cases this allowance is being paid in addition to the special long-term allowance.

Mr. Dean: At November, 1970, 196,000 allowances were in payment ; and in 181,000 cases the long-term addition, which covers special needs up to the level of 50p a week, was payable as well. Further figures reflecting the recently improved levels of heating allowances will be available in the Spring.

Mr. Blenkinsop : Is the Minister aware that in some cases of which I have evidence the extra allowance for heating is being denied because the long-term addition is being paid? Will he make clear his Department's welcome of the efforts made by bodies such as the trades council and others in my constituency to try to bring to the attention of old people the allowances available for them?

Mr. Dean : I am grateful for what the hon. Gentleman says. We are doing that in the review of benefits now taking place. Each book, each individual case, is being looked at carefully to see whether more help may be available. But the extra heating allowances are special allowances available over and above the long-term addition for those who have special needs for them.

Dame Irene Ward : This is a very important matter which has already been raised from the North. When will my hon. Friend be in a position to let us have some information? I am very grateful to him for the inquiries being made. Other people have been concerned with the matter for a considerable time.

Mr. Dean : I am much obliged to my hon. Friend for the details of cases she has sent me, which are being reviewed. It is clear from them that there is a great deal more to learn about this age-old problem than we yet know.

Mr. R. C. Mitchell : Is there not a need for a big extension of the heating allowances to a much wider range of pensioners on supplementary benefit, particularly in view of the increase in the price of gas and electricity, and possibly of coal?

Mr. Dean : My right hon. Friend the Secretary of State will certainly consider that. But it is a wider problem, because in some cases having more money available for heating merely means heating the street or damp walls. We must tackle bad housing as well.

HANSARD 22 February 1972

The issue was taken to the floor of the House of Commons.

From: The Rt. Hon. E. Fernyhough MP

HOUSE OF COMMONS

LONDON, SW1

22nd February 1972.

Dear Jack,

<u>Mrs. ███. ████████</u> Princess Street, Jarrow.

You will recall that you passed on to me a letter you had received from the above constituent of mine who had applied for a fuel allowance and had been turned down.

I approached the Department of Health & Social Security on her behalf and I am afraid I have been no more successful than you were. I am, however, enclosing a copy of the reply I received to my representations from which you will see that Mrs. ████████ received some little extra benefit as a consequence of having, in the first place, written to you.

Sorry I could not stay any longer last Saturday. I was due in Newcastle at 6.30 pm.

Very best wishes,

Yours sincerely,

Ernie

Mr. J. Grassby,
South Shields Trades Union Council.

Local MPs supported the campaign making representation to the DHSS and the Secretary for Health and Social Security (Keith Joseph).

HOUSE OF COMMONS
LONDON SWIA OAA

23rd February, 1972

Dear Jack,

I enclose copy of the reply I have
had to a question in the House yesterday.

Although the figures are out of
date it seems to suggest that 90% of
those getting heating allowances were
also in receipt of the long-term addition.

I have therefore sent the Minister
a copy of the determination in the South
Shields case. I will also follow up the
Block Release cases.

Yours sincerely,

*Where in effect the
heating allce was denied,
because a long term addition
was in payment.*

Arthur Blenkinsop

Mr. J. Grassby,
Red House,
Westoe Village,
Co. Durham.

TRADES UNION CONGRESS

GENERAL SECRETARY: VICTOR FEATHER CBE

CONGRESS HOUSE · GREAT RUSSELL STREET · LONDON WC1B 3LS

Telephone 01-636 4030   *Telegrams* TRADUNIC LONDON WC1

March 22   1972

DEPT   Social Insurance
OUR REF PJ/SHC
YOUR REF

Mr J Grassby
Secretary
South Shields Trades Union Council
Ede House
143 Westoe Road
South Shields
Co Durham

Dear Mr Grassby

Supplementary Benefit: Heating Allowance

Thank you for your letter of January 26, 1972 about
the above.

As you will know, the General Council have been
pressing for changes in the Supplementary Benefit
scheme, so that extra allowances are not offset
against the long term addition. They are continuing
their efforts in this field as part of the National
Council of Labour's campaign 'Care of the Elderly'.

The root of the problem is, of course, the need for
nearly one in three pensioners to rely on means tested
Supplementary Benefit. By it's very nature the scheme
is largely discretionary. As a matter of interest,
the S.B.C. has resisted attempts by many organisations,
including the TUC to publish their Codes, particularly
the 'A' Codes. The nearest we have got, is the S.B.
Handbook which for all its limitations, is, in my
view, extremely useful.

We shall be writing separately on the question of
finance to produce leaflets.

If I may say so, your leaflet is very good indeed.

Yours sincerely

Secretary, Social Insurance Department

*The TUC letter which revealed the existence of secret DHSS codes of
practice – the 'A' Codes.*

HOUSE OF COMMONS
OFFICIAL REPORT
(HANSARD)

I turn now to special heating needs for old people and others on supplementary benefit. As from 1st October extra heating allowances will be paid on top of the new rates of supplementary benefit, instead of being offset against the long-term addition. Thus, for the first time, supplementary benefit recipients will be entitled to the full amount of any additional heating allowance awarded because of their individual circumstances. The Supplementary Benefits Commission intends to apply this provision to all cases where a need for extra heating has been identified but offset in the past. This will be done as they come up for normal review. It is estimated that over 400,000 supplementary benefit recipients may benefit, at a cost in a full year of about £6 million.

HANSARD 7 March 1973
The Secretary of State for Social Security (Sir Keith Joseph)

Keith Joseph succumbed to the pressure and agreed that the heating allowance would not be offset against other benefits.

The 1972 & 1974 Miners' Strikes

The 1972 and 1974 miners' strikes afforded the opportunity for the Trades Union Council to engage in action in accordance with its policy of direct action.

The Trades Union Council provided all the traditional forms of support in its expression of solidarity. Public collections were made, public meetings were addressed and local trade union branches were called upon to respect the miners' picket lines. The public were urged to send cash, clothing and food to the miners' strike committee, and local traders were encouraged to provide cheap goods to striking miners.

More unconventional support was provided by the Trades Union Council's campaign to maximise energy use. In 1974 national coal stocks were running low and the Heath government, in something like desperation, introduced a government campaign to save fuel using the slogan – 'Switch it off'. Local town councils were urged by government to save fuel by switching off street lights and lights in public buildings. Few councils in the North seemed to respond. The Trades Union Council sought to encourage the public to use <u>more</u> energy and introduced its own campaign – 'Switch it on'. The public were urged to switch lights on and to leave them burning at night.

The 1974 strike was, in many ways, a re-run of the 1972 strike, and lessons learned then were applied to a range of industrial disputes. The most unconventional and most direct intervention from the Trades Union Council came in the form of help to striking miners to maximise their claim to social security supplementary benefits. This was achieved by facilitating and legitimising, the services of the Claimants Union to the miners' 'Strike Claims Committee'. This action was important to provide the financial help to strikers to survive, but also to boost their moral by allowing each miner to feel that he was playing a direct role in the strike process.

The Department of Health and Social Security officials had set up a claims sub-office in the miners head-quarters, the Armstrong Hall, in South Shields. The miners had been persuaded by the SSTUC to set up a 'Strike Claims Committee' to assist each miner in his claim for benefits. The Claimants Union acted as 'advisers' to this Committee and helped to provide a personal adviser (technically 'a friend') to accompany each miner when claiming. In this way precedents were set for the payment of 'urgent needs' benefits for rent, fuel, clothing, etc. The news of any new payment was quickly spread to all miners, locally and nationally.

The confrontation between miners and DHSS officials became fraught at times and on one notable occasion, with unconscious irony, the DHSS officials withdrew their labour.

A measure of the success of the co-operative action came after the 1972 strike when, in reply to a parliamentary question by Arthur

Westoe Colliery, South Shields, in 1972.

Armstrong Hall, Stanhope Road, South Shields.

Blenkinsop MP, it was revealed that, per capita, single miners in South Shields had received five times more in payment of supplementary benefits than in the rest of the coalfields.

In December 1973 the Heath government desperate to preserve coal stocks introduced a national 3-dayworking week. In an accompanying campaign the Trades Union Council and the Claimants Union encouraged all workers on the 3-day week to claim unemployment benefit for the period they were 'laid off'.

The miners' strikes united the whole Labour movement with the mining communities and, as the 1974 general election was to show, with the majority of the country.

An informed account of the demise of the British coal industry has been written by a then member of the Trades Union Council, Mike Peel, *Westoe: The Last Pit on the Tyne*. The book was commissioned by Westoe Colliery Campaign Group and is available from South Shields Central Library.

THE COAL STRIKE

Security staff is accused of 'callous denial'

A COMMITTEE which represents thousands of coal strikers in South Shields and outlying areas today accused Department of Health and Social Security officials in South Shields of "a deliberate, callous refutation" of the letter and spirit of a section of the 1966 Social Security Act. But the Department denies this:

The Strike Claimants' Committee — set up on behalf of strikers from Westoe and Boldon Collieries and Monkton Coke Works — claims that single strikers, who have proved urgent need are not being paid immediately and that this is contrary to the Social Security Act.

And it demanded an end to the practice of the local Department through which single men are told to get support from their family; facilities in strike centres for immediate payment to anyone "in urgent need," and publication of "secret regulations constantly referred to by local staff."

Same procedure

The statement has been answered by Mr Reg Thompson, manager of the Department of Health and Social Security in South Shields, who told the Shields Gazette:

"The same procedure for payment of benefit is being followed in all strike claim centres. There is a limit to what this office can do within the staff and accommodation available.

"To have provided immediate payment facilities at the strike centre would have created administration and security problems and resulted in delays in payment generally. In fact, all payments due on claims made last week, including those made by single men, were posted by Friday evening at the latest.

There have been difficulties over the last week due to action at the centre and problems of communication, but now the system is settling down. Additional experienced staff from other areas have been drafted in and delays are being reduced to a minimum.

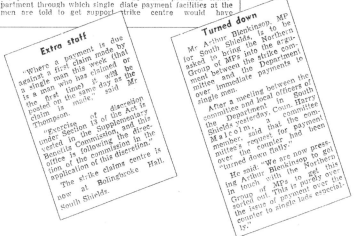

Extra staff

"Where a payment is due against a first claim made by a single man this week (that is a man who has claimed or the first time) it will be posted on the same day as the claim is made," said Mr Thompson.

"Exercise of discretion under Section 13 of the Act is vested in the Supplementary Benefits Commission, and this office is following the direction of the commission in the application of this discretion."

The strike claims centre is now at Bolingbroke Hall, South Shields.

Turned down

Mr Arthur Blenkinsop, MP for South Shields, is to be asked to bring the Northern Group of MPs into the argument between the strike committee and the Department over immediate payments to single men.

After a meeting between the committee and local officers of the Department in South Shields yesterday, Coun. Harry Malcolm, a committee member, said that the committee's request for payment over the counter had been "turned down flatly."

He said: "We are now pressing Arthur Blenkinsop to get in touch with the Northern Group of MPs to get this sorted out. This is purely over the issue of payment over the counter to single lads especially."

Striking miners soon experienced the same problems as single parents in claiming 'urgent need' social security payments.

The government had thought it had effectively stopped the right to social security payments to strikers by their 1971 Act. The miners and the Claimants Union, showed they had got it wrong. The 'urgent needs' clause gave a loop-hole which was vigorously exploited.

Shields Gazette
and Shipping Telegraph

HOME

No. 33246 (Established 1849)   Saturday, January 29, 1972   2½p.

MP JOINS BATTLE

He tackles dispute on benefits

THE COAL STRIKE

MR ARTHUR BLENKINSOP, MP for South Shields, has stepped into a controversy over striking miners' social security rights and is taking up the men's case "both locally and nationally."

Mr Blenkinsop told the Shields Gazette today that last night he met representatives of the miners' claimants committee set up as part of the strike committee and discussed some of the complaints the men had made.

"The first thing is that this strike is the first major dispute where the new 1971 Tory Social Security Act and the tighter regulations affecting Social Security allowances, so far as strikers are concerned, have been in force.

"This is the first major test for the operation of these stricter rules that were applied recently. Nevertheless, it should still be made quite clear that single men on strike can still claim an allowance 'where they are in urgent need.

MP CONCERNED ABOUT RULES

By Our Political Staff

SOCIAL SECURITY officials paying out special allowances to miners in urgent need as a result of the strike, are interpreting the rules differently in various parts of the country, according to Mr Arthur Blenkinsop, MP for South Shields.

He has written to Social Services Secretary, Sir Keith Joseph, expressing his concern about difficulties that have arisen in South Shields.

"It appears," he wrote, "that many of those who are being granted allowances in view of their urgent need, are being told that these payments must be refunded.

"While I can understand that repayments can properly be asked for where there is some element of duplication of payment, it does not seem to arise in these cases, nor do I gather that in other parts of the country, this requirement is being made.

MUCH HIGHER

"Refunds are required in connection with payments made after a return to work. That is not the present position."

One of the main items for which specific allowances were being claimed was rent—often due to the local authority. An arbitrary sum of £4 or £4.50 was being allowed, even although in many cases the rent might be a good deal higher.

There seemed to be no general ruling on this matter said Mr Blenkinsop.

"It does seem to be that some difficulties that have arisen in South Shields may have developed from heavy pressure that I can quite understand your staff having to face at this time," added Mr Blenkinsop.

NO LIMITATION

"I hope that in these circumstances there will be no limitation on the need to recruit extra staff where this is required."

Mr Blenkinsop told the Shields Gazette that he understood that, in Derbyshire, for instance, Social Security officials were not insisting on repayment.

"I have been in touch with the chairman of the Parliamentary Labour Party, Mr Douglas Houghton, in the hope that the matter can be taken up officially by the Shadow Cabinet and the Opposition," he said.

"I have also applied to the Speaker, Mr Selwyn Lloyd, for permission to raise the matter myself in a special debate at an early date."

Shields Gazette 3 February 1972

The local M.P, Arthur Blenkinsop, appreciated the significance of benefit payments to strikers, and strongly supported the campaign.

about £1 million a week, to subsidise the creation of additional unemployment? Will my hon. Friend look again at the workings of the 1971 Act and consider the case for returning to the Labour Government's 1948 Act and the provision for the establishment of need?

Mr. Dean: We intend to keep the working of the 1971 Act under close review, but I must remind my hon. Friend that, because in most cases there is no strike pay or tax refund, the main part of the Act does not apply. The part which will apply in a few months' time, namely, no payment after people have gone back to work, is also not relevant to the figures I have given because the men are still on strike.

Mr. Ashton: Will the hon. Gentleman enlarge on the position of single miners who are on strike, particularly those whose parents are retired and who are receiving no income although they have previously paid a substantial proportion of their wages in tax? Will he give an assurance that single miners who are suffering genuine hardship will receive assistance and not be told to become strike breakers and go back to work?

Mr. Dean: The law for many years now, administered by Governments of all political colours, has been that money should not be available to single men who are on strike unless hardship is proved. Where hardship is proved, money is available, and I quoted a figure of over £3,000 which has already been paid during this strike under that category.

Mr. Hiley: Will my hon. Friend consider the means by which this money can be repaid after the strike is over?

Mr. Dean: The 1971 Act has considerably tightened the conditions on which money can be made available. Before any further review, I think we should wait a little longer to see how the Act works.

Mr. Fernyhough: Does not the hon. Gentleman realise that there has never been a miners' strike which has had such public support as this one has and that he must turn a deaf ear to his hon. and right hon. Friends who would like to repeat the experience of 1926? The

11 H 28

miners will not go back until they get justice, and it is up to the hon. Gentleman to see that they get as generous treatment as anyone else from the Supplementary Benefits Commmission.

Mr. Dean: The hon. Gentleman will not draw me into discussing the merits of the strike. The job of my Department is to administer the law, and I am sure the whole House will agree that the officers of my Department have been doing a very effective job under difficult circumstances in administering the law and giving the due assistance to the wives and children of strikers.

Mrs. Castle: Is the hon. Gentleman satisfied that other sections of his Department are not being mobilised to help strike breaking? Is he aware that local medical committees have been informed by his Department that regional medical officers are to speed up the scrutiny of claims for sickness benefit from miners as a group, and that they will call miner's for medical examination without waiting for a report from the miner's own doctor? Is not this an intolerable interference in the clinical judgment of doctors and the rights of miners under the health service in support of a policy designed to break the strike?

Mr. Dean: That is an entirely different question. I will of course consider what the right hon. Lady said, but I hope that she will agree that the special arrangements we have made to administer the law and to see that strikers' families receive their due benefit under the law are deserving of tribute to the officers concerned.

Mr. Bruce-Gardyne: On a point of order. In view of the terms of my hon. Friend's reply, I beg to give notice that I shall seek to raise the matter on the Adjournment at an early opportunity.

Dental Services

16. **Mr. Dormand** asked the Secretary of State for Social Services whether he will take steps to arrange for the provision of facilities for emergency dental treatment over holiday periods.

49. **Mr. Edward Lyons** asked the Secretary of State for Social Services whether he will take steps to provide funds for the operation of an emergency dental service in Bradford.

HANSARD 1 February 1972

Barbara Castle raised the question of sickness benefit rights of strikers – an area also exploited by the miners and the Claimants Union.

THE COAL STRIKE

Minister assures:
'No secrecy on benefit'

MINISTER for industry, Sir John Eden, denied in the Commons that secret instructions had been issued by the Government for miners on strike to get less supplementary benefit than other claimants.

The allegation was made during the coal industry debate by Mr Ernest Fernyhough (Lab. Jarrow). who raised the subject on behalf of Mr Arthur Blenkinsop (Lab. South Shields).

"There is a feeling in mining areas that the Government are so bitter and annoyed by the miners' action that they have issued instructions that they are to be treated less fairly and justly in their applications for supplementary benefit than ordinary citizens," said Mr Fernyhough.

Were any special instructions sent out? "I should like the Minister to make clear whether any secret instructions were sent out to the Supplementary Benefit Commission regarding payment to strikers," he challenged.

Rent benefit

In Jarrow and South Shields a strike claimants committee had done a remarkable job advising claimants who were unable to make adequate representations.

"That committee has made some discoveries. For instance, why was a limit put on the amount of rent benefit that a striker could claim when such a limit did not apply to other applicants? Why were single miners treated less generously than other single men applying for benefit?" asked Mr Fernyhough.

"What are the secret regulations?. There is the deep seated feeling that somebody with authority is so prejudiced and bitter towards the miners that he is determined to make them go through the experience of 1926 by harsher, less generous treatment through the Supplementary Benefits Commission than other applicants."

Some way

Replying, the Minister assured Mr Fernyhough there had been no special instructions sent out and that nothing of the kind had been done at all.

"I have made inquiries since he raised this matter and I can assure him that no special instructions of any kind have been given. These strikers are being treated in exactly the same way as strikers in any other industry would be treated," asserted Sir John.

In his speech, Mr Fernyhough declared it was obvious that the Government had miscalculated the temper and spirit of the miners, and they had also misled the general public. It was said that

SIR JOHN EDEN
"Same treatment"

there were mountains of coal, that no one would suffer and that the miners would gradually be compelled to return to work because no one would notice the effect of the strike.

The Government could no longer hide from the public how very serious and damaging to the nation the strike was becoming, and they could not absolve themselves from all blame.

"The Government know that if there is any body of workers which has been socially responsible through the post-war years, it is the miners. There was a time when coal was as precious as jobs are today. The miners never took advantage of their power to squeeze from the consumer, or the country, what market forces would have enabled them to do.

Arduous work

"They held back. They were responsible. No body of men has ever stood by and seen an industry run-down as rapidly as the miners without any sit-ins and great industrial upheaval."

It was a poor tribute to what the miners had done for the Government to act so bluntly, harshly and indefensibly.

"If the miners could have had what the motor car workers had received in pay rises this week, there would have been no strike, but the Government had no power to interfere with the car workers' settlement, and they had got a wage increase twice as big as that offered to the miners.

Shields Gazette 9 February 1972

The Jarrow M.P., Ernie Ferryhough, joined the argument enthusiastically.

HOUSE OF COMMONS
LONDON SWIA OAA

12th April, 1972

Dear Jack,

I enclose copy of a letter I have
had from the Town Clerk which does suggest
that the miners' pressure with regard to
housing allowances during the strike has
at last forced a decision through on the
long standing question of the level of
housing allowances for people on
supplementary benefit. I think it is
worth noting that action taken especially
for the miners does seem to have helped
this much wider group of people.

Yours sincerely,

Arthur Blenkinsop

Mr. Jack Grassby,
The Red House,
Westoe Village,
South Shields

*An example of the spin-off benefits from the direct action taken during
the 1972 miners strike.*

THE COAL STRIKE

Voucher gifts to the strikers

DURHAM miners facing hunger through their month-old strike are to be given a weekly supply of 50 £1 food vouchers by sympathetic among the most deserving fellow trade unionists.

Members of the General and Municipal Workers Union at the Royal Ordnance factory at Birtley are to give the Durham NUM vounchers which will be distributed cases of miners suffering under the strike.

They told miners' leaders that the weekly supply of vouchers would continue as long as the strike lasted

Pupils at Jarrow's Hedworthfield Secondary School, were back today in the expectation of coal being delivered to add to the small supply left.

Coal supplies have been delivered to Hebburn's Clegwell and St. James RC SChools and it is hoped that pupils will be able to return within a few days when heating systems are back to normal.

COMMITTEE DEMANDS REJECTED

MINERS claim that the Department of Health and Social Security has "snubbed" a committee which represents thousands of strikers in South Shields and outlying areas of the town.

Last Friday a busload of men visited the regional headquarters of the department at Gosforth and members of the local Strike Claimants Committee put three demands to the regional controller and his assistants.

They were—an end to the departments' practice of instructing single men to get their family to support them; facilities in Bolingbroke Hall, South Shields for immediate payment to those in urgent need, and the publication of "secret" regulations which the committee claims give local managerial staff power to "systematically refuse" to meet urgent needs in full.

The department has now replied. It says 'no' to the first and second demands and that the question of publicity was under consideration nationally.

A spokesman for the committee said: "As far as we're concerned that's another snub. We will discuss it."

Free soccer at Shields

SOUTH SHIELDS Football Club have decided to admit all local miners on strike free of charge to Saturday's Northern Premier League game against Lancaster City at Simonside Hall.

Says club chairman, Coun. Jack Leighton: "We know that many of our suporters are miners and that at this time they haven't much money to spend. We feel the least we can do is to help out by letting them into Saturday's match free of charge on production of their union card,

Shields Gazette 9 February 1972

Any payments, in cash or in kind, to striking miners, could be deducted from social security payments. Creative accountancy by the miners found ways around this problem.

MINERS OFFERED REDUCED PRICES

MANY shopkeepers and traders in South Shields have started to offer reduced prices and other concessions to striking miners and their familes. This action is in reponse to a call from the South Shields Trade Union Council strike liaison committee asking them to do what they can for the strikers. Several working men's clubs are providing free soup and are considering ways of giving cheap beer.

Other offers range from cheap hair styling to reduced price fish and chips. One hairdresser's shop is offering half price permanent waving and shampooing, and men's haircuts for 10p in the afternoons.

UNION CARDS

A spokesman for the liaison committee said: "Many shopkeepers have offered reduced rates to their own miner customers but others have offered concessions to all miners and their families on the presentation of a National Union of Mineworkers trade union card."

He advised miners and their families to take their union cards with them when shopping and to ask if special terms are being offered to miners.

He also asked local shopkeepers to notify the committee at 143 Westoe Road if they are prepared to offer special terms.

Shields Gazette February 1972

Public sympathy and support was massive. The Trades Union Council encouraged local traders to allow concessionary rates to miners.

SOUTH SHIELDS TRADES UNION COUNCIL
STRIKE LIASON COMMITTEE

PRESS STATEMENT 7TH FEB .1972

SMALL SHOPKEEPERS HELP STRIKERS

Many small local shopkeepers and traders answered the
call made by the Strike Liason Committee to help striking miners
and their families by offering special reduced prices or concessionary terms.
Several Working Mens Clubs are providing free soup and are
considering ways of making available cheap beer.
Other offers range from cheap hair do's to reduced price
fish and chips.
Many shopkeepers have offered reduced rates to their own
miner customers but others have offered consessions to all
miners and their families on the presentation of an N.U.M trade
union card.
Examples include :-
   J.&.M. Reynolds , 260 Green Lane - reduced price
       groceries and special offeres.

   Vera Bulmar , 212 South Frederick St., - half
       price permenant waving & shampooing
       Mens hair cutting - 10p.
       Afternoons only.

   Webbs Fish Shop, 1 Redhead St., - reduced price
       fish & chips.

All miners and their families are advised to take their union
card with them when shopping and to ask if special terms are
being offered to miners.
Local shopkeepers are asked to notify the Liason Committee
at 143 Westoe Rd., if they are prepared to offer special terms.

        Jack Grassby
        Secretary
           Strike Liason
           Committee.

*Ultimately, most private businesses offered concessionary rates to striking miners
on production of their union card.*

FREE-MEALS OPERATION HELPS KEEP THE COUNTY SCHOOLS OPEN

Heating restored

AN EMERGENCY operation to ensure that the children of striking miners get free school meals has helped to keep County Durham schools open despite fuel shortages. Ald. John Coxon, the County Education chairman, reported that an extra 11,000 youngsters were taking free meals after parents had been told that loss of income due to the strike qualified them for the concession.

He explained, at a Press conference after the meeting of the education committee that he believed their efforts had played a part in getting clearance from pickets at Dawdon Colliery for coal supplies to schools closed due to fuel shortages.

Earlier in the meeting he said the possibility of getting a supply of drift coal for the worse-hit schools on South Tyneside had faded when they were told this had been earmarked for hospitals. But now they were hoping to get clearance for coal from Dawdon.

Ten tons of coal had been taken to Hebburn Clegwell and St. James's RC secondary school and it was hoped the other secondary schools could be similarly reopened. If supplies continued they would also be able to open the eight primary schools affected.

TENANTS of more than 300 flats in sky-scraper blocks and maisonettes at Sunderland are to have their heating and hot water supplies restored.

The miners' liaison committee has agreed to release coal supplies from Dawdon Colliery for the district heating system at Gilley Law which went off more than a week ago when the coal ran out.

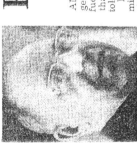

DR LEITCH
"Emergency centres"

Plan to ease the plight of sick and aged

EMERGENCY centres for pensioners and sick people in South Shields may be set up to alleviate any hardship caused by the miners' strike. Dr Ian Leitch, Director of Social Services for the town, said today he would be reporting to the Social Services Committee tonight about the prospect of setting up emergency centres.

Shields Gazette 10 February 1972

Shields Gazette, Friday, February 4, 1972—13

THE COAL STRIKE

Shields unions call for big one-day walkout

SOUTH SHIELDS trade unionists have called for a national one-day general strike in support of the miners' strike. Trade union officers from 48 local branches made the call at a special meeting convened by the South Shields Trades Union Council Strike Liaison Committee, at Armstrong Hall. They unanimously passed the resolution as the first step towards supporting strike action by all trade unionists.

The branch officers agreed to take action through their individual unions to get support for the call.

The meeting also appealed to all trade unionists to isolate all building and plants picketed by the miners, by refusing to cross any picket lines.

The treasurer of the liaison committee, Mr Fred Pringle, told the meeting that support for the miners had been "widespread, generous and enthusiastic."

Many gifts

"It reflects a common interest in the miners' struggle and a strong traditional sympathy by workers in the region with the mining community. It is now necessary to co-ordinate and channel this support on a sustained basis," he said.

Mr Pringle reported many donations and gifts of food for the strikers including £100 from Readhead's shop stewards' committee, £25 from Reyrolle's shop stewards' committee, £10 from the Labour Party West Ward, £10 from the Marsden Inn Folk Club and £10 from the South Shields No. 1 branch of the Amalgamated Union of Engineering Workers.

Many other donations had been sent direct to the NUM national strike fund, he said.

Volunteers in bid to help the old folk

SOME old and infirm people in Jarrow and Hebburn entitled to priority supplies of fuel during the miners' strike are unable to make personal applications. So volunteer organisations in the two towns have decided to lend a hand.

The organisations involved are the Inner Wheel, Ladies' Circle, WRVS, Round Table and Rotary Club — and Jarrow Council has agreed to let the organisations use facilities at the town hall.

Members of these groups will visit the homes of the old and infirm and ensure that forms are completed and submitted to the appropriate authority. Where there is evidence of failure to meet genuine priority claims they will also make representations to the National Coal Board and the National Union of Mineworkers.

The organisations are also hoping that churches, over-60's Clubs and other voluntary bodies in Jarrow and Hebburn will join the project.

Names and addresses of those needing help should be submitted by letter or telephone to WRVS, c/o Town Hall, Jarrow, (tel. Jarrow 898271). Volunteers will then visit the people listed and help to complete the claim form.

The call for a national one-day strike was thwarted by victory to the miners—and the end of their strike.

Miners boost strike cost

Sunday Telegraph Reporter

SOCIAL Security payments to strikers may rise sharply if an experiment successfully applied during the miners' strike, which cost £6 million in state benefits, is widely adopted by the big trade unions.

The South Shields office of the Department of Health and Social Security paid out five times more in supplementary benefits to single men with no dependants than any other office in the country, including some with many more miners in their area

The reason for the discrepancy, union officials say, is that the Westoe Lodge of the National Union of Mineworkers was the first to set up a strike claims committee to give its members expert advice on how to prepare their applications.

As a result £4,864 was paid to 308 single men without dependants as well as £76,269 to 1,777 men with families.

Sunday Telegraph 26 March 1972

An unusually frank endorsement, from an unusual source, recording the success of the miners in co-operation with the Trades Union Council and the Claimants Union to pioneer 'Strike Claims Committees.'

Westoe Lodge was the first in the country to set up such a committee. The result was 5 times more paid to single men than elsewhere in the country.

Shields Gazette 27 February 1974

Row breaks on 'miners denied benefit' claim

THE ROW over supplementary benefit payments to single miners on strike in Durham blew up into a national issue last night, after it was claimed that Kent miners were being paid benefit denied to North-East men.

The Prime Minister was asked to step in to the dispute in a telegram sent by Mr Arthur Blenkinsop and Mr Ernest Fernyhough, Labour candidates for South Shields and Jarrow.

In their weekly strike bulletin the South Tyneside Claimants' Union say that miners of Snowdon Colliery in Kent are being paid supplementary benefits which are being refused to the Durham men.

The Claimants' 'union leaflet says that single strikers in Kent are being paid under section 13 of the Social Security Act.

This section says that no other provisions of the Act shall prevent the payment of benefit in an urgent case.

The Claimants' Union says that single strikers who are in urgent need are being denied the same benefits as those in Kent.

Complaints

A mass meeting of single miners was held in the Labour and Workingmen's Social Club, Victoria Road, South Shields, yesterday, to voice complaints about unfairness in the payment of benefits Mr Blenkinsop and Mr Fernyhough were at the meeting.

Afterwards Mr Blenkinsop told the Gazette: "We had put to us a large number of personal problems, where single strikers helping to maintain elderly or disabled parents, paying rent for lodgings or paying maintenance allowance in the case of a separated husband and wife, were denied benefit.

Hardship

"We have promised to take these cases up locally and nationally in order to get a proper interpretation of the Act. There has been a tightening up of the regulations since the 1972 strike, with-

drawing initiative from local and regional officials, done on national instructions.

"In all these cases there is real hardship in our view, and this issue will be followed up nationally in order to ensure that, where there is hardship, the case will be speedily dealt with."

Mr Fernyhough, who suggested sending the joint telegram to Mr Heath, added: "Most of the cases are single people who are being assessed on the basis of their last wage slips, which vary from £19 to £24 gross.

Retain

"They have already exhausted their limited reserves, and the young people in particular are now basically dependent on the charity of relatives and friends.

"At a time when more than ever we need to retain young people in the mines, many of them will be driven to seek alternative employment, with all the dire consequences that that could have for a country which now desperately needs coal.

"It would be tragic if these lads in their late teens and their early twenties decide to leave the mining industry because of the harsh treatment meted out to them during this strike."

Dossier

Most of the questions at the meeting were about the definition of an "urgent case."

Mr Jim Slater, chairman of Harton and Westoe lodge, asked: "Have we to look like someone from Belsen before they'll believe we're hungry?"

The miners' claims committee are compiling a dossier of hardship cases. Examples given at the meeting were of a man and wife who both work for the Coal Board being assessed as single people, a household living on the wife's maternity benefit, and a man supporting his disabled brother.

The arguments over payment of social security benefits to striking miners erupted again in the 1974 strike.

SOUTH TYNESIDE CLAIMANTS UNION   23RD.FEB. 1974

STRIKE BULLETIN No. 1

EMERGENCY PAYMENTS

Already many strikers have been done out of their first weeks benefits. Every striker was entitled to a payment one week after the receipt of their last pay.
YOU COULD HAVE DEMANDED AN EMERGENCY PAYMENT LAST WEEK. SOME STRIKERS DID - AND GOT A PAYMENT. MANY DID NOT EVEN KNOW ABOUT IT.

THIS SHOWS HOW IMPORTANT IT IS TO KNOW YOUR RIGHTS!

SINGLE STRIKERS

Single strikers CAN claim benefits NOW. Some have already got them.
SINGLE MEN AT SNOWDOWN COLLIERY IN KENT HAVE ALREADY BEEN PAID.
THE DHSS LEAFLET SB2 ADMITS THIS . BUT YOU HAVE TO SHOW "URGENT NEED".
You CAN show urgent need - but you will need help and advice as how to do this - and you will have to be prepared to fight the DHSS officials to get them to adopt a reasonable attitude. This CAN be done - the men of Snowdown Colliery have done it already!

The Claimants Union will hold a special discussion meeting to consider the needs of single strikers :
Sat. 23rd Feb.
12.00 Noon
Peoples Place, Derby Ter.

DISCRETIONARY PAYMENTS

The Official Supplementary Benefits Handbook states that the DHSS .."may increase an award of supplementary benefits where there are exceptional circumstances .."
This includes such things as ...HEATING COSTS, H.P. INSTALLMENTS, FOR ESSENTIAL ITEMS,DIET ALLOWANCE, HANDICAPPED DEPENDANTS, NURSERY FEES, GAS AND ELECTRICITY BILLS...PLUS RENT AND RATES IN FULL ..PLUS INSURANCE ,.. PLUS MORGAGE INTEREST.

You have a RIGHT to these and other benefits ... see the Claimants Union leaflet for strikers available at the Peoples Place. BUT ULESS YOU PRESENT YOUR ARGUMENT FOR BENEFITS IN THE PROPER WAY THERE IS A GOOD CHANCE THEY WILL BE REFUSED. IT IS BEST TO GET ADVISE BEFORE YOU MAKE A CLAIM.

CHECK YOUR BENEFITS

A recent survey carried out by Edinburgh University found that 55% of claimants were not receiving correct benefits.
YOU CAN CHECK YOUR BENFITS BY DEMANDING FORM A124A. This sets out how THEY have calculated your benefits. You are entitled to this as a right. When you get this statement of the calculation of your benefits check it yourself against what you think you should be getting. If in doubt consult your Claims Committee or the Claimants Union.

THE SOUTH TYNESIDE CLAIMANTS UNION MEETS TUES. 2.0 -4.0 P.M.
SAT. 11.0 A.M - 1.0 P.M.
PEOPLES PLACE, DERBY TER. SOUTH SHIELDS Tel. 66062.

The CU and SSTUC continued to encourage and aid all strikers' Claims Committees. This leaflet was the first of many 'Bulletins'.

NEW BENEFITS LINE-UP STYLE FOR MINERS

THE Department of Health and Social Security today issued details of 13 special centres set up in the Northern Region to pay benefit during the miners' strike. Miners at Westoe, Boldon and Monkton should report to the Bolingbroke Hall, South Shields, from Thursday morning onwards, as set out below. Men affected by the strike at Hylton, Usworth, Wearmouth, Whitburn Headquarters and Whitburn workshops, should report to the TA centre, Dykelands Road, Roker.

Those from Easington, Elemore, Hawthorn, South Hetton and Thornley should go to the DHSS offices in St. Cuthbert's Road, Peterlee. Those from Vane Tempest, Herrington, Houghton - le - Spring, Eppleton, and coal preparation gangs, to the Vane Tempest Miners' Hall, Seaham.

Those from Dawdon Colliery, Seaham and Murton should call at Dawdon Parish Church Hall, Princess Road, Dawdon.

Avoid queues

For the first time in miners' disputes, a revised alphabetical listing will be used to avoid large queues of miners at benefit claim centres.

Those making claims should attend as near as possible to the half - hour period given below. Claims can be registered from 10.30 a.m. on Thursday.

For that day the claimants with the following surnames should attend at the times in brackets.

Aab - Arc (10.30), Ard - Bam (11.0), Ban - Ben (11.30), Ben Bos (12.0), Bot - Bro (1.30), Bru -Cam (2.0), Can -Chi (2.30), Cho - Con (3.0).

On **Friday** the times and surnames are as follows: Coo - Cro (9.30), Cru - Del (10.0).

Shields Gazette 11 February 1974

To help deal with the growing problem of social security claims the DHSS set up special claims centres.

2—Shields Gazette, Saturday, March 2, 1974

'Strikers being given proper state benefit'

'MORE IN KENT' REPORT DENIED

THE Department of Health and Social Security today denied claims by trade unionists, striking miners and two Tyneside MPs that supplementary benefits were not being paid correctly.

The South Tyneside Claimants' Union has alleged that striking miners in Kent are being paid more benefit than those in County Durham.

And South Shields and Jarrow MPs, Mr Arthur Blenkinsop and Mr Ernest Fernyhough, had written to Mr Heath asking him to sort out the mix-up.

Same rules

The Westoe Claims Committee for the striking miners in South Shields also claims that officials are flouting the rules laid down for paying benefit to single men who are hardship cases.

But a spokesman for the Department of Health and Social Security in Newcastle told the Gazette today: "We have checked these allegations thoroughly and there is no truth in them.

"The same rules apply no matter what part of the country you are in. We have checked with the Kent offices and the claim about extra benefits there is not true."

"If the Kent system was different we would have objected The Supplementary Benefits Commission has told us how to pay the striking miners and we apply those rules," he said.

The arguments over payment of social security benefits continued though the whole period of the 1974 miners strike.

LEAFLET ON HOW TO PUSH CLAIMS

SIX-THOUSAND leaflets are being distributed in South Shields telling workers to press for full benefits if they are on short-time working.

The leaflet was produced by the Claimants' Union, and financed by mechanics at Westoe Colliery.

The Claimants' Union said today that many workers had been "swindled" out of supplementary benefits to which they were entitled.

And it advised workers to set up their own works claims committees to help them get their full benefits.

WHERE IT BELONGS

The leaflet says that short-time working "is an attempt by the Government to put pressure on workers and their families and so blackmail the miners, power, rail and Health Service workers into dropping their demands.

"This leaflet is designed to throw the responsibility for the economic crisis back where it belongs — on the Government's economic policy."

The leaflet explains how to claim unemployment and supplementary benefits, and says: "Often your rights will be refused. This because the officials do not understand their own regulations.

STUDYING IT

"They are overworked and undertrained — and some of them are just bloody-minded. Also they are being manipulated at the top by their political masters for political ends... To beat them we have to know our rights, and organise to get them."

Officials of the Department of Health and Social Security were studying the leaflet today before making any comment.

Shields Gazette 9 June 1974

The Claimants Union revealed that all workers on a 3-day week could claim unemployment benefit for those days they were 'laid off' – an entitlement not foreseen by the government, and which they tried to head off.

(THE RIGHTS OF WORKERS AFFECTED BY INDUSTRIAL ACTION.)

Many workers have now been placed on short time working with a reduction in pay. This is an attempt by the government to put pressure on workers and their families and so blackmail the miners, power, rail and health service workers into dropping their wage demands.

Over the past months wages have been clamped down while prices have soared. The government itself has put up rents, school meals, etc. Meanwhile some profits and dividends have doubled. The miners and others are fighting this unjust policy on behalf of all other workers.

This leaflet is designed to help workers fight off the government's attack, to help the miners and other workers resist the government's blackmail, and to throw responsibility for the economic crisis back where it belongs—on the government's economic policy.

"WORKERS SHOULD DEMAND FROM THEIR EMPLOYER 5 DAYS WORK OR 5 DAYS PAY AND SHOULD PREPARE TO FIGHT FOR THIS BY STRIKES OR FACTORY OCCUPATIONS. MEANWHILE THE FAMILIES OF LOWER PAID WORKERS CAN BE PROTECTED BY CLAIMING THE MAXIMUM SOCIAL SECURITY BENEFITS WHICH ARE THEIRS AS A RIGHT".

Many workers on a reduced working week will now be eligible for a wide range of benefits. THIS LEAFLET TELLS YOU WHAT THEY ARE AND HOW TO GET THEM. It has been produced by the Claimants Union.

UNEMPLOYMENT BENEFIT

ANY person available for work can claim Unemployment Benefit for any period he is not working. If you are laid off 2 days a week say, because of government or other workers action, you can claim 2/6 of the weekly rate of Unemployment Benefit. (This starts after 3 days but Supplementary Benefits can be claimed **immediately**—see below). If you work on a Saturday you can claim 3/6 of the weekly rate.

To claim Unemployment Benefit you should have at least 26 Class One Stamps paid or credited over the past year. If you have 50 stamps you will get full benefits. If you have fewer stamps you will get a reduced benefit. If you are unemployed for TWELVE days you can qualify for extra earnings related benefits.

The basic weekly rates for Unemployment Benefit are set out below:

	£
Single person	7·35
Married woman	5·15
Person under 16	4·05
Wife or other dependant	4·55
First dependant child	2·30
Second dependant child	1·40
Third and other dependant children ...	1·30

How to claim

You should register at an Employment Exchange—AS SOON AS YOU START A PERIOD OF UNEMPLOYMENT.

In **addition** you will also qualify for Supplementary Benefits if your Unemployment Benefit is below the amounts of Supplementary Benefit allowances given below. When you register for Unemployment Benefit you should also apply for **Supplementary Benefit at the same time** by asking for FORM BI. It is important that you do this—particularly if a system of payment of Unemployment Benefit is made by your employer.

ORGANISE

TO GET YOUR FULL ENTITLEMENT IS COMPLICATED AND DIFFICULT. THE ABOVE FIGURES GIVE ONLY AN OUTLINE AND FURTHER DETAILED CALCULATIONS ARE NEEDED IN EACH INDIVIDUAL CASE. FOR EXAMPLE NO ACCOUNT IS TAKEN IN THE ABOVE OF OTHER SOURCES OF INCOME SUCH AS FAMILY ALLOWANCE. ON THE OTHER HAND THE FIRST £2 OF PAY COULD BE DISREGARDED WHEN CALCULATING SUPPLEMENTARY BENEFITS. ALL WORKERS ARE ADVISED TO SET UP THEIR OWN **WORKS CLAIM COMMITTEE** TO HELP THEM SORT OUT THEIR CLAIMS— and then to demand these rights from the Employment Exchange, Social Security Office or Tax Office.

OFTEN YOUR RIGHTS WILL BE REFUSED. This is because the Officials do not understand their own regulations. They are overworked and undertrained—and some of them are just bloody minded! Also they are being manipulated at the top by their political masters for political ends. They will put pressure on you and your family in the hope that YOU will put pressure on the miners and other workers.

TO BEAT THEM WE HAVE TO KNOW OUR RIGHTS—AND ORGANISE TO GET THEM.

If you are not satisfied with your allowance—SAY YOU WANT TO **APPEAL**—and then get help. Further information, assistance and advice can be obtained from South Shields Claimants Union, Peoples Place, Derby Terrace, South Shields. (Tel.: South Shields 65062). Members are available to attend Works meetings to give advice. Works Committees are invited to duplicate this leaflet. Further copies are available, 50p per 100 from Peoples Place.

January, 1974.

Published by the South Shields Claimants Union, Peoples Place, Derby Terrace, South Shields, Co. Durham, with the financial assistance of Westoe Colliery Mechanics (N.U.M.)
Printed by Dean Printing Works, South Shields.

Workers misled on 3-day week claims Union

A CLAIM that employment department officials had attempted to mislead workers over benefits available on a three-day week was strongly denied today in South Shields. An official of the Shields Claimants' Union told the Gazette: "The Government and the Department of Employment have conspired to swindle thousands of working class families out of up to £10 a week during the first weeks of short-time working."

Shields Gazette 28 December 1973

The claimants say that information given in the press and on television suggests that no benefit can be got for at least a fortnight after short-time working starts.

And they say that department officials could have told the public that supplementary benefits can be paid as soon as short-time begins.

Swift reply

The claimants' union cites the example of a family with three children, where the man earns £25 for a five-day week.

He could claim £10 a week immediately from the Department of Health and Social Security, and this amount on top of three days wages could bring his total income up to or even above his normal wage.

But the claimants are concerned that many workers would not know that this benefit was immediately available. Their attack brought a swift reply from Mr John Gillespie, area manager for the Department of Employment in South Shields.

"I deny we have misled anyone. We have given and will give the correct information about drawing unemployment benefit. The payment of supplementary benefit is a matter for the Department of Health and Social Security.

"They assess what is called "approved needs" but we are not in a position to decide what people's needs are. It is not our job. I will admit it might be better if there was some centralisation of these benefits, but anyone can collect a form for supplementary benefits and it is not hard to apply for them," he said.

In motion

Claimants union officials are suggesting that workers in three-day industries should set the wheels in motion now for claiming maximum social security and other benefits.

They suggest that works and factories should set up claims committees to deal with this on a co-ordinated basis, and they are offering their help through People's Place, Derby Terrace, to any group who wants further help.

How to work less and collect more

WORKERS facing a three-day week have been told how to make a profit out of the country's current crisis.

Their secret is to rake in cash from social security which could top even their normal take-home pay.

So instead of losing on the short-time working, they can spend days at home and be better off than working flat out for a week.

The "legal fiddle" has been designed by the South Shields Claimants Union, one of a number of groups throughout the region dedicated to beating the welfare system's red tape.

Their activities have led to several head-on clashes with Government departments and another is brewing rapidly.

For apart from telling workers how to beat the three-day week, they have accused dole officers of deliberately misleading workers over their rightful claims for benefits.

This is how they say a worker can fatten his thinner wage packet during the short working week.

They give as an example a family with two 13-year-old daughters and a younger child whose father brings home £25 for a five-day working week.

As soon as he is put on a three-day week he can rightfully claim that he is not fully employed and sign the unemployment register at the dole

His unemployment benefit will not be available for up to two weeks but "after signing on" he is entitled to fill in a B1 form avail-able at the dole counter which can be taken round to the Department of Health and Social security.

This would entitle him to £11.65 for himself and his wife, £7.40 for two daughters and £3 for the young child, plus for example £4 rent.

This adds up to £26.05 Since he takes home for three days working only £15 social security is, therefore, obliged to make up his wage to £26.05.

They'll give him £11.05, making him £1.05 better off than if he was working a normal five-day week.

A C.U. spokesman said: "Thousands of people will be entitled to these benefits so they need not suffer during the short working week.

"If they are earning a pittance for three days, the money from social security is rightfully theirs."

But he said dole officers repeatedly failed to inform workers about the avail-ability of the B1 form.

A South Shields Department of Employment spokesman said his staff did not inform workers about social security claims. "We deal only with unemployment claims.

"But social security benefits belong to the Department of Health and Social Security and it is not up to us to advise people about a different department."

Sunday Sun 30 December 1973

The argument on payment of unemployment benefits to workers on the 3-day week became a major national issue.

Dole men didn't 'tell all' on cash

By Journal Reporter

A NORTHERN dole official admitted last night that his staff has not "told all" to three-day-a-week workers trying to claim extra cash to make up their thin wage packets.

But he denied that his department deliberately withheld the information to mislead workers put on a short working week during the power crisis.

"My department is only concerned with unemployment benefits. We advise people fully on their rights for these claims," said a spokesman for the Department of Employment at South Shields.

"Workers could make supplementary benefit claims —it depends on their circumstances — but supplementary benefits belong to the Department of Health and Social Security and we cannot offer advice on claims from a different department," he said.

The town's Claimants Union has bitterly attacked the department for allegedly misleading families about their eligibility for social security benefits.

It said thousands of workers had missed out on up to £10 a week during the first weeks of short working time.

"Workers have not been told by the staff of their rights to claim these benefits," said C.U. member, Mr. Jack Grassby.

"We know that there are two departments, but there is obviously no effort between them to co-operate to help a person make up his reduced wage packet."

Newcastle Journal 28 December 1973

The Department of Employment sought to pass the buck to the Department of Social Security.

Heath ponders benefit cuts for strikers

By IAN AITKEN, Political Correspondent

As the nightmare prospect of a two-day or even one-day working week looms ahead, Ministers were yesterday examining a new formula for reducing social security benefits paid to the families of strikers short of cutting them off altogether.

The odds are that such a plan, which has been strongly resisted by the Department of Health and Social Security, would involve special legislation and therefore could not be introduced in time for the start of the threatened strike.

RALLYING ROUND: A march to Trafalgar Square yesterday in support of the miners

The Guardian 28 January 1974

The government, recalling its experience during the 1972 strike, sought a solution by benefit cuts.

'Switch on' call by new action group

A NEW South Tyneside trade union group today urged members of the public to support the miners' strike by switching on electrical appliances and lights. South Tyneside Action Group, made up of trade union officials and council-house tenants, has written to the Town Clerk of South Shields, Mr Robert Young, over what it considers to be over-enthusiasm in complying

Shields Gazette 11 February 1974

Britain's ills send 38,000 packing

AUSTRALIA will have all the migrants it wants this year thanks to the crisis in Britain, according to Australian Immigration Minister Albert Grassby.

But he warned that Australia did not want Britons who were simply escaping from bad conditions.

Arriving home from a six-week overseas trip — which included visits to Britain, Ireland, Holland and Italy — Mr Grassby said in Sydney today the prospects of meeting the 110,000 migrant quota for 1973-74 had been "pretty dismal" before his visit overseas.

"Interest in migration from Europe had died down and it is the situation in Britain that will allow us to reach our target," he said.

Some 38,000 Britons are expected to come to Australia this year. "If there is unemployment in their field and it is likely they can't get jobs they won't be coming," added Mr Grassby

with the Government's emergency heating and lighting restrictions.

The letter calls on Mr Young to order the normal use of electrical power in schools, colleges and offices, and street lighting, consistent with the legal requirements of the emergency regulations.

BUCKET OF COAL

A spokesman for the group said the letter was "the first shot in a campaign to persuade the public not to co-operate in voluntary electricity saving but to "Switch On Something."

"Due to either over-enthusiastic interpretation of the regulations or to a misguided sense of public duty, local authority establishments are implementing electricity savings greater than those called for by the emergency order," the spokesman said.

"Every electric fire or light switched off is equivalent to another bucket of coal being delivered to the power stations, and this is a technical breach of the miners' picket. It is a form of back-door blacklegging.

"It weakens the effect of the miners' action and prolongs the industrial strife," he said.

A town hall spokesman said today that no comment could be made as they had not yet received the action group's letter.

South Shields Trades Council will decide tonight what action it will take to support the miners' strike.

Miners rap dole staff

DOLE office counter staff h a v e been accused of b e i n g incompetent a n d "bloody-minded."

And the accusation has been printed on 6,000 leaflets d i s t r i b u t e d throughout South Shields.

The criticism comes from a group of miners who have bitter memories of their battle with dole officials during their strike last year.

So, to help 1,800 workers in South Shields who have been put on short-time, they have produced their own leaflet — on how to beat Department of Employment "red tape."

And their regard for the staff is bluntly expressed in the leaflet. T h e y say: "Officials do not understand their own regulations. They are over-worked and under-trained and some of them are just bloody-minded."

The guide has been produced and financed by the mechanics' branch of the miners' union at the town's Westoe Colliery.

Leaflet

Miners and volunteers were yesterday handing out the leaflets on local indus-trial estates and at Depart-ment of Employment offices.

Said ex-miner Mike Peel: "I remember vividly how hard it was for our men to get any sort of benefits from the dole when we were on strike 12 months ago.

"And what little we did get seemed to be handed over grudgingly — as if it was the counter staff's own money.

"Workers shouldn't have to upt up with this treat-ment and miners feel they can use last year's experi-ence to help others."

The leaflet urges workers to go to the counter clerk ni organised groups and not leave until they are satisfied that they will get their claims.

It also calls upon shop floor workers to organise f a c t o r y committees to organise factory committees to advise on benefit rights.

Last night the employ-ment staff's organisation, the Civil and Public Service Association was not avail-able for comment.

Newcastle Journal 9 January 1974

The arguments continued until...

The miners' strikes united the whole British Labour movement. Edward Heath fought the 1974 general election on the question 'who governs Britain?'. He got an answer – 'not you!'.

The Rent Strike

The 1972 Housing Finance Act (the Rent Act) instructed local authorities to collect an extra £26 per council house in the period April 1972–73. It was, for many poor families, a real extra burden at the time.

The Act sought to raise money from council rents to pay for other housing costs including a rent rebate for tenants in private housing whose rents were to be decontrolled. This was seen by the South Shields Trades Union Council as a switch of funds from council tenants to private landlords.

Further increases in council rents to a 'fair level' were in prospect. This was seen, correctly as events were to show, as the beginning of the end of cheap council housing.

The SSTUC saw this as an opportunity to engage in a campaign of grass-root direct action to confront the political establishment.

The objectives of the campaign were to engage local tenants in direct action against the Rent Act; to join with similar action on a national basis; to defeat the implementation of the Act, and with it the Heath government.

If, from the vantage point of 1999, this seems fanciful, it should be recalled that some 15 years later the Poll Tax was to be defeated by similar tactics and that, in 1974, the miners' strike did indeed bring down the Heath government.

The objectives of the SSTUC were displayed (for those who choose to read between the lines) in the leaflet produced by the South Shields Federation of Tenants Association:

'Fight back, refuse to pay the rent increase and you can change the law...the miners did...the dockers did...and so can you!'

A secondary objective (of some) was to expose what they saw as the right-wing tendencies of the local council Labour Group and local Labour Party leadership. Some revolutionary comrades had a wider perspective.

The tactics adopted were first to draw the constituency Labour Party and the Labour Group (soon to be the majority town council political party) into opposition to the Act (then a Bill) with a view to heightening public awareness and maximising tenant response.

It was never the expectation of the SSTUC that the Labour Group would refuse to implement the Act (although they would have been happy to support them if they did!). With a pragmatic, conservative tradition, and with many councillors who were careerist rather than idealist, the eventual implementation of the Act was never seriously in doubt.

With the government threat of surcharges (and possible jail) few councillors could be imagined as socialist martyrs – with the possible exception of one, Michael Campbell, a staunch member of the SSTUC, who led Labour Group opposition to the Bill.

The tactic was, at first, more successful than expected. Initially the local Labour Party and Labour Group leadership were encouraged to speak out publicly against implementation. The Labour council election leaflets (May 1972) publicly expressed resistance to the Act. It has been argued that this election policy was a major contributory factor in securing Labour 8 gains and consequent control of the local council.

Tenant opposition to the Act was evident in a mass rally of over 600 tenants in the town's Bolingbroke Hall – a meeting addressed, ironically, by the Labour Council leadership.

On 4th October in the face of bitter public opposition, the now Labour-dominated town council voted to implement the Act. The voting was;

22 Labour councillors against implementation.

11 Labour councillors for implementation.

3 Labour councillors abstained.

The vote for implementation was carried with the aid of 20 Progressive councillors (nominally independent).

The reality behind this vote was more complicated than the figures suggest. This has been brilliantly exposed by Ian Malcolm (son of the then Chair of Housing) in his dissertation on the Rent Strike – currently held in South Shields Central Library.

On 20th November 1972 the SSTUC triggered off the Rent Strike. The campaign was based on the formation of 14 Tenants Associations in the main council estates of the town. A Federation of Tenants Associations was formed to co-ordinate their activities. The responsibility for the formation of these Associations was delegated to Jim Riddle, a Communist member of the SSTUC – a task he performed brilliantly and enthusiastically.

At one time the town council admitted to 460 tenants on strike. Based on Tenants Association reports the SSTUC estimated the figure at its peak to be near 1200.

At this point the SSTUC viewed the local strike as moderately successful. However, nationally, only a handful of councils had refused to implement the Act (Clay Cross was a notable exception) and rent strikes nationally were sparse, sporadic and poorly organised. Labour councils hinted at evictions.

On 10th December 1972, following a meeting of the Tenants Federation, the SSTUC called off the strike.

As an issue the Rent Strike failed, yet in South Shields alone some thousand tenants were engaged in direct political action. Certainly it was a defining moment for relationships between the South Shields Trades Union Council and the Labour Group and constituency Labour Party – and a watershed for many individual members of the Labour movement.

The lessons learned from the Rent Strike were to be applied directly to the fight against the Poll Tax. This time the action was to prove more successful. Tenants had learned of the impotence of the main political parties – and the necessity to construct their own grass-root organisations. Town councillors had learned of the dangers of bravado rhetoric. Not only was the Poll Tax to be defeated but many saw this as the beginning of the end of the Thatcher project.

Photo: Shields Gazette

South Shields Town Hall in 1970 – the bureaucratic base of local democracy.

MARSDEN WARD

UNDER THE CONSERVATIVE

"RENT ACT"

YOU FACE

MASSIVE INCREASES

in Rent whether you be a Council Tenant or a Tenant of the Sutton Trust. Do you believe that any legislation on Rents brought out by the Tories is of benefit to ordinary people . . . **of course it is not.**

The Tory Party like its Progressive imitation in South Shields is the Party of the investor and speculator. I ask you on **THURSDAY, 4th MAY** to

Reject this Unjust Act

VOTE LABOUR

JIM DONEGHAN - X

Published by Jim Doneghan, 143 Westoe Road, South Shields, and
Printed by F. & A. Tolson, Ltd., Bede Industrial Estate, Jarrow.

The standard Labour Party's local election address, May 1972.

£1
on your rent in October
and many rents to Double over the next Five Years.

TENANTS need to ORGANISE to fight against these large rent increases and the Means Test which will result from the Government's Rent Act. The standard of living of tenants will be cut repeatedly over the coming years, starting this October . . . . UNLESS RESISTANCE IS ORGANISED **NOW.**

SOUTH SHIELDS TRADES UNION COUNCIL, representing over 10,000 local trade unionists, is prepared to help existing TENANTS' ASSOCIATIONS to plan and to co-ordinate resistance to the rent increases and to promote the establishment of Tenants' Associations on estates where they do not already exist.

A PUBLIC MEETING
on TUESDAY, 27th JUNE, 1972
at 7.30 p.m.

in the MIDDLE CLUB, VICTORIA ROAD
Speaker : JACK GRASSBY (Secretary of South Shields T.U.C.)

Members of existing Tenants' Associations, and members of the public interested in taking part in these organisations, are cordially invited to attend.

Published by the South Shields Trades Union Council, 143 Westoe Road, South Shields.

DEAN PRINTING WORKS

The beginning of the formation of the Tenants Associations. Each Association elected their own chairperson and secretary – an example where 'leadership' arose from the action.

Shields Gazette

and Shipping Telegraph

HOME

3p.

No. 33323 (Established 1849)   Wednesday, June 28, 1972

BIG RENTS ROW
We'll strike, say tenants

A RENT and rates strike involving at least 1,000 council house tenants in South Shields is planned in protest against the Housing Finance Bill.

This follows a public meeting of more than 100 tenants, councillors and unionists held at the Middle Club, in Victoria Road.

They voted unanimously in favour of the strike and to form tenants' associations on all of the town's housing estates.

The protest also includes a request to the Labour-controlled council to stick to its promise not to implement the Bill, and to instruct the council's local government officials to refuse to help the Government's Housing Commissioner who may be sent to the town to implement the Bill when it becomes law.

Mr Jack Grassby, secretary of South Shields Trades Union Council, who called the meeting, said that it was only through direct action of the kind taken by the miners, the Liverpool dockers and the railway workers that the Bill could be defeated.

Mr Grassby told the meeting that all council rents would rise by £1 in October and by 75p every year after that until in most cases they were double their present level. Even those in low-income brackets who could get a rebate after a means test would still be paying some increase, he said.

"It would be very foolish and dangerous if individuals refused to pay rent increases. It must be a concerted attack of at least 1,000 tenants in this town," he added.

RESIGN

The trades union council would help groups to form tenants' associations, or strengthen existing ones, and it called on the local Labour party to honour Ald. Ernest Mackley's election pledge to refuse to implement the Bill.

Mr Grassby also asked the council to instruct members of NALGO (the town hall officers' union) to refuse to help any Commissioner sent in by the Government to enforce the law.

Coun. William Malcolm (Lab, Rekendyke) said he would resign as chairman of the Housing Committee before he would be a party to mass evictions of those who took part in a rent strike.

Representatives of tenants' associations from Woodbine Street, West Harton and Victoria Road, also supported the call for a strike.

The press, perhaps conscious of public support, always reported this campaign objectively – even sympathetically!

16—Shields Gazette, Friday, August 11, 1972

CRISIS COUNCIL MEETING ON RENTS IS URGED

A CALL for an emergency meeting of the town council was made today by Coun. Stan Smith, leader of the South Shields Progressive group, following the decision of the controlling Labour Party to refuse to implement the Housing Finance Act, but at the same time not to obstruct officials in their work.

As reported in the Shields Gazette last night, the decision was carried by 13 votes to 12 — but only after a lengthy and acrimonious meeting.

Coun. Smith told the Gazette today: "We had a meeting of the Housing Committee on the Monday before the last council meeting and my understanding at that meeting was that the committee were not going to have anything to do with the Rents Bill, but that we would not impede the officials or the civil servants from carrying out their duties."

"It comes as a bolt from the blue, therefore," said Coun. Smith, "to read in last night's Gazette, that some of the Labour councillors wish to flout the law."

Coun. Smith said that the Housing Committee was held at a time when the minutes of that meeting could not go before the full council two days later. They would be presented at the next council meeting on October 4.

Instructions

"It seems quite improper that our town hall officials have not any instructions as to what to do and none can be given until the next council meeting."

"If the Labour Party is so divided over this issue that they are thinking of flouting the law, the proper thing would be to call an emergency meeting of the town council, so that tenants and the community know where they stand and, perhaps more importantly, the council officials know what their instructions are," said Coun. Smith.

He warned that the Progressive group "completely dissociate ourselves with any talk or suggestion that the law should not be obeyed."

To wait until October 4 was a far too long period to wait and the emergency meeting should be called immediately.

Ald. Ernest Mackley, leader of the council, said today: "There will be no special meeting of the town council. The Management Board is quite capable of looking after any emergency problems."

COUN. STAN SMITH
"I was amazed"

The 'Progressive' party took fright – and sought to make political advantage.

Call for Rents Act showdown

A MEETING of all Labour party councillors should be held on the implementation of the "Fair Rents" Act, to avoid a betrayal of pre-election pledges. South Shields Trades Union Council made this call today to the secretary of Shields Labour party.

In a letter to Coun. Bob Growcott, the executive committee of the local TUC expresses its disgust and indignation at the Labour councillors' decision "to stand detachedly to one side while the rent commissioner is permitted to increase unimpeded the rents of this town."

Hypocritical

"We believe that the logic of the Labour group's original decision to refuse to implement the Rent Act because of its unjust character leads to the conclusion that it would be hypocritical to assist with its administration or to collaborate with any government administrative agent.

"The Labour group's decision could well mean that the Labour party is accused of collaboration with the Tory rent commissioner and a betrayal of its pre-election pledge.

"The executive feel that for such an important policy decision to be taken, all of the Labour councillors should have had the opportunity to be present.

Opposition

"We call upon the South Shields Labour party to exert its maximum influence with the Labour group to ensure that it returns to its former commitment for vigorous opposition to the Rent Act."

Mr Jack Grassby, secretary of the TUC, told the Shields Gazette today: "We hope that the Labour party will persuade the Labour group of councillors to reconsider their decision not to obstruct the introduction of rent increases by the government commissioner."

Shields Gazette 14 August 1972

The Trades Union Council sought to bring pressure on the local Labour Party and Labour Group to maximise the impact of what they always suspected would be their eventual surrender.

4—Shields Gazette, Friday, August 18, 1972

Solid front is tenants'aim to defeat 'fair rents' Act

DEFIANT council tenants fired a broadside at the Government's "fair rents" Act at the first meeting of Whiteleas Tenants' Association, South Shields.

"If we stick together, we can beat it," said one of nearly 200 tenants who met in St. Oswald's School hall last night.

Now plans are going ahead for a massive meeting next month, when the ward's three councillors will be asked to add their voices to the tenants' protest.

BREAK THEM

The association, one of a number being formed throughout the town, was launched with talk of a rent strike and a South Shields referendum on the Act.

Guest speaker Coun. William Malcolm (Rekendyke), chairman of the Housing Committee, said the Act was aimed at "breaking" council estates.

"The Tories have decided that council housing as we know it is to be destroyed. They look on council estates as bastions of Labour, and they are determined to break them.

"No longer will council houses be provided with rents within easy reach thanks to subsidies."

He said the Act, the "most vicious piece of class legislation since the war," was an attempt to shift the burden of housing subsidies on to council tenants.

COUN. ALBERT ELLIOTT

The Government had promised "generous" rebates for those who could not afford the higher rents — "But they can afford to be generous with other people's money. They will be providing the rebates with your rents."

Coun. Malcolm said it was still the local Labour Party's policy not to implement the Act, but he warned that tenants that councillors would need strong support when they defied the Act.

FULL SUPPORT

The "formidable" penal clauses meant that councillors could be fined up to £400, charged hundreds of pounds a week to cover lost rents, and even jailed if they failed to pay up.

"It's essential that tenants realise exactly what councillors face if this council

doesn't implement the Act. I would hope that every support will be given by this association when that stage is reached," he said.

Asked what effect a rent strike would have, he said: "It could help to put the pressure on I can't see anyone evicting a whole estate, but what the result would be I don't know. Even if the whole town protests, it could be picked off."

MAIN PURPOSE

The association's secretary, Coun. Albert Elliott (Brinkburn), said he would continue to oppose the Act "whether I go to jail or not."

He called on the ward's three representatives — Councillors Ken Scrimger, Thomas Bell and Robert Donkin — to attend the next meeting to give their positions on the Act,

Mr Jack Grassby, secretary of the local Trades Union Council, said that a rent strike was the main purpose in his council's promotion of tenants's associations,

"This is the only way you will beat the Act. Half-a-dozen people refusing to pay will achieve nothing — you would have to have at least 1,000. With numbers like that, they couldn't work the Act.

"It's what people do that makes the law — not the passing of an Act. If enough people in this town refuse to pay, the Act will be changed."

STRIKE A BLOW

"Five dockers were jailed — and the law was changed. If we can get five councillors in jail they could strike a blow against the Act and be instrumental in having it removed."

Mr Grassby said he thought the whole council should resign and "go to the people" for a decision on the Act. "I think the people of the town should decide what the councillors should do."

Mr Harry Waggett, the association's chairman, said that while the Rent Act was the main target at present, the association was aimed generally at fostering a community spirit.

He said that now that the association was formed, the next meeting could make concrete decisions.

A REFERENDUM

Among ideas put forward by tenants was a Town Hall referendum on the Act, the production of a leaflet explaining how people's rents would be affected, and the forging of links with other tenants' association.

A protest meeting on the Act is also planned for Biddick Hall Ward next month. It will be held in Biddick Hall Junior School on Wednesday, September 6.

Names and addresses of the Whiteleas association's officials are: chairman, Mr Harry Waggett, 45 Whiteleas Way; secretary, Coun. Albert Elliott, 67 Rubens Avenue) treasurer, Mr Robert Stidolph, 37 Rodin Avenue.

Surprisingly, many Labour councillors pledged non-implementation of the Act.

I'll face jail, says tenants chief

THE chairman of the newly-formed White-leas Tenants' Association, South Shields, said today he was ready to go to jail in defiance of the " Fair Rents " Act.

Coun. Albert Elliott, Labour representative for Brinkburn, told members: "I will continue to oppose the Act whether I go to jail or not."

He called on other councillors to state their positions on the Act and stick to their guns in the future.

Protests

Plans are being made for a meeting next month when the three Whitelea wards councillors will be asked to add their voices to the association's protest.

The association is to consider a rent strike and a referendum in the town on the Act.

Other estates in the town are planning protest meetings. The next is planned for September in the Biddick Hall ward and the Whiteleas association has appointed bus driver Mr. Harry Waggett as chairman and Mr. Robert Stidolph as treasurer.

Newcastle Chronicle 21 August 1972

BIDDICK HALL TE·NANTS ASSOCIATION

A PUBLIC MEETING OPEN TO ALL BIDDICK HALL TE·NANTS WILL BE
HELD:-
WED. 30TH. AUG.
ALL SAINTS CHURCH HALL, GALSWORTHY RD.
7.0 P.M.

THE PURPOSE OF THIS MEETING WILL BE TO FORM THE BIDDICK HALL
TE·NANTS ASSOCIATION AND TO ELECT ITS OFFICERS AND COMMITTEE.
THE MEETING WILL HEAR A REPORT ON WHAT THE RENT ACT WILL
MEAN TO COUNCIL TENANTS IF IT IS IMPLEMENTED. THIS INCLUDES :-

* A means test of husband and wife's income

* A £1 a week rent increase in October

* Further rent increases each year until
rents are MORE THAN DOUBLED.

* A possible rent increase for every wage
increase.

* A possible £1.50 increase in rents when
a child leaves school to start work.

ACTION TO BE TAKEN BY THE TENANTS ASSOCIATION ON THIS AND
OTHER MATTERS WILL BE DISCUSSED AT THE MEETING.

ALL BIDDICK HALL TE·NANTS ARE URGED TO ATTEND

Tenants Associations were formed each of the 14 main council estates. This was the format of the initiating leaflets.

Tenants pledge to hold back rents as new Act protest

MORE THAN 150 people at the inaugural meeting of Cleadon Park Tenants' Association, South Shields, pledged their unanimous support to withhold rents in protest against the new legislation.

And the chairman of the newly-formed association, Mr Horace Raper, urged that a countrywide rent strike among tenants should be organised with South Shields leading the way. At the school hall in Park Avenue, tenants were asked how many would refuse to pay increases under the Housing Finance Act.

Mr Raper said that all the tenants' associations in South Shields should unite and then get the support of similar organisations throughout the country.

He said that all the country's tenants could not be put in prison or fined. "This action is our answer to the Government's policy," he added.

Earlier, the chairman of South Shields Housing Committee, Coun. William Malcolm (Rek.) had been received with impatience by some tenants when he described the implications of the Act.

Coun. Malcolm described the Act as "a vicious piece of legislation" through which the Government was "getting at council-house tenants." He warned the tenants that the Act was the most important thing which affected their homes at present.

Asked by tenants what Government action would be taken on a rents strike, he said it would be wrong for him to advocate such action but people must act on their own conscience.

Assistant secretary of South Shields Trades Union Council, Mr Michael Peel, said the tenants must direct their own affairs, and the association should be self-governing. No outsider should muscle in and take control.

One tenant said it was important that if the association withheld the extra rent it knew South Shields' Labour Party and the Town Council was behind it.

Tenants were anxious to criticise the modernisation of their homes. Mr Raper said it was disgraceful and that windows, bathrooms, doors and gates, for example, were in a terrible state.

It was agreed that tenants should write down their complaints and hand them in to Mr Raper at 94 Ashgrove Avenue.

The meeting was adjourned, but Mr Raper said another would be held soon and he asked tenants to tell their neighbours about what had been decided.

Coun. Malcolm

Others formed

Organised by South Shields Trades Union Council, the meeting was one of several being held to form tenants' associations in the town. There will be others during the next few weeks at Marsden, Simonside and Brockley Whins.

The council's secretary, Mr Jack Grassby, told the Shields Gazette that the associations would join to form the South Shields Federation of Tenants' Associations.

Officers elected were: Chairman. Mr Raper; secretary, Mr Arthur Wann; treasurer, Mrs W. Ditchburn. Committee: Mrs I. Sidey, Mrs I. Sword, Mr A. Hardy and Mr C. Worthington.

Special meeting on the question

THE Executive Committee of South Shields Labour Party, has decided to refer the whole question of the Fair Rents Act to a special meeting of the General Management Committee next Thursday.

It is understood that this decision was reached after discussion lasting about an hour-an-a-half.

STRONG FEELING

Inquiries by the Shields Gazette today revealed that at yesterday's meeting, the committee and all affiliated delegates, will be told that there is a strong feeling among members of the executive that not only should the Labour-controlled Town Council not implement the Act, but that instructions be given to Corporation officials not to help the housing commissioner who may be sent in by the Government.

No member of the executive, contacted by the Shields Gazette, would comment officially on the meeting.

Shields Gazette 25 August 1972

Tenants Associations continued to be formed – meanwhile the constituency Labour Party executive showed the first signs of cold feet.

Workers Press, Wednesday August 30, 1972 PAGE 3

Fighting the Tories' Rent Bill

South Shields unionists plan rearguard rent action

BY OUR OWN REPORTER

SOUTH SHIELDS Labour Council now stands alone in the Tyneside area in its refusal to implement the Tory Rent Act.

All other Labour controlled councils in the North East area have declared they will implement the Act and raise council house rents.

These include Teesside, Jarrow, Hebburn and Boldon, as well as Sunderland, which have applied to Tory Minister Julian Amery for a reduction in the size of the increase because of the economic position and high unemployment.

In South Shields, however, trade unionists are suspicious that the local Labour council will fall in line with other Labour councils soon.

The Labour group won back control of the town council in May after their election pledge not to implement the Act.

The Labour group, however, has ignored the housing committee's move not to take on extra staff to assist the Tory-appointed rents commissioner if he was sent in.

At their last meeting, called when one-third of the group was on holiday, the group decided 13-12 not to hinder rent-raising agents, but to continue its policy of non-implementation.

This apparent climbdown has incensed local tenants and trade unionists who feel the action is hypocritical and an omen of further somersaults.

The local trades council has tried to counter this with a rigorous crash programme to organize tenants' associations on council estates, promote a rent strike and continue the struggle in the event of a complete climbdown by the Labour group.

Whitelease and Cleadan Park associations have voted unanimously for rent strikes.

Three of the area's 12 estates have now been organized and a fourth meeting is planned for tonight on the Biddic Hall estate.

Here the trades council hopes to chalk up its biggest success, especially after being snubbed by Labour councillors in the ward who refused to mount a joint campaign for the meeting.

National Union of Mineworkers delegate, Mike Peel, trades council assistant secretary, who has been involved in the campaign, told us:

'Following the unfortunate decision of the South Shields trades council to delay the discussion on the setting up of a Council of Action, the trades council itself has had to take on the role of sole organizers of local opposition to the Tory Rent Act.

'We are grossly undermanned and ill-equipped financially to ensure its success.

'A caucus of ten people have undertaken this mammoth task of organizing the tenants. While their efforts are commendable, a lack of a long-term view to bring down the Tory government will contain the struggle purely within the bounds of economics.

'Whilst I realize that much valuable experience will come out of this struggle, the narrow objectives of the trades council in confining this issue to rents, ensures that if the hoped for rent strike collapses, there is a danger that a lot of activists will be disillusioned because the much broader issues of all-round Tory attacks on the working class will have been neglected.'

As unemployment in the north east rockets towards 100,000, the means test of the Tory Rent Act poses in a concrete way the road of the 1930s.

The rights of the working class, its standard of living and trade unions can only be defended today in the complete mobilization of the working class in a General Strike to remove the Tory government from office.

The All Trades Unions Alliance demand for the building of a Council of Action in South Shields must be taken up as the only means of halting the craven retreat of Labour councils before the Tories' offensive.

This also means bringing together tenants' associations, trade unionists, unemployed and all working-class political organizations onto the Councils of Action.

Mike Peel, assistant secretary South Shields Trades Council

Regional support for the rent strike – never strong – began to fade.

SOUTH SHIELDS TRADES UNION COUNCIL

HOUSING COMMITTEE REPORT
SEPT. 1972.

        In accordance with the instructions of the Council
this Committee has organised 10 meetings of Tenants
and 4 more are in the process of being convened.
        10 Tenants associations have now been formed with
the policy of opposing the Rents Act and about 2,500
people have attended tenants meetings.
        The Officers of the existing 10 Tenants Associations
met in Ede House on Sat.16th Sept together with members
of the Housing Committee.   It was agreed to recommend to
the Council the following :-

        1. That a South Shields Federation of Tenants Associat-
           ions be formed and that a meeting of all Associat
           ions be convened for Sat. 23rd Sept. for this
           purpose.

        2. That the Federation be invited to send delegate
           representatives to the Trades Union Council
           as Associate Members.

        3. To establish a Liason Committee with represent-
           atives from the Federation and the Trades Union
           Council with the purpose of co-ordinating
           opposition to the Rents Act.

*The report of the Trades Union Councils' Housing sub-committee showing
progress in setting up the Tenants Association.*

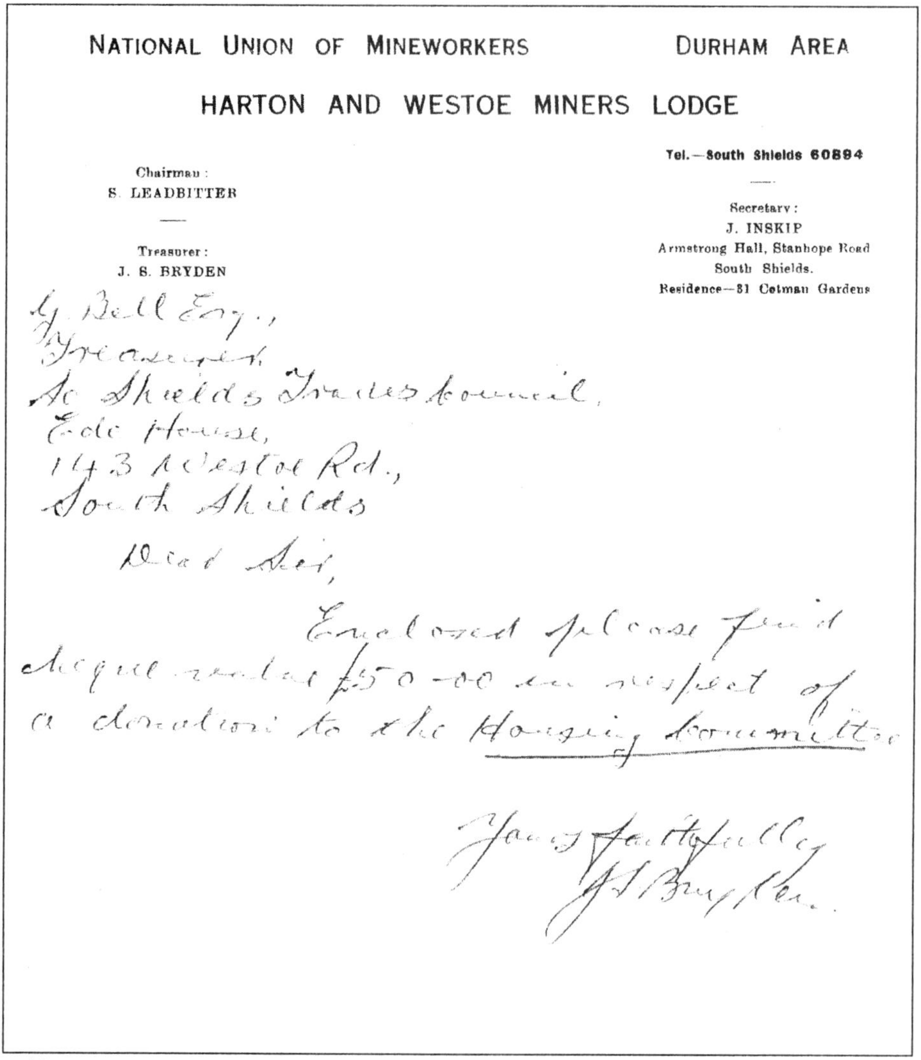

NATIONAL UNION OF MINEWORKERS   DURHAM AREA

HARTON AND WESTOE MINERS LODGE

Tel.—South Shields 60894

Chairman :
S. LEADBITTER

Secretary :
J. INSKIP
Armstrong Hall, Stanhope Road
South Shields.
Residence—81 Cotman Gardens

Treasurer :
J. S. BRYDEN

[handwritten letter]

G. Bell Esq.,
Treasurer,
So Shields Trades Council,
Ede House,
143 Westoe Rd.,
South Shields

Dear Sir,

Enclosed please find cheque rental £50-00 in respect of a donation to the Housing Committee.

Yours faithfully,
J. S. Bryden

Strong support was received from local trade union branches – particularly the NUM – a debt which was to be repaid by the Trades Union Council in the 1974 Miners Strike.

THE AMALGAMATED SOCIETY OF BOILERMAKERS, SHIPWRIGHTS, BLACKSMITHS and STRUCTURAL WORKERS

Nobel

NAME OF BRANCH *South Shields I* 7 Oct 19 72

ADDRESS *127 Tunfield Gdns South Shields*

Boilermakers, Shipwrights, Blacksmiths and
SOUTH SHIELDS No.1
T.B.2 ACCOUNT No. 368
BRANCH STAMP

Our Ref.

Your Ref.

To *Mr J Bell*
Eden House
Westoe Road
South Shields

Please confine each letter to one subject

Worthy Treasurer,
Dear Friend,
The circular requesting a donation to the Housing Committee, to enable them to form Tenants Associations to fight the Rents Act, was read at our September Monthly Meeting and I was instructed to foreward three pounds (£3) as our donation.
Find enclosed P. o for the above amount,

Yours faithfully,
F. E. Mowat,
B. Sec

Amalgamated Union of Engineering Workers
(ENGINEERING SECTION)

Received with satisfaction

Please confine each letter to one subject

Seal ↓

Secretary's Address

W. DONKIN,
122, VINE STREET,
SOUTH SHIELDS,
CO. DURHAM,
NE 33 4RG.

Our ref

Your ref

Corres. No. 54 S.E.

Date 18/11/72

MR. J. GRASSBY
SECRETARY
So SHIELDS TRADES UNION COUNCIL

Dear Sir & Brother,

At our branch meeting held on the 28th of October 1972 our members reaffirmed their complete support for the tenants in South Shields in opposing the Housing Finance Act.

The members of this branch further decided to donate the sum of Ten Pounds to the Trades Union Council Housing Committee Rent Strike fund.

Arrangements are being made for the payment to be made to the treasurer of the above fund.

Yours fraternally
W. Donkin
Branch Secretary

AMALGAMATED UNION OF ENGINEERING WORKERS (Engineering Section)
J Conway, General Secretary, 110 Peckham Road, London SE15 Telephone 01-703 4231

Received

General and Municipal Workers' Union

Registered Office: Ruxley Towers, Claygate, Esher, Surrey

from the ...PLESSEY..., Branch

Secretary...W. D. DAVIS....

Address 89, GAINSBOROUGH AVE
...WHITELEAS S/S

TRADE UNION DEPARTMENT

6·10·72 19

To Mr J Grassby
Secretary TUC
Ede House

One Letter One Subject

Quote your Regional Office reference here....................

Dear Sir & Bros,

Contribution.

From Mr J.G. Mercer the Branch Chairman of the Plessey Branch of the G.M.W Union, And myself. The Branch Secretary, Also our fellow members,

We would like you to accept the modest sum of £ 20·00.

This is to help you in your cause, Regarding the tennants association,

Thank you,

yours Sincerely,

W. D. Davis,

17 Stanhope Rd
Jarrow.

Dear Sir,

May I on behalf of Jarrow Federation of Tenants also Simonside Tenants Ass. offer you our congratulations on the great fight South Shields as putting up against the Rent Act & our best wishes for the future to you all may you fight this fight all the way, united as you are now, Good Luck to you all.

I remain
yours sincerly

Mrs J. Fulcher.

(Sec) Fed of Tenants Ass at Jarrow.

Resistance to the Act by neighbouring Jarrow tenants was short lived.

FIGHT BACK . . .

the attack on YOUR rents has started!

- ON MONDAY 2nd OCTOBER THE RENT ACT will be applied to all NORTH EASTERN ESTATE HOUSES in South Shields. Their Rents will all be increased by £1.

- THIS IS JUST THE BEGINNING of the RENT ACT increases for them and the start of the attack on the rents of all tenants, Council and Private, in South Shields.

- TENANTS of the North Eastern Estates have said they will REFUSE to pay the rent increase. In doing so they risk EVICTION.

- THEY are prepared to fight back for themselves and for every tenant in South Shields.

- What happens in the North Eastern Estates NOW will effect what happens to YOUR FAMILY in the months ahead.

THEIR FIGHT IS YOUR FIGHT

They need and deserve your support .. ANY family threatened with eviction MUST be defended by 1000 other tenants!

- THE FIGHT BACK STARTS WITH A PUBLIC MEETING FOR ALL TENANTS TO PLAN THE ACTION FOR DEFENCE OF N.E. ESTATES.

- ## SUNDAY 1st OCTOBER 1972
  At 6-30 p.m.

- ## BOLINGBROKE HALL
  Bolingbroke Street (Near Town Hall)

All tenants are urged to take this first step to defend their own homes by attending this vital meeting

Issued by South Shields Federation of Tenants Association, 143 Westoe Road, South Shields
DEAN PRINTING WORKS · SOUTH SHIELDS · 2826

This meeting was a landmark in public resistance.

FIGHT-THE-ACT GROUPS ARE SNOWBALLING

THE tenants' association movement is snowballing in South Shields, as the date for the operation of the "fair rents" Act approaches. Seven associations have so far been formed on council estates, and more are planned before the end of the month. Meetings have been attracting between 150 and 300 tenants — exceptional numbers for public meetings of this type.

About 200 people turned up for the first meeting of the Simonside and Brockley Whins association in Monkton Junior School last night. Mr John Shaw, a long-stance lorry driver, of 58 Stoker Avenue, was elected chairman after calling in tenants to refuse to pay rent increases imposed by any housing commissioner sent to the town.

A committee of six was elected, and will be choosing a secretary later.

Two meetings of already - established associations are planned for tonight, those of the Whiteleas association and the Cleadon Park group. South Shields Trades Union Council, which has been promoting the associations, is trying to persuade them to consolidate their organisation before deciding on action to oppose the Act.

A spokesman said the associations were "champing at the bit," but he hoped that they would wait until a federation had been formed to take action.

Definite

He said that now that the town council's Management Board had made a definite decision not to implement the Act, attention should be directed to means of preventing a housing commissioner putting it into operation.

"We shall continue to advocate a rent strike, but in addition other methods of opposition are being studied, and other forms of direct action to obstruct the commissioner will be proposed."

Shields Gazette 7 September 1972

Whiteleas Tenants' Association

THE NON-IMPLEMENTATION OF THE
HOUSING FINANCE ACT, 1972

This week, throughout the country, Council tenants will be receiving notices informing them that their rent is to be increased by £1 per week because of the Conservative Government's Housing Finance Act.

In South Shields, however, Council tenants will not receive such notices. This is because of the local Labour Party's refusal to implement the Act—on our behalf—thus saving us from the £1 increases.

By defying the Act, our Councillors may face heavy penalties, including huge fines, imprisonment, etc.

On Thursday, our three Ward Councillors, K. Scrimger, T. Bell and H. Donkin, will speak on the Rent Act and will outline the consequences of defying the Act, both for themselves and for us, the tenants.

The meeting begins at 7.00 p.m. this Thursday, 7th September, in St. Oswald's School Hall, Nash Avenue.

Please attend to give our Councillors moral support. After all, what's one hour of your time compared to what our Councillors could be facing shortly !

After the meeting, tenants may take up complaints with their Councillors over a cup of tea.

Published by Whiteleas Tenants' Association (Coun. A. Elliott, Sec., 67 Rubens Avenue, South Shields), and printed by The Dean Printing Works.

Shields residents to band together

A FEDERATION of tenants' associations is to be formed in South Shields on Saturday, it was announced today. The town's MP Mr Arthur Blenkinsop will address the inaugural meeting to be held in Ede House, said a spokesman for South Shields Trades Union Council.

The meeting was called by officials of eight tenants associations, who met at the weekend,

Nine associations are now in existence, sponsored by the trades union council with the main aim of opposing the "fair rents" Act,

COORDINATE

A tenth association will be formed tonight for tenants of the North-Eastern Housing Association, and the eleventh will be set up for Laygate and Victoria tenants at a meeting on Wednesday evening.

The new federation may be invited to send delegates to the trades union council as associate members, and a liaison committee is planned between the federation and the council to coordinate opposition to the Rents Act.

REFUSE

The weekend meeting of association officials also agreed to appeal to South Shields members of Nalgo, the town hall staff union, to refuse to cooperate with any Government housing commissioner sent to the town.

The local branch of Nalgo has recommended members to comply with a housing commissioner's instructions.

Shields Gazette 18 September 1972

Arthur Blenkinsop M.P. addressed the inaugural meeting of the Federation of Tenants' Association.

Shields Gazette

and Shipping Telegraph

HOME

No. 33430 (Established 1849)   Saturday, September 30, 1972   3p.

Coun. Stan Smith, who says that rent revolt Labour JPs should resign from the Bench.

RENT REBEL WARNING BY MR WALKER

By Malcolm Scott,
Our Municipal Reporter

SOUTH SHIELDS Town Council is breaking the law if it upholds the decision not to implement the "fair rents" Act. This is the message spelled out by the Environment Minister, Mr Peter Walker, in a letter to the council.

He ends his letter with an appeal to the council to implement the Act after all. But the Management Board reaffirmed its policy of defiance after discussing the letter this week. The 630-word letter is printed in full in the council minutes, which were received by members today.

The Environment Minister interviewed.

Shields tenants 'man barricades' against rent rise

A MASS meeting of tenants in South Shields overwhelmingly decided last night not to pay rent increases under the Housing Finance Act.

More than 600 people crowded into Bolingbrooke Hall to show their support and solidarity in fighting the Act and undertook to break the law by not paying any increases if they were called to do so.

They unanimously pledged their support to the North-East Housing Association tenants who are refusing to pay the £1-a-week increase as from today.

Five points

The meeting, called by the South Shields Federation of Tenants' Associations — there are ten associations in the town — agreed to a five-point plan put forward by executive committee member, Mr Jim Riddle.

1 — Formally to record opposition by the Federation of Tenants' Associations to the Housing Finance Act.

2 — To give every kind of help to the North-East Housing Associations' tenants.

3 — To launch petitions against the Act on every estate in the town, and led by jazz bands to parade to the Town Hall to present them to the Mayor, Coun. Vincent Fitzpatrick.

4 — To express appreciation the Labour group of councillors who have decided not to implement the Act.

5 — To rally at the Town Hall on Wednesday night, when the council meets to discuss the implementation of the Act, and show their disapproval of it.

Union backing

Mr Riddle was given loud support when he said tenants in South Shields should not be "hijacked" into paying the increases and called on any Labour councillor, who was having second thoughts about not implementing the Act, to resign before Wednesday to avoid betraying himself and his ward.

South Shields Trades Union Council, and union branches in the town, who sent financial aid ranging from £5 to £20, also gave backing to the tenants in their fight.

The Mayor, Coun. Fitzpatrick, in an unofficial capacity, told the tenants that it would be the town, with 16,000 council tenants, which would be in default by the £1-a-week in refusing to implement the Act, not the tenants. He urged everyone to pay his normal rent and to refuse to pay only the increases.

"You will not be responsible for saving £1 week by week. It will be arrears against the authority, not the tenant.

Action plan

"It has never been the British way of life to break the law, but this is a situation each and everyone of you has to consider," said Coun. Fitzpatrick.

Mr Jack Grassby, secretary of South Shields Trades Union Council, proposed that an action liaison committee of South Shields Trades Union Council, the North-East Housing Association tenants, and representatives of the Federation of Tenants' Associations in South Shields be set up to plan action for the defence of the North-East tenants.

Not accepted

He said that the Trades Union Council would gather financial support, get legal advice and give aid to the councillors refusing to implement the Act.

He said South Shields unions would seek a national strike from the TUC if any councillor were threatened or a tenant evicted. He said the dockers and miners had broken the law in getting their pay rises, and the Act could be defeated by tenants breaking the law with the trades unions behind them.

Speakers addressing the public meeting of over 600 tenants on the 1ˢᵗ October 1972 in the Bolingbrooke Hall – including, ironically, the Labour Group leadership.

'FREE VOTE' SHOCK

Row over Labour decision on Act

By A Municipal Reporter

LABOUR COUNCILLORS WILL HAVE A FREE VOTE ON THE "FAIR RENTS" ACT AT TOMORROW NIGHT'S MEETING OF SOUTH SHIELDS TOWN COUNCIL.

The authority to vote "according to their conscience and not according to majority decision" was given by 17 votes to 15 at a stormy meeting of the Labour Group on the council last night.

The policy of non-implementation — shouted from the "roof-tops" during the post months and the subject of two decisions of South Shields Labour Party, two decisions of the Labour Group and one from the Management Board — now rests in the hands of eight people.

If eight Socialists, whether they be councillors or aldermen, raise their hands tomorrow night with the Progressives, it will mean that as far as the town council is concerned, the Act will be implemented in the town.

But that does not mean the battle has been won; that the fighting will stop. The numerous tenants' associations which have mushroomed in the town, will continue the battle.

As a spokesman of South Shields Trades Union Council told the Gazette today: "This betrayal of their election pledge means that Labour councillors have abdicated the right to speak on behalf of the people of South Shields."

"The only hope now for non-implementation lies in a massive demonstration by tenants' associations."

Shields Gazette
and Shipping Telegraph

No. 33432 (Established 1849)   Tuesday, October 3, 1972

HOME

3p.

The decision for a 'free vote' on the Act allowed the Labour Group off the hook. This was the defining moment in their 'resistance' to the Act.

WE WILL NOT PUT SHIELDS RENTS UP —LABOUR LEADER

COUNCIL house rents in South Shields will definately NOT go up on October 1 under the "fair rents" Act. Four weeks notice has to be given before rents are put up, but no notices have yet been issued by the town hall. Notices would have had to go out over the weekend if the Housing Finance Act was to come into operation on schedule on October 1. When and how the notices will now be issued was not clear today.

The Management Board, the council's policy-making body, has decided not to implement the Act. And while it has agreed not to obstruct council officials in preparing for the Act, the officials have had no instructions to issue notices of rent rises.

DELAYED NOTICES

Ald. Ernest Mackley, leader of the Labour group, said: "As far as we are concerned, it is now in the hands of the Government. We are on the outside looking in."

Ald. Mackley said he did not know how the notices would be issued. "The officials presumably need orders from someone — but they will not come from us," he said, adding that the Minister of Housing could eventually issue instructions.

The longer the notices are delayed, the longer council tenants will be reprieved from rent rises, which will be not more than £1 a week.

But the increases will be imposed at some stage, possibly by a Housing commissioner sent in by the Government to take over the corporation's housing.

COMPLYING

Formal notices have been sent out to council tenants in Jarrow and Hebburn. Rents will go up by 55p in Hebburn, while Jarrow is asking the Government to allow increases below £1.

ALD. MACKLEY
'Out of our hands'

The 648 South Shields tenants of the North Eastern Housing Association have been given notice that their rents will go up by £1. An association spokesman said today: "We have complied strictly with the Act."

The increases under the Act are the first step towards "fair" rents.

Shields Gazette September 1972

'The order [to implement the Act] will not come from us.'
But, reading between the lines, the writing was on the wall.

REMEMBER THE DATE .... 4TH OCTO... 1972

.... this day the Labour Council broke its election pledge
NOT to implement the Rent Act, and betrayed the people of South Shields.
.... this day the Labour Group of Councillors tried to hide
behind the mockery of a "free vote " to allow some councillors the
luxury of voting against implementation safe in the knowledge that their
own colleagues voting with the Tories would implement the Act and save
their skins from the consequences of their vote.
.... this day the Labour Council treat with contempt the
demands of thousands of tenants and local trade unionists.

THIS PROTEST BY TENANTS AND TRADE UNIONISTS IS DESIGNED TO
DEMONSTRATE THAT THE LABOUR COUNCIL HAS FORFEITED THE RIGHT TO ACT
ON BEHALF OF THE PEOPLE OF SHIELDS AND HAS LOST THE AUTHORITY AND
RESPECT DUE TO THEM AS COUNCILLORS.

We call upon the people of South Shields to show their rejection of
these councillors by refusing to accept any rent increases that they
will now try to force upon tenants.

FUTURE RESISTANCE TO THE RENT ACT IS NOW IN THE HANDS OF THE
PEOPLE OF SHIELDS, TENANTS AND TRADE UNIONISTS , FIGHTING AGAINST
A LABOUR COUNCIL WORKING IN CO-OPERATION WITH THE TORY GOVERNMENT.

SUPPORT THE RENT STRIKE

The Council voted to implement the Act on the 4th October (with the aid of 20 'Progressive' councillors). This SSTUC leaflet marked the occasion – and acted as a trigger for the rent strike.

Journal picture special

It was a night of strong words and emotions at South Shields.

BELOW: A handclap and a hug for Coun. Malcolm Campbell who represents Rekendyke ward. A section of the 500 banner-carrying tenants who crowded outside the Town Hall to reaffirm their determination to oppose the Fair Rents Act.

ABOVE: Coun. Thomas Bell, who resigned the party whip, leaves the meeting still smiling. He represents the Whiteleas ward.

Newcastle Journal 5 October 1972

'Resign' pair speak out

BIDDICK HALL residents were today urged to persuade two of their councillors not to resign over the rent Act decision.

Labour Party secretary Coun. Bob Growcott appealed to the ward's electors to "rally round" Coun. Jim Davison and Coun. John Wakeford, and press them to keep their seats on the council.

"It is disastrous that these two good Socialists should resign, leaving behind the turncoats and the traitors."

Coun. Wakeford, who has represented Biddick Hall since 1965 and is vice-chairman of the Finance Committee, said today he would be handing in his letter of resignation as a councillor tonight.

"What I intend doing is to have a meeting with the tenants. I will ask the tenants of Biddick Hall to meet me and I will explain the

reasons why I took the actions I did. I think I owe it to them."

'UNRULY MOB'

Coun. Davison, elected last year, told the Gazette that he would put his resignation in tonight.

Coun. Davison, who voted against implementation, said: "My vote was influenced by what I thought the people of Biddick Hall wanted as well as my own conscience. I cannot find it in my heart to accept this Act."

He added: "The crowd which gathered at the town hall had no influence on me whatsoever. In fact, their actions should have driven me the other way.

"They were just an unruly mob. Mob rule gets no-one anywhere. Mob law only leads to the gun, brick and the bomb.

"I was prepared to be put on the rack, but I will not accept the rule of mob law. Their behaviour was terrible."

Crowd chaos at Act debate

POLICE reinforcements had to be called to South Shields Town Hall last night, after chaos had broken out in the public gallery during the Town Council's debate on the "fair rents" Act.

About 200 people — mostly council-house tenants — had packed into the gallery, which normally holds 60, and more were straining to hear on the staircases outside.

The Mayor, Coun. Vincent Fitzpatrick, finally ordered the gallery to be cleared when Coun. Jim Doneghan,

Labour chairman of the Education Committee was drowned out during his speech.

About 20 police moved in to clear the gallery, but it was nearly half-an-hour before the debate could continue.

Some of the tenants, although angry, moved away quickly as a police inspector explained "this is no longer a public meeting."

But others stayed put, and as a chorus of "We shall not be moved" broke out.

Angry tenants shout at councillors as they arrive for the vital rent Act meeting.

WHAT THE COUNCILLORS SAID

ALD. George Gibson (Lab.): "Council house tenants have been let down—they have been left to carry the can. It's a sad day for the Labour Party Shields."

COUN. Thomas Bell (Lab.): "There are other battles to fight yet, and the best way to fight them is by staying on the council."

COUN. Gerry Graham (Lab.): "I voted against the Act, but still admire the stand of Coun. Doneghan. It took a lot of courage . . . the "fight is now inside the group."

COUN. Malcolm Campbell (Lab.): "Ald. Mackley is the one who is completely to blame for the result. He could have tipped the balance by not supporting a free vote in the group."

ALD. Enerest Mackity (Lab.): "I am upset with what happened last night and the resulting resignations. However, the members voted according to their conscience and I won't criticise them for that. The Labour group will survive."

Shields Gazette 5 October 1972

The divisions in the Labour Group began to show. Two councillors resigned and 8 gave up the Labour whip.

THE JOURNAL

NEWCASTLE UPON TYNE   THURSDAY   OCTOBER 5   1972   No. 39,292   3p

Two quit, 8 resign whip after tenants storm council

Police break up town hall demo

BY DAVID PRICE and FRED HACKWORTH

FAIR Rents Act protesters wave placards as the Mayor of South Shields, Coun. Vincent Fitzpatrick arrives for the meeting.

Pictures: Peter Thursfield

COUN. Malcolm Campbell is cheered after resigning the Labour whip on South Shields Council.

TWO Labour members resigned from South Shields Council and eight others resigned the party whip after a near riot at South Shields Town Hall last night.

They walked out of the meeting minutes after the council voted to end their three-day defiance of the Fair Rents Act and increase council house rents.

The decision caused uproar when 500 angry tenants waiting outside the Town Hall were told of the news. Squads of police with a police dog were called in to control the crowd and protect councillors leaving the building.

Earlier 250 tenants had been thrown out of the public gallery after they had forced the council meeting to be abandoned. They tried to climb over the barriers separating the public from the council chamber to get at councillors.

Hundreds of leaflets were hurled at councillors, and several men had to be forcibly restrained by friends after they heard three Labour councillors speak in favour of implementing the Fair Rents Act.

One tried to force his way into the council chamber, but was held back by a councillor and a bundle of leaflets were snatched from his hands before he could throw them.

Cries of "scab" and "traitor" were chanted as the councillors left the chamber to wait in the lobby until things cooled off.

The Mayor, Coun. Vincent Fitzpatrick asked police to clear the gallery but despite an inspector's pleas for the tenants to go quietly they sat down and chanted "We shall not be moved."

After 35 minutes the gallery was cleared and councillors resumed the debate — which had already lasted two hours.

But the tenants tried to storm through the Town Hall's main entrance. Police held them back and they held an impromptu meeting on the Town Hall steps.

But their protests were in vain. Within 30 minutes of the gallery being cleared the debate ended and a vote was taken.

Shields Gazette

and Shipping Telegraph

HOME

No. 33434 (Established 1849)   Thursday, October 5, 1972   3p.

COUNCIL START MASSIVE RENTS ACTION

By Malcolm Scott and Steve Levinson

SOUTH SHIELDS corporation officials today began work on serving 16,000 council tenants with notices of rent increases in the wake of rowdy scenes at the town hall last night.

But it will be at least six weeks before the rises take effect. And in the meantime the Finance Committee is left with the problem of finding £112,000 — the deficit that will arise because of a seven-week delay in implementing the "fair rents" Act.

The Labour Party was also counting the cost — in resignations — of the council's decision to operate the Act.

Two councillors will tonight resign from the council, and at least six others have said they will resign the Labour whip.

And in the aftermath of last night's decision — which followed a noisy display of tenants' anger, accusations of betrayal and broken election promises were directed at the Labour members who voted with the Progressives.

Eleven Labour members sided with the minority group, and three others abstained, to enable the Act to go through.

Immediate reaction from tenants associations was that they would probably be putting up their own candidates at the next elections.

"OFFICIAL"

Councillors John Wakeford and Jim Davison are the two men to resign. The six who have broken away from the Labour group are Couns. Malcolm Campbell, Bob Growcott, James Hodgson, Paddy Cain, Albert Elliott and Ald. George Gibson. It is believed Coun. John Dent may join them.

Couns. Thomas Bell and Gerry Graham denied reports that they had resigned the whip. Coun. Campbell said that he and others who had broken away now considered themselves the official Labour group.

"We regard ourselves as the only representatives of the Labour Party," he said.

Deputy Town Clerk, Mr Alan Stansfield, said today that it would be at least a week beofre the first tenants receive notice of rent increases, and details of the rebate scheme.

BACKDATED

There would then be a four-week delay before the increases take effect.

"We are starting on this work today, but it is a long process and it will take at least a week to get the notices printed," he said.

He said that tenants need not worry about receiving bills backdated to October 1 — the day the Act should have been implemented.

Coun. John Wakeford and (below) Coun. Jim Davison, who are resigning from the council in protest.

LETTERS

THE OLD FIGHT HAS GONE

I WAS one of the 250 people who crammed into the public gallery of the town council chamber and witnessed the sell-out by our Labour councillors. What has happened to the old Socialist fighting spirit which has taken the party through many battles in the past? Apart from a few it has obviously gone.

I admire the two councillors who have resigned from the party and those who have formed a breakaway group. It seems a shame that those who have said they will resign will not change their minds and join the rebels.

If they can get the support of the trade unions and Federation of Tenants' Association, I am sure that they could become the only real Labour Party in the town.

I cannot see that council house tenants will have short enough memories to re-elect the Labour Quislings who voted in favour of implementing the Tory Act. Nor can I see them being too keen on the fence sitters who voted in favour of refusing to implement the Act, knowing fine well that there were enough of their colleagues prepared to commit political hara kiri to get it introduced. I am sure that many of them deep down did not want to oppose the Act's implementation, but they were too afraid of their political future to stand up and be counted. They wanted to get the Act enforced, but at the same time they did not want to jeopardise their future on the council, and in my eyes they are equally guilty.

BRIAN LISTER
44 St.Cuthbert's Avenue,
South Shields.

Shields Gazette 11 October 1972

This public response to the Labour councillors 'betrayal' was widespread.
The threat of the formation of a breakaway Labour Group was premature.

NATIONAL ASSOCIATION OF TENANTS AND RESIDENTS,
283, Grays Inn Road, London. WC1.

D E C L A R A T I O N

FOR NON-IMPLEMENTATION AND DEFEAT OF

THE HOUSING FINANCE ACT

THIS CONFERENCE of representatives of tenants' associations, trade union branches, trades councils and other organisations of the labour movement, declares its complete opposition to the Housing Finance Act and its intention to campaign for collective and individual non-implementation.

THE AIM OF THE ACT is not to solve Britain's housing problem. It is to transfer the cost of council housebuilding from the Government to council tenants, cut Government housing subsidies, raise rents of millions of council and private landlord tenants, subsidise private landlords and extract huge profits for moneylenders, speculators and the Government.

CONFERENCE REJECTS the idea that the national rent rebate and rent allowance scheme will bring "massive benefits" to tenants. In fact, any rebate paid to one council tenant, will be paid for in the form of increased rent. by other council tenants.

THE NATIONAL RENT ALLOWANCE scheme is a subsidy to private landlords who will receive - by 1975 - an annual subsidy of nearly £50 million. The cost of administering the national rent rebate and rent allowance scheme will be paid for by the ratepayers who will also contribute to the rebates and allowances. Thus, tenants and owner-occupiers will be subsidising private landlords.

BY DENYING ELECTED COUNCILLORS their democratic right to fix council rents and transferring that right to non-elected, Government appointed Rent Scrutiny Boards, the Government intends to speed up and consolidate this profit-making process.

THE HOUSING FINANCE ACT maintains the upward spiral of land and property prices, cuts new council housebuilding, increases rents of furnished accomodation, maintains the horrors of homelessness, the degradation of living in sub-standard dwellings and the massive council house waiting lists. It completely rejects the idea of housing as a social service.

National opposition to the Act was patchy and poorly organised.

192

Shields Gazette
and Shipping Telegraph

No. 33431 (Established 1849)   Monday, October 2, 1972

HOME

3p.

RENT DEBT IS ON
Defiant Shields tenants

By Our Municipal Reporter

SOUTH SHIELDS TODAY BEGAN TO RUN UP ITS FIRST DEBTS UNDER THE "FAIR RENTS" ACT.

Standing alone in the North-East in defiance of the Act, the Town Council faces a weekly loss of at least £16,000 from today.

- Labour Party reverses decision
- More join protest in North

The great rents rebellion

By BILL DOULT

LABOUR'S rank and file successfully revolted against Party chiefs at Blackpool yesterday.

They demanded guarantees of money for councillors who defy the Tories' Fair Rent laws.

This was a complete reversal of the decision which Party chiefs believed—and had been hoped — taken on Monday.

But it offers no real prospect to rent rebel councillors that a future Labour Government will pay them for penalties incurred in refusing to put up rents.

Yesterday's reversal followed confusion and anger on the first day of the conference when the Party debated hard-line resolutions on land, housing and rents.

Meanwhile, the grass-root Labour movement showed that national opposition to the Act could have been possible. In the event no central Labour support was forthcoming.

TRADES UNION CONGRESS

GENERAL SECRETARY: VICTOR FEATHER CBE

CONGRESS HOUSE · GREAT RUSSELL STREET · LONDON WC1B 3LS

Telephone 01-636 4030   *Telegrams* TRADUNIC LONDON WC1

October 6 1972

DEPT Economic
OUR REF DL/BC/VG
YOUR REF

Mr J Grassby
Secretary
South Shields Trades Union Council
Ede House
143 Westoe Road
South Shields
Co. Durham

Dear Mr Grassby

Housing Finance Act

Thank you for your letter of September 27. The General Council appreciate the hard work which your Council has undertaken in coordinating opposition to the Housing Finance Act in South Shields.

If you have any particular questions on the Act which you need information on this Department will be able to help you. The Secretary of the TUC Northern Regional Advisory Committee is Mr J W Harper, CBE and his address is, Angus House, 13, Northumberland Square, North Shields, telephone N. Shields 78225. He may be able to help you in organising duplicating and publicity facilities.

If you require further information please let me know.

Yours sincerely

*Mr Woodbridge
Nel 21425*

Secretary
Economic Department

The Trades Union Congress recognised the strong grass-root sentiments and, surprisingly, offered support – at a distance – but carefully avoided mentioning a rent strike.

The Unfinished Revolution

No mass Shields evictions pledge

AS hundreds of council house tenants staged a Rent Act revolt today, the chairman of South Shields Housing Committee assured them there would be no confrontation between the tenants and the council over eviction.

Coun. William Malcolm (Lab., Rekendyke) said there would be no mass evictions, but this did not absolve anyone who acted irresponsibly by not paying the rent increase.

A call was made to Coun. Malcoln by more than 200 tenants at a meeting last night to reaffirm his previous statement saying that tenants on a rent strike would not be evicted.

Coun. Malcolm told the Shields Gazette today that his original statement had said there would be no mass evictions.

"But of course that doesn't underwrite anyone being irresponsible. There will be no mass evictions obviously because it would not solve any problems.

"If there were a considerable number of people going on a rent strike then obviously this is something the Labour Group would have to look at, but the final decision would have to be taken by the Council.

"We have to wait and see what happens, because after all is said and done, there are something like 18,000 houses, less those that have been sold. This is quate a lot of people, a tremendous amount more people than has ever attended any meetings."

He said many people who were being persuaded to go on a rent strike could benefit from the Housing Finance Act by way of rebate.

"Whilst none of us like the Rent Act, we want people to take every advantage of it. It would be tragic if they go on a rent strike and lose rebates which they could quite possibly qualify for.

"It is a case of watch and see. It is not a case of confrontation between tenants and the Council," said Coun. Malcolm.

Shields Gazette 20 November 1972

'No mass evictions' – 'but this did not absolve anyone who acted irresponsibly'. This veiled threat was repeated in more direct terms by the Labour Group leadership.

Shields Gazette

and Shipping Telegraph

No. 33472 (Established 1849)   Saturday, November 18, 1972

HOME

3p.

'PAY RENT RISE OR BE EVICTED'

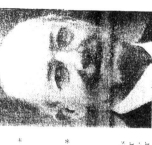

Ald. Mackley

TWO THOUSAND council tenants in South Shields were told that if they failed to pay rent rises coming into Force on Monday they could well be evicted.

This warning — from Ald. Ernest Mackley, Labour leader of the town council — came on the eve of a planned rent strike during which many tenants are expected to refuse to pay rises under the Housing Finance Act.

And Ald. Mackley was critical of South Shields Trades Union Council, which is advocating a rents strike

He said: "I would urge all council tenants to ignore the advice of these people who are asking them not to pay he increases.

"It's no good people thinking that the local Trades Union Council can protect them against their action."

The council leader claimed that tenants were being led on by the Trades Union Council.

By Pauline Hepburn

*   *   *

LED UP HILL

He said: "These people are leading tenants up the hill, and they certainly won't lead them down again."

And Ald. Mackley said that the Trades Union Council was conducting a campaign against the local Labour Party instead of the Government.

"This whole campaign is being directed at the Labour Party instead of the Government who are responsible for this Act.

*The local Labour leadership tried to pass the buck to national government –
'reluctant implementation' became the political life-jacket of that period – and after!*

The Unfinished Revolution   **197**

RENT STRIKE

On the 4th October, 1972, the South Shields Labour Council broke its election pledge and voted to implement the Rent Act in South Shields.

Previously **17** Labour Councillors had supported a "free vote" in the Council to allow 11 of their members to vote with the Tories and bring in the Rent Act.

The Labour Council is now collaborating with the Tory Government to operate the Act. You will have been notified of the first £1 increase in your rent to come into effect on the 20th November. Even if you qualify for a rebate **your rent has been increased unnecessarily.**

REMEMBER .... you will lose £1 of your rebate if you look after an aged parent
.... you will lose £1·50 of your rebate if your child leaves school for work
.... you will lose 34p for every £2 wage increase or overtime.
AND REMEMBER .... your rents will go up another £1 in 1973
.... and another £1 in 1974
.... and then the process will start all over again !
AND ALSO REMEMBER .... you get NO rebate on rates (see the front of your rent book), and these will shoot up next year due to the Rent Act.

THE ONLY WAY LEFT TO RESIST IS TO REFUSE TO PAY THE RENT INCREASE

Twelve Tenants' Associations have been formed in Shields to support a Rent Strike. Over 1,000 tenants have already said they will NOT pay the rent increase.

If sufficient tenants say they will not pay—NOTHING CAN BE DONE TO FORCE THEM TO PAY.

What YOU can do :
When the rent collector calls for the increased rent—**PAY YOUR NORMAL RENT BUT REFUSE TO PAY THE INCREASE.**

Be polite but firm—remember the rent collector is only carrying out his orders—and he might even be on your side.

Don't enter into an argument with him. If he does try to argue with you, call for your neighbour—or just close the door. Report it later to your Tenants' Association.

What will happen :

Nothing can happen if you refuse to pay the rent increase for at least four weeks. You will have to be the equivalent of at least one full week in arrears before any action is taken—AND THE CHAIRMAN OF THE HOUSING COMMITTEE HAS SAID HE WILL NOT EVICT ANY TENANTS BECAUSE OF A RENT STRIKE.

If anyone TRIES to take action against ANY tenant they will be defended by the combined strength of :
Their Tenants' Association
The Federation of Tenants' Associations
The Trades Union Council
.... and every other tenant on rent strike.

If even ONE tenant is threatened the Trades Union Council will call for industrial strike action by local unions.

Victor Feather and the T.U.C. have pledged their full support. We will demand THEIR help if YOU are threatened.

The Claimants' Union, for those claiming Social Security Benefits, has offered its full support for the strike. They will be available five days a week and ANY tenant on rent strike can call to see them any afternoon Monday to Friday :
1.00—3.00 p.m.
THE PEOPLE'S PLACE (ex-Unitarian Church, Derby Terrace, near public baths).

DON'T WORRY, YOU ARE NOT ALONE, AND YOU WILL NEVER BE LEFT TO FIGHT FOR YOURSELF.

If your rent is paid by Social Security you will NOT be asked to join the rent strike (but you can if you want to help the fight). **But don't pay any increase until you have got it from Social Security.**

What else YOU can do :
SIGN THE PETITION TO THE TOWN COUNCIL—someone will call at your door.
DISPLAY THE POSTERS "SUPPORT THE RENT STRIKE"—available from Tenants' Associations.
ATTEND YOUR NEXT TENANTS' ASSOCIATION MEETING—further details and information about the rent strike will be given there.

ATTEND THE MASSIVE PUBLIC PROTEST DEMONSTRATION TO BE HELD :

SUNDAY 19th NOVEMBER at BOLLINGBROKE HALL
6.00 p.m.

FIGHT BACK .... REFUSE TO PAY THE RENT INCREASE AND YOU CAN CHANGE THE LAW .... The Miners did .... The Dockers did .... SO CAN YOU !

SUPPORT THE RENT STRIKE

Published by the South Shields Federation of Tenants Associations. Printed by Dean Printing Works, South Shields.

Alderman rapped as rents revolt gets under way

THE threatened rent strike by hundreds of council house tenants in South Shields is on from today. A meeting of more than 200 tenants representing 15 tenants associations in the town decided at a mass meeting last night not to pay increases under the Government's Housing Finance Act.

Representatives from the associations told the meeting in Bolingbroke Hall that their members had unanimously voted not to pay the increase, and the meeting endorsed the decision.

'Change advice to tenants', Mayor urged

A PLEA has gone out to the Mayor of South Shields, Coun. Vincent Fitzpatrick, to reconsider the advice he gave to council house tenants last month not to pay rent increases which come into operation today.

The plea is in a letter to the Mayor from Coun. Stan Smith, the leader of the Progressive Group in South Shields, and he reminds Coun. Fitzpatrick: "Because you are Mayor many people may be inclined to follow your advice.

"Now that Ald. Mackley has told the tenants they will be evicted from their homes if they do not pay the increased rent, will you reconsider the advice you gave the council house tenants last month?"

The letter continues: "Many people feel as Mayor you have led the people up the hill and now it is your duty to lead them down again."

DEFAULT

Coun. Smith points out that Coun. Fitzpatrick gave this advice at a mass meeting of council house tenants on October 1, when he claims the Mayor said: "It would be the town with 16,000 council tenants which would be in default by the £1 a week in refusing to implement the (fair rents) Act, not the tenants."

Coun. Smith says the Mayor "urged everyone to pay his normal rent and to refuse to pay the increases" adding: "You will not be responsible for saving £1 week by week. It will be arrears against the authority, not the tenant."

Footnote: The Gazette report of the mass meeting of October 1 points out that Coun. Fitzpatrick was acting in an "unofficial capacity" when he gave this advice.

Statement on eviction clarified

THE headline in Saturday's Gazette: "Pay rent rise or be evicted" over a story concerning the meeting of South Shields council house tenants has caused some misunderstanding.

Ald. Ernest Mackley, leader of South Shields Labour Group said today that he had had many phone calls during the weekend. "I said that if tenants refused to pay the rent increases they could well be evicted. This is different from what the headline stated," he said.

"The question of eviction or the policy in relation to evictions will be decided by the Labour Party and the Labour group on the council."

In doing so they criticised the leader of Shields Labour Group, Ald. Ernest Mackley, for his statement, reported in the Shields Gazette, in which he said tenants who refused to pay the increase could well be evicted.

Resigned

One woman asked: "How can we get these traitors out? Are they going to be put out at the elections?"

The tenants called on the Labour Group to repudiate the statement made by Ald. Mackley and called on the chairman of the Housing Committee, Coun. William Malcolm (Lab. Rekendyke) to pledge again that no tenants on a rent strike would be evicted.

Three Labour councillors who resigned the Party whip over the implementation of the Act attended.

No authority

Coun. Albert Elliott (Lab. Brinkburn) said if he went back to the whip, "it will be with the sole object to vote against Ald. Mackley as leader of the Labour Party in South Shields.

"I'm positive, and I'm on the Housing Committee, that there is no danger that Ald. Mackley is going to evict anybody."

Coun. Paddy Cain (Lab. Bents said: 'I don't know what Billy Malcolm will think about this (the statement) as chairman of the Housing Committee. I don't know where Ald. Mackley gets his authority from. I am sure it's not from the Labour Party or Group.

Shields Gazette 20 November 1972

The Rent Strike started – with confusion and recriminations in the Labour Group.

EVERY TENANT & TRADE UNIONIST INVOLVED IN THE RENT STRUGGLE
IS INVITED TO THE

RENTS STRUGGLE CONFERENCE

SUNDAY the 26th
NOVEMBER

STARTING PROMPTLY AT 11am
AT THE STUDENTS UNION
OXFORD RD, MANCHESTER

COME IN COACHES
BRING YOUR BANNERS
LIMITED CATERING FACILITIES
WE WILL SET UP A CRECHE

THE CONFERENCE HAS AN
INDUSTRIAL SECTION

FOR MORE INFORMATION
contact P.F.ROBINSON
74, Sussex St.
Lower Broughton,
Salford 7.
Tel 061-834-4406

RENTS STRUGGLE
needs news... Place
your orders, & your
info. with CHAMELEON,
5, WEST STREET,
LOWER BROUGHTON.
(834-4406)

LEEDS OLDHAM ROCHDALE YORK
CHADDERTON SHEFFIELD
MIDDLETON BARNSLEY
CLAY
CROSS
WHITEFIELD

STOCKPORT
BIRMINGHAM
LONDON

GLAMORGAN
CHELTENHAM
KNUTSFORD

11.00
STUDENTS
UNION
OXFORD
RD.

anson, ardwick
collyhurst, sale
droylsden, hulme
fallowfield, moss side
waterslea, burnage

gorton,
moston, spath
lane, benchill
altrincham, hartfield
wythenshawe, shefard
partington, calchon
farm, rusholme

BLACKBURN
BURNLEY BOLTON
LANCASTER SWINTON
ATHERTON
ECCLES
SALFORD

WIGAN
LEIGH
KIRBY
LIVERPOOL
WARRINGTON

PRODUCED BY
MANCHESTER
TENANTS ACTION
GROUP (95-29359)
which is made up
of over 30
associations in the
GREATER MANCHESTER
& SALFORD areas.

PRINTED BY
MOSS SIDE PRESS Ltd.
(226-3458)

Nationally, resistance to the Rent Act was strongest in the Midlands area. But even here, with the exception of Clay Cross, resistance soon faded when national Labour Party support was not forth coming.

Another Shields councillor quits over rent Act

A SOUTH SHIELDS councillor walked out of a housing meeting — and announced his resignation from the town council over the "fair rents" Act. Coun. Malcolm Campbell (Rekendyke), condemning Labour colleagues for their attitude to a tenants' rent strike, said: "I am serving no purpose here."

He told members of the Housing Committee: "Promises were made by the Labour Party, and are not being kept. I am very disappointed with my colleagues. There is no point in being here when the Act is being carried out by Labour councillors."

Coun. Campbell said he was the only councillor advocating a rent strike as the way to fight the Housing Finance Act. After his walkout, the committee was told that at the end of last week 295 out of more than 16,000 tenants had refused to pay the £1 increase, 2.4 per cent of all tenants. The total a week earlier had been 408.

The committee decided that tenants who did not pay the increase should be treated in the same way as others in arrears.

A proposal by Coun. Albert Elliott (Lab., Brinkburn), that none of the tenants on rent strike should be evicted, found no supporters. Coun. Elliott revealed that he was withholding the increase as a protest.

Chairman, Coun. William Malcolm (Lab., Rekendyke), said that there would be no mass evictions. But the council could not "underwrite" individuals who were in arrears.

COUN. CAMPBELL

'Very sincere'

"We cannot meet tenants to discuss the question of evictions. The decision on that is ours and ours alone. But we are very reluctant in South Shields to evict anyone, because of the hardship it causes and the problems it gives to social service departments," said Coun. Malcolm.

He said he was sorry Coun. Campbell had decided to resign. "He was a very sincere councillor, although some people thought he was a little extreme. I have always had a certain regard for him, and in time he would have been a valuable member."

Coun. Malcolm said the Labour Party had opposed the Act, but when the majority of local authorities decided to implement it, South Shields could not stand alone in defiance.

Came back

Coun. Douglas Ridley (Lab., Simonside) said the tenants on rent strike had been badly advised and badly led. "I appeal to them to use a bit of sense."

Coun. James Hodgson (Lab., Cleadon Park) said the council had been "held over a barrel" by the Tory Government. He did not support the Act, but had no intention of backing a rent strike. "People have got to pay the increase whether they like it or not."

Coun. Campbell, member for Rekendyke, is the third Labour councillor to resign over the Act. One of them, Coun. Jim Davison, changed his mind and is back on the council, but Mr John Wakeford stuck to his decision.

● The Housing Committee has decided to suspend the waiting list, to help solve the problem of a shortage of houses.

Shields Gazette 7 December 1972

77 Lisle Rd.,
South Shields.

The Town Clerk,
Town Hall,
South Shields.

30th Dec. 1972

Dear Sir,

You will know that at the last meeting of the
Housing Committee I indicated that I felt that I could no
longer continue as a Labour Councillor because of the
attitude of my Party colleagues to the Tory Rent Act.

It must have been clear for some time that I have
been unhappy in my role as Labour Councillor and deeply distres-
sed by the about-face of the leader of the Labour Group
and certain Labour Councillors on their election pledge
and public statements.

It has become obvious to me that the power structure
of the Party political system on the Town Council allows
a small clique to dictate policy contrary to the democratic
decision of the majority and in opposition to the expressed
views of the electors of the Town. Indeed it has become clear
that the political structure has been designed and maintained
with this intention.

It has become impossible therefore for me to continue to
participate in a system which makes denies the possibility
for me to act in accordance with the socialist principles
which I hold and upon which I was elected to the Council.

I could be grateful if you would present this letter
of resignation to the Council.

Yours faithfully,

M. Campbell.

Coun. Malcolm Campbell's letter of resignation

The advert the "Shields Gazette" refused to print . . .

RENT STRIKE

TO ALL TENANTS ON RENT STRIKE—
KEEP IT UP — AT LEAST FOR
THE NEXT FOUR WEEKS

TO TENANTS NOT ON RENT STRIKE—
START NOW — IT IS NOT
TOO LATE !

ALL TENANTS CONCERNED ARE INVITED TO

A PUBLIC MEETING

7.0 p.m.

Sunday December 3rd

Bolingbroke Hall

REPORTS, INFORMATION AND ADVICE ON THE
RENT STRIKE WILL BE GIVEN.

THE "ESTABLISHMENT" IS WORRIED ABOUT THE POWER OF
THE TENANTS ASSOCIATIONS.

THE PRESS, THE TOWN COUNCIL AND THE POLITICAL PARTIES
ARE TRYING TO CENSOR NEWS AND BAN INFORMATION.

ATTEND THE MEETING

AND GET THE FACTS !

Published by the South Shields Federation of Tenants Associations.
Printed by Dean Printing Works, 11 Franklin Street, South Shields.

Support for the Rent Strike at this time was still strong but faltering.

Rent strike ends —with 'Phase 2' action to follow

THE South Shields rent strike, which a fortnight ago was predicted as lasting another month, has ended and tenants are to pay back their arrears in instalments. This "dignified retreat" was made last night at a meeting of the South Shields Federation of Tenants' Association when voting was 38 to 11 in favour of ending the rent strike now, as advised by a liaison committee formed by representatives of the federation and the South Shields Trades Council.

The decision brings to an end what the federation has termed "phase one" of the South Shields council tenants' battle against the Housing Finance Act — the refusal of a number of them to pay the new £1 rent increases. Now, the federation is looking forward to next year when the Act will affect private tenants and those living in furnished accommodation, so they can begin phase two of their opposition to what are expected to be further rent increases.

Shields Gazette 11 December 1972

Rents protest dropped

COUNCIL HOUSE tenants have called off a protest over rent increases, four days after a councillor resigned on their behalf.

Coun. Malcolm Campbell stormed out of a South Shields housing committee meeting and announced he was quitting the town council.

He said it was because the committee had refused to give assurances that they would not evict council tenants who refused to pay rent increases demanded by the Housing Act.

By Journal Reporter

But after his gesture of support to the tenants, the cause has ended following a decision by South Shields' federation of tenants' associations.

Coun. Campbell said last night that he was not going to reconsider his resignation decision.

"I have quit the council for good and I am not going back on my word. The rent strike may have ended but it has not been a failure."

He added: "For some time now I have been dissatisfied with the attitude of my fellow Labour councillors. They have made promises to the people and betrayed them.

"And at that housing meeting they said they were prepared to evict tenants who were fighting a cause which they believed in."

The federation voted by 38 to 11 in favour of calling off the protest action because the number of tenants withholding rent had fallen each week.

But those tenants determined to continue their stand will still get the backing of the local trades council, a tenants' spokesman said.

Newcastle Journal 7 December 1972

The Rent Strike ends. Contributory factors were the collapse of the national campaign and the uncertainty as to whether the Labour Council would implement a programme of evictions. The Trades Union Council advocated the end of the strike in a collective unified manner. The Poll Tax was to be the next conflict with 'reluctant' Labour councils implementing Tory legislation.

Troops Out Movement &
Anti-Recruitment Campaign

From the perspective of the year 1999 it might seem surprising that in the mid-70s, the British trade union movement should be actively engaged in a campaign involving Northern Ireland.

The reasons for this involvement lie both with the confidence of the trade union movement at that time, and with its traditional international perspective.

Also for more specific reasons:–

1. Many Irish workers immigrated to England in the 19th and early 20th century. These were often unskilled or semi-skilled workers and were naturally attracted to the largely manual worker trade unions of that time.

2. Many trade union activists came from a political view which identified the British presence in Ireland as imperialist exploitation.

3. The British trade union movement had close fraternal contacts with Irish trade unions at local and national level.

In 1972 the Trades Union Congress (TUC) reported that many trades unions had expressed concern about developments in Northern Ireland. The General Council of the TUC approved a policy calling for:–

An end to civil disobedience.

An end to imprisonment without trial.

A bill of human rights.

This official TUC policy was soon translated into an anti-internment campaign calling for:–

Release of internees.

Withdrawal of British troops.

Many local contacts were made between English Trades Councils and their Northern Ireland counterparts, and between English and Irish Claimants Unions.

South Shields TUC made contact with several Northern Ireland Trades Councils, and sought to intervene in what they saw as a misguided conflict involving common fraternal interests. In answer to a national TUC call they made contact with interned trade unionists-as did many individual trade union branches.

In retrospect the 'Troops Out' movement can be seen as a totally inappropriate response to the problems of that time. Nevertheless, this sort of political action, supported by different political groups, for different political reasons, can also be seen as one of the many contributing pressures placed on successive British governments which ultimately led to what became known as the 'peace process'of the late 90s.

The international dimension to trade union thinking led the South Shields TUC to be involved in other international issues. Their anti-imperialist stance led them to campaign against army recruitment which they saw as an exploitation of the unemployed youth in the region. Certainly, recruitment statistics for that time indicate that a high proportion of servicemen (and women) were recruited from areas of high unemployment such as the North East. Although it was officially denied that recruitment campaigns were directed to the NE it is certainly the case that recruitment officers regularly visited local schools and colleges. It would be naive to have expected otherwise. Then, as now, some 50% of all forces recruits were only 16 years of age.

This Anti-Recruitment Campaign was one of the more controversial of the SSTUC projects. It resulted from a view that:–

1: Northern unemployed youths were being targeted by recruitment campaigns for the armed forces; and the region was being neglected for job opportunities.

(In spite of strong denial by parliament, official statistics were eventually to reveal that there was in fact a direct correlation between unemployment and recruitment. In retrospect not a surprising conclusion.)

and 2: Some members of the SSTUC were of the then conventional 'left' view that the armed forces were acting as agents of imperial repression. The use of the army in Northern Ireland did, for some, confirm this opinion.

The controversy arising from this campaign bitterly divided the SSTUC – but not, surprisingly, entirely on political lines. Some revolutionary comrades thought this was a fight too far.

Nevertheless, the campaign was fully in time with the spirit of an age that could still believe the slogan – 'make love not war'.

The national and local anti-apartheid movement was also strongly supported by the Trades Union Council and many joint campaigns were mounted with anti-apartheid groups active on Tyneside at that time.

TRADES UNION CONGRESS

GENERAL SECRETARY: VICTOR FEATHER CBE

CONGRESS HOUSE · GREAT RUSSELL STREET · LONDON WC1B 3LS

Telephone 01-636 4030   *Telegrams* TRADUNIC LONDON WC1

IN REPLY PLEASE QUOTE:
CIRCULAR NO.145 (1971-72)

DEPT International
OUR REF VF/MW/SA
YOUR REF

TO THE SECRETARIES OF
TRADES COUNCILS AND
FEDERATIONS OF TRADES
COUNCILS.

March 29, 1972.

Dear Colleague,

Northern Ireland

Many trades councils have written recently expressing concern about developments in Northern Ireland. For your information I am enclosing a copy of a circular with other enclosures which was sent to unions on Friday, March 24.

Yours sincerely,

VICTOR FEATHER

General Secretary.

ENCLS: Circular and
attachments.

At the time 'Ireland' featured prominently on the trade unions' official agenda.

TRADES UNION CONGRESS

GENERAL SECRETARY: VICTOR FEATHER CBE

CONGRESS HOUSE · GREAT RUSSELL STREET · LONDON WC1B 3LS

Telephone 01-636 4030   *Telegrams* TRADUNIC LONDON WC1

IN REPLY PLEASE QUOTE:
CIRCULAR NO. 144 (1971-72)

DEPT International
OUR REF VF/MW/SA
YOUR REF

TO THE GENERAL SECRETARIES OF
ALL AFFILIATED ORGANISATIONS

March 24, 1972.

Dear Colleague,

Northern Ireland

The General Council have decided as a matter of urgency to ensure that union Executive Committees should be informed of developments in regard to Northern Ireland, and of the lead which the General Council has given. You will know that this morning the Prime Minister announced the steps the government are to take, and I attach a copy of the statement issued on behalf of the TUC. You will see that it calls on every union to give maximum support in restoring calm and reason in Northern Ireland.

In the trade union field the recent background to these events is that on February 2 the Northern Ireland Committee of the Irish Congress of Trade Unions held a special delegate conference in Belfast which endorsed proposals (copy attached) for immediate steps preparing the way for reconciliation in the community. A strong observer delegation of the General Council attended this conference, and the General Council have since approved the proposals.

On March 12 General Council representatives discussed the proposals in detail with representatives of the Executive Committee of the Irish Congress of Trade Unions and its Northern Ireland Committee. Subsequently they informed the Home Secretary of the agreed view that a swift political initiative by the government was necessary if the drift towards civil war in Northern Ireland was to be halted, and that it should include steps designed to reduce and eventually terminate imprisonment without trial, accompanied by a transfer of responsibility for security in Northern Ireland to Westminster, and a guarantee that the constitutional status of Northern Ireland as part of the United Kingdom would not thereby be brought into question.

Throughout the period of civil disturbance in Northern Ireland the General Council have maintained close contact and consultation with the Northern Ireland Committee, which is the sole central trade union organisation in Northern Ireland and represents working people of every opinion. The General Council consider that at this critical stage they should give a lead to trade unionists in both Great Britain and Northern Ireland, and they have endorsed the proposals of the NIC as a moderate and balanced approach to the long-standing social and political problems of Northern Ireland.

I now ask that the statement issued this morning by the TUC should be given the widest publicity and that it should be brought to the notice of your Executive Committee, together with the NIC proposals, with a view to firm and prompt endorsement.

I should be grateful to know what action your organisation takes on this recommendation.

Yours sincerely,

VICTOR FEATHER

General Secretary.

ENCLS:
Statement
Proposals

The TUC is maintaining the closest contact and consultation with the Northern Ireland Committee of the Irish Congress of Trade Unions, which is the sole central organisation in Northern Ireland able to represent working people, and the only body capable of judging and supporting their united interests. Their proposals for the future, which have been approved by the General Council of the TUC, have included an end to civil disobedience, a phased end to imprisonment without trial, a bill of human rights, the fulfilment by public representatives of their duties, and agreement on measures to protect lives and property, understanding that the constitutional status of Northern Ireland as part of the UK would not thereby be brought into question.

The TUC statement was open to interpretation and was translated by some as 'anti-internment' and 'troops out'.

Troops Out Movement

IRELAND: TROOPS OUT NOW!
SELF-DETERMINATION FOR THE
IRISH PEOPLE

For centuries successive British Governments have announced several "final solutions" to the "Irish Problem".

Famine, Partition, Home Rule, Direct Rule, concessions and Black and Tan style repression have all been tried and all have failed.

Any British "solution" must fail, because the basic problem in Ireland is British presence there.

The only solution Britain's rulers have never tried is <u>GETTING OUT</u>.

We, the undersigned, believe that only the people of Ireland should have the right to determine the future of Ireland.

Therefore, we call upon the Labour Party to break now from its bi-partisan role on Ireland with the Tories, and implement a policy of withdrawal of Troops from Ireland now.

Name	Address	Occupation/Position

For information, activities and speakers contact:
EALING, LONDON, W.5.

Troops Out Movement

THE ARMY

The first regular British Army was raised in the seventeenth century. "Suppression of the Irish" coupled with "Defence of the Protestant religion" was given as the reason for its existence.

Since 1945 the post-war "Professional" British Army has taken part in 35 "little wars": Malaya, Kenya, Cyprus and Aden are just a few. The overwhelming majority of these operations were struggles by the peoples of British colonies for the right to rule their country by themselves.

The British press and mass media were used to mislead the people of this country about the exact nature of the role of the Army during these actions, often portraying the troops as a kind of peace-keeping force. A look at the casualty figures for any of these operations makes nonsense of that conception: i.e. in Kenya during the "Emergency" the total white deaths, civilian and military were less than 100, while more than 11,500 African "terrorists" sic, were killed during operations by the British security forces.

IRELAND

Britain invaded Ireland 800 years ago. That's when the "Irish problem" started. There's been no peace in Ireland ever since.

In 1921 partition of Ireland was Britain's solution to this "Irish problem". (Ireland was cut in two and civil war immediately followed.)

But Ireland is one country - and that's why there is war in the North of Ireland today.

Since the Tories have been in power they have tried direct rule, internment, CS gas, water-cannons, rubber bullets, lead bullets, torture, a so-called "reform programme", a White Paper, a farcical revival of Stormont and special criminal agents like the Littlejohns. They've all hopelessly failed.

THE ONLY THING THEY HAVEN'T TRIED IS GETTING OUT!

The Troops Out Movement is determined to secure the withdrawal of British troops from Ireland. If you support this demand and want to help us in our activities, please fill in below:

NAME: _____   TEL NO.: _____

ADDRESS: _____

_____

████████████████ Ealing, London, W.5.

THE ANTI-INTERNMENT LEAGUE
FOR THE IMMEDIATE RELEASE OF ALL INTERNEES IN NORTHERN IRELAND

Our Ref. I64 *a* ,

Jack Grassby,
Secretary,
South Shields Trades Union Council,
Ede House,
Westoe Rd.,
South Shields.

Basement Flat,
████████████,
London W. I4.
Feb. 22nd.

Dear Mr. Grassby,

████████████ gave me your name. He tells me that you would be
interested in the names of any A.T.T.I. members who are interned.
Unfortunately I have at the moment not got the names of any
A.T.T.I. members who are interned but will try to find
out for you and will write again if I am successful.

████ also suggested to me that you might be interested in
our conference for Trade Unionists on the Irish crisis being held
in London on March 5th. I enclose a copy of the initial
invitation. There will be three sessions covering firstly the
history of the relationship between the Irish and British Labour
movement and the enemies they have in common. Secondly the present
crisis in particular the effects it has had on the working-class in
the North. Thirdly what action can British Trade Unionists take.

I also enclose a copy of our bulletin which might be of interest.

Yours fraternally,

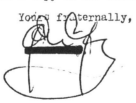

B2, IO.

*The Troops Out Movement and The Anti-Internment League had wide
support in the Labour movement.*

INTERNMENT TO BE CHALLENGED FROM SHIELDS

SOUTH SHIELDS Trades Union Council is to co-operate with the Belfast Trades Council in an attempt to free trade unionists interned without trial in Northern Ireland.

At a special meeting delegates heard that the Belfast council had offered to provide South Shields TUC with a list of interned trade unionists.

Mr Jack Grassby .secretary of the South Shields TUC, told the meeting that the council could bring pressure on the Government through the Trades Union Congress and also through individual trade unions whose members were interned.

He said the ending of internment was the "first step" before a solution would emerge in Northern Ireland.

Mr Jim Riddle, of the Tailors and Garment Workers Union. supporting the plan, said he hoped delegates would be concerned if ever, trade unionists were put in jail in Keppel Street police station without trial.

"The day may come when you or I will be picked up because whatever happens in one part of the British Isles can happen in other parts," he said.

Shields Gazette 26 April 1972

COUNTY DURHAM CONNOLLY ASSOCIATION
(including Tyneside)

████████████,
Pelton Fell,
Chester-le-Street,
DH2 2PE.

tel. 3916

17th April, 1972

Dear Jack,

I am writing to ask your Trades Council to support our delegate conference in Newcastle on Saturday, 13th May, from 2 p.m. to 5 p.m. The conference is being held in the Connaught Hall, under the chairmanship of Desmond Greaves, editor of the Irish Democrat, and the reporter from Ireland will be Miss Ann Hope, E.C. member of Belfast Trades Council on which she represents the Clerical Workers; she is also on the E.C. of the Civil Rights Association, and has just returned from a tour of European capitals, east and west, sponsored by the Irish Union of Students.

The conference is being organised jointly by the Irish Democrat and the Co. Durham branch of the Connolly Association. The subject is the crisis in Ireland and the British Labour movement. Sponsors to date include the following M.P.s: Geoffrey Rhodes, Ted Garret, Edward Milne, Ted Fletcher, Fred Willey, and John Horam; and Arthur Scott and Jack Carr of the National Executive of AUEW (TASS), plus the Teesside Divisional Council of the same union.

We would welcome your official sponsorship, but, above all, delegates. The delegate fee is 25p. Credentials can be had from myself or from the Irish Democrat (283 Grays Inn Road, London W.C.1.).

It would be most helpful if you could draw the attention of your affiliated branches to the conference.

Yours fraternally,

Michael
████████,

Broadway Claimants Union

c/o ━━━━━━━━━

Belfast

19th June 1978.

Dear Friends,

We would appreciate your help in publicising the enclosed statement from the Workers Resource Centre. During the said the R.U.C and British Army went through our Claimants files and, as they have, up to the minute, refused to give us a list of what they have taken, it is more than likely they have stolen some of our past files. This is a new departure from the usual level of repressive tactics used here and we feel is a dangerous precedent which must be exposed publically and fought.

Hoping you can help us in doing that

We Remain

Yours in solidarity.

━━━━━━━━━

Contacts in N.Ireland included exchanges between Claimants Unions.

BELFAST & DISTRICT TRADES' UNION COUNCIL

ESTABLISHED 1881

TELEPHONE 26283

Please Address all Communications to Secretary
MISS B. SINCLAIR

WARING HOUSE,

4 WARING STREET,

BELFAST, 1

19th May, 1972

Mr. Jack Grassby,
Secretary,
South Shields Trades Council,
Ede House,
143 Westoe Road,
South Shields.

Dear Jack,

I am enclosing the names and trade unions of internees and detainees. Some may have been released but there are still some 600 there.

I received the collection taken for the Council by the members of the AEUW (TASS Section) Tyneside Divisional Committee of £3.50. My Council was very pleased with this aid as we have suffered much because of the 'troubles' and also the mergers that have taken place within the trade union movement.

Our attendances at Council meetings have been increasing and we hope this trend continues. Although, at the moment things are pretty grim. And, in such conditions, the working class suffers.

Yours sincerely,

Betty Sinclair

Hon. Secretary.

PEACE, EMPLOYMENT & RECONSTRUCTION IN NORTHERN IRELAND.

The following is an extract from the Address of the Chairman of the Northern Ireland Committee, Irish Congress of Trade Unions, Mr. Brendan Harkin, to the Special Delegate Conference held in Belfast on 2nd February, 1972.

WE STAND TO-DAY AT THE EDGE OF A DEEPENING ABYSS WITH NEITHER SIDE APPARENTLY PREPARED TO TAKE THE NECESSARY STEP TOWARDS PEACEFUL SOLUTIONS.

For this reason I wish to put the following suggestions in the hope that they may be found helpful.

    1. A DATE SHOULD BE AGREED BY WHICH:—

    a. CIVIL DISOBEDIENCE SHALL CEASE.

    b. IMPRISONMENT WITHOUT TRIAL SHALL END.

    c. ALL PUBLIC REPRESENTATIVES SHALL RETURN TO THEIR REPRESENTATIVE DUTIES, AND

    d. ALL-PARTY TALKS SHALL COMMENCE.

    2. IT SHOULD BE AGREED THAT A BILL OF HUMAN RIGHTS SHALL BE ENACTED IMMEDIATELY WHICH WILL PROVIDE FOR EQUAL RIGHTS FOR ALL CITIZENS.

    3. A MAMMOTH ECONOMIC AID PROGRAMME SHOULD BE EMBARKED UPON TO REDUCE THE DREADFUL LEVEL OF UNEMPLOYMENT.

    4. THE THREE GOVERNMENTS IN BELFAST, DUBLIN AND WESTMINSTER SHOULD AGREE IMMEDIATE AND APPRO-PRIATE STEPS TO PROTECT THE LIVES AND PROPERTY OF INNOCENT PERSONS, TO PREVENT THE RE-EMERGENCE OF VIOLENCE.

I AM ONLY TOO WELL AWARE THAT IN MAKING THESE PROPOSALS I AM RUNNING THE RISK OF ATTACK FROM MANY QUARTERS BUT FOR ALL OF US THE RISK OF DOING NOTHING IS EVEN GREATER. THERE IS NO VICTORY FOR ANYONE IN WHAT I HAVE SUGGESTED BUT THERE MAY BE AN OPPORTUNITY FOR A RETURN TO SANITY.

These proposals were adopted by the Conference, and we invite your support.

Irish Congress of Trade Unions,
Northern Ireland Committee,
Congress House,
236 Antrim Road,
Belfast, BT15 2AN.

The Irish TUC was actively involved in seeking a solution.

TYNESIDE ANTI-INTERNMENT LEAGUE

Dear Bro Grossly,

    The Anti-Internment League was formed last August to campaign for a just settlement of the Irish crisis. It has the immediate aims: (1). RELEASE INTERNEES
                (2). WITHDRAW BRITISH TROOPS.

The killings in Londonderry on January 30th. and the recent deaths in Aldershot have emphasised the deep involvement of this country with events in Ireland. We feel it is particularly important for the Labour movement to be well informed on the situation, so that clear and principled demands can be made.

The Tyneside branch of the A-I.L. would welcome an invitation to speak on any aspect of the Irish situation in which your members would be interested. For instance we would be prepared to give a general survey or talk about British policy in Ireland, political and economic discrimination in the Six Counties, the Civil Rights movement, events in Derry, the history of the I.R.A.

I would be most grateful if you would return the form below as a first step to arranging a meeting.

You may also be interested in the National Conference for Trade Unionists organised by A-I.L. this Sunday (March 5th.) at N.U.F.T.O. Hall, Jockey's Field, London WC1.

                    Yours Fraternally,

We would also be grateful of further information on how best to campaign in your area

To be returned to: Tyneside Anti-Internment League,

              Newcastle-upon-Tyne, 4.

NAME OF ORGANISATION:

NAME, ADDRESS AND OFFICE OF OFFICIAL:

TELEPHONE NO.:

    We would like more information about the A-I.L. and its aims.
    We would like to arrange a meeting with speaker.
        Provisional time, late and place:-

      Subjects we are most interested in:-

                 (Please delete where inapplicable.)

The SSTUC leaflet which introduced the campaign against armed forces recruitment.

The advertising campaigns for the Forces show a life of beer, birds and bingo. They never mention killing - the main purpose of the Forces. Why not do you think?

In the Forces you may be expected to use physical violence and to kill ordinary people like yourself, your family and your friends.

Could you do this? You won't be given a chance to refuse!

You will have to learn to obey orders - any orders. If you are ordered to shoot you will have to shoot - even if it means the death of innocent women and children as has happened recently in Northern Ireland.

Could you really do this without question? Do you really know what the war in Ireland, say, is all about?

Can you really take sides and kill to order.

Much of the equipment and many of the tactics you will be trained to use in the Forces are intended for use against the people of this country when they are wanted. They will be used against so called "trouble-makers" - trade unionists, strikers, pickets and students - people like yourself and your friends.

By joining the Forces you will be helping to develop the tactics and weapons, the experimental guns and gas, which will be available for use against workers here. It has happened in the past, it is being planned again. The Army chiefs, Brigadier Callvert and Brigadier Kitson, are already preaching a policy of training the armed forces to be used against strikers, students and other "Trouble-makers". The Tory pamphlet "In Defence of Peace" says that "The techniques of political terrorism must now be an integral part of every soldiers career."

There is a famous question asked of soldiers:-

When your officers order you to shoot

GOOD PROSPECTS

at your own people - in what direction will you point your rifle?

Your own people are your family and friends and the working class of this country, of Ireland, and the world. If you were asked this question what would be your answer?

★　　★

Your life in the Forces will be mainly one of boredom, redtape and bull. You will be bullied and browned off. There is no place to question authority. Are you prepared to be bossed around and never answer back?

And don't be conned by Army propaganda about "Training for a trade". Ask at the Employment Exchange how many vacancies they have for Field Gun Mechanics or Chieftain Tank Drivers! And if you do get a civvy job it will cost you £150 to buy yourself out before your time's up!

Why is the government prepared to spend thousands of pounds to train a gunner or a tank driver while the training of a brick-layer or plumber is left to the chance forces of private profit?

Why can millions of pounds be spent to train missile-technicians while cancer and kidney research has to depend largely of voluntary support from charity donations?

★　　★

When you look for a job make sure you demand a real job with proper training and good prospects. You cannot be forced to take just any job that's going - although pressure might be put on you to do this. It's not your fault there are no decent jobs. Don't feel guilty about it.

Remember there are alternative to joining the forces - even if you cannot get a job:-

a) You go to the Technical College and take a GCE or a technical course in Engineering, Electronics, commerce etc...or study a hobby. You can draw Social Security while doing this provided you are prepared to take a suitable job if one turns up and you attend college for not more than 3 days a week.

b) You could go back to school. Many schools now put on special non-examination subjects and include hobbies and sport etc. If you return to school, your parents can claim tax allowance and perhaps Family Allowance. Also the local authority says you can claim "Maintenance Allowance" - but your family will have to be near the starvation level to get this - so don't depend on it.

c) Until a suitable job turns up you could do some of the things you've always wanted to do but never had the time. You could join the trade union campaign for better job training, more apprenticeships, and more educational opportunities.

(continued overleaf)

GOOD PROSPECTS

Parents will want you to do the best you can for yourself – to see that you get a good training and a job. In desperation they might be mis-guided to advise you to join the Forces. They might tell you about the good times they had – they will have forgotten the bad times.

Ask them if they really want you to be trained to kill as a profession.

Ask them if they really want you to be used in a war that you don't un-derstand which is only in the inter-ests of capital.

If you feel that undue pressure is being placed on you to join the For-ces or to take a rotten dead end job – contact your local Trades Union Council. If you feel that you are being done out of Dole or Social Security benefits – contact your local Claimants' Union. Their adress-es are given below.

These organisations will help you to resist pressure and to fight back. This is where your fight is.

Remember the army's interests are not your interests or the interests of the working class. Let the Bosses and the Politicians do their own dirty work. Their life is not at risk...Yours will be!

Join the growing body of opinion for the withdrawl of troops from Northern Ireland.

If you are thinking of joining the Forces...........

...Think again!

South Shields Claimants Union:

Peoples Place, Derby Terrace, South Shields, (Tues. 1.30–3.30pm)

Newcastle Claimants Union:

25° Westgate Road. Newcastle (Tues. 2pm)

Published by the South Shields Trades Union Council, 143 Westoe Road, South Shields.

Printed by Moss-side Press, Manchester.

UNIONS ARE SPLIT, BUT DOCUMENT APPROVED

SOUTH SHIELDS trade unionists—though bitterly divided — have approved a document condemning local Armed Forces recruitment and British Army presence in Northern Ireland.

Mr Campbell — used his casting vote.

The decision split the town's Trades Union Council down the middle and it took two votes by the president, Mr Malcolm Campbell to force the document through — one as a council delegate and his casting vote as chairman.

The final vote in favour of the document was 10-9.

Disagreement was so intense that at one point Mr Campbell's chairmanship was challenged, and he was forced to stand aside while a vote of confidence was taken. He retained the chair.

Innocent

Delegates were generally ready to accept an anti-recruitment document; the dissenters objected to references about Northern Ireland. Some also claimed that the document was anti-Army.

As amended, it includes the phrases: "You will have to learn to obey orders — any orders. If you are ordered to shoot you will have to shoot — even if it means the death of innocent women and children as has happened recently in Northern Ireland."

At another point the phrase: "You should join the growing lobby of people against the war in Northern Ireland," was added to the statement. In both instances Mr Campbell used his casting vote to force them through.

In favour

Reaction by opposing delegates was bitter. Mr Jim Riddle (Tailor and Garment Workers' Union) said that the document had been referred from a sub-committee as anti-recruitment, not anti-Northern Ireland. He later dissociated himself from it.

MR FLORENCE

Mr Joe McAlroy (Technical and Supervisory Services) said that he was "100 per cent in favour of an anti-recruitment campaign. We have had soldiers killed in Aden, Columbia and even India if you go back far enough." But statements in the document were not accomplished facts.

At one point Mr Jim Florence (Amalgamated Union of Engineering Workers) interjected: "This is an extremely divisive policy we are creating, and you are pushing democracy to the brink. When you find yourself in a partisan situation like this, it is not worth tuppence."

First time

However, Mr Jack Grassby (Association of Teachers in Technical Institutions) told opposing delegates: "Our views are just as strongly held as yours. We are not just against recruitment, but also against the purposes for which the Forces are being used."

Mr Campbell stated that it was not unknown for a trades council chairman to use his casting vote, but it was the first time he had to do so. "I am not attacking the Army, but the ways in which it is used," he added.

Mr John Bradley (National Association of Schoolmasters) later said: "My union

Mr Riddle — dissociated himself from the document.

meeting last night disagrees with it. No-one was aware of any undue propaganda presented within the schools service. The Armed Services receive the same treatment as do recruiting officers from industry."

Her Views

When printed, the document will be circulated among school-leavers who might be tempted to join the forces.

Asked for her views Miss Maureen Robertshaw, head of the Youth Employment Service office in South Shields, said:

"The idea is to give young people and their parents ideas for careers. We won't exclude anybody. Our purpose is to provide observation and discussion of various careers — not recruitment."

She did not feel that moral issues were involved.

Shields Gazette 27 June 1973

The anti-recruitment leaflet proved to be controversial from the onset.

Unions fight to prevent recruiting

By Journal Reporter

THE first shots have been fired in a battle to stop the armed forces recruiting jobless teen-agers in a North town.

South Shields Trades Council has written to the education director demanding that recruiting officers should be barred from schools.

Members have also asked for all posters enticing youngsters to join up to be removed from classrooms and school corridors.

Other plans have been drawn up but have not been divulged.

The letter, which was also sent to the Town Clerk, says the armed forces are putting unfair pressure on to jobless young people by stepping up recruitment campaigns.

Many young people, it says, are enticed into a life in the forces because they see no attractive alternative.

Newcastle Journal May 1973

"To help remove this pressure we ask that the local authority should ban recruitment campaigns in the South Shields area."

Mr. Malcolm Campbell, a Trades Council president, a taxi driver said: "We believe that this area has sacrificed more than its fair share of young people as the casualty list from Northern Ireland shows.

"We don't want our lads to become cannon fodder just because they haven't a job to go to."

The town's Education Director, Mr. Geoffrey Denton, said he could not comment because he had not received the letter.

The Army's Divisional Press Officer refused to comment last night.

THE JOURNAL Thursday May 17 1973

'Cannon fodder' blast
Dole boys warned against joining Army

A TRADES COUNCIL is to picket Army recruiting centres in a bid to stop unemployed youngsters joining up.

For council members fear that the youths will be used as "cannon fodder" in Ulster.

Taxi driver Malcolm Campbell, president of South Shields Trades Council, said last night: "Unemployed youngsters are easy targets for the Army.

"They get so bored being without a job that they will take anything that comes up."

And he added: "We shall try to persuade young people not to join the armed forces, particularly lads about to

By Journal Reporter

leave school this summer. We will picket recruiting centres throughout Tyneside.

"Recruits will be used as cannon fodder in such situations as Northern Ireland."

Tradition

Mr. Campbell said that the government was well aware of the high unemployment among youngsters on Tyneside and was willing to exploit the situation to get more people to join the forces.

An Army spokesman said: "There is no direct evidence to show that unemployment in South Shields has led to an upsurge in Army recruiting.

"The area has always had a fine military tradition proved by the record of the famous Durham Light Infantry and their successors, the Light Infantry.

"The Army has always had careers offices in most large towns and cities where young men and women can go for advice about an Army career.

"Joining is entirely voluntary and the potential recruits are given ample time to consult their families or any other outside agency before committing themselves."

The Tyneside press were (from the vantage point of today) surprisingly sympathetic to the campaign.

Recruiting in schools —no action on letter

FORMER South Shields Education Committee chairman Ald. Mrs Margaret Sutton has said that youngsters risk having their futures blighted because they are pressurised into joining the Armed forces by recruiting visits to schools. She said that even if the youngsters came back out of the forces there lay ahead only "blind alley occupations."

Shields Gazette June 1973

The chair of the local Education Committee was a strong (and surprising) supporter of the campaign.

MACKLEY RAPS 'BAN RECRUITMENT' PLEA

SOUTH Shields Trades Union Council has fired its first shot in a war against Armed Forces recruitment in the town. It is demanding that the town council bans any recruitment for the Forces because of the local economic situation.

A letter to the Town Clerk, and Mr Geoffrey Denton, Director of Education, says: "The South Shields Trades Union Council is concerned with the combination of high unemployment and intensive recruitment as placing unfair pressure on young unemployed persons in this area.

"We believe that as a consequence many young people are enticed into a life in the Forces because they see no attractive alternative. To help remove this pressure and to help our young people to make a more balanced and objective choice we ask that the local authority should ban recruitment campaigns in the South Shields area."

ALD. MACKLEY

The demands met with instant opposition from Ald. Ernest Mackley (Lab.), chairman of the Management Committee.

"I don't agree with this. I don't agree at all. Young people are not sheep. They should be given the chance to make a choice, and they should be given the choice to make the Army a career," he said.

Shields Gazette 24 May 1973

Enticed

Ald. Mackley said he opposed the letter's demands, but it would be up to the Management Committee and the Labour Party to make their own decision.

Mr Malcolm Campbell, trades council president, said that the campaign against recruitment would be directed mainly at young men who are enticed into the Army and could end up in Northern Ireland.

"We believe that this area has sacrificed more than its fair share of young people as the casualty list from Northern Ireland shows," he said in a statement.

No comment

Demands for a ban on recruitment publicity in the town's schools drew no comment from Mr Denton, who had not received the letter today.

The Army's diivsional Press officer declined to comment today.

The anti-recruitment drive was launched a week ago, when executive members voted 10-5 in favour of the campaign.

A trades council spokesman, Mr Jack Grassby, said their "further activities" were planned, but could not yet be divulged.

The local Labour Party was split – with the leadership coming out against the campaign. The local and national press remained surprisingly sympathetic.

Army wins campaign

A BID to expel Army recruiting officers from school classrooms split the ranks of South Shields Education Committee last night.

Councillors could not agree with Ald. Mrs. Margaret Sutton's claim that the glamour of a uniform was tempting jobless youngsters to join up.

She asked: "Do we really have to have the Army in the schools? Leave the children alone until they are about 20 and let them decide for themselves."

She said when a boy had no job on leaving school he was bound to see a bit of glamour in the armed forces, but if he joined his future would be blighted. "If he doesn't like it he will have to leave and end up with a blind-alley occupation."

Backed by Coun. Albert Elliott she supported the town's Trades Council who want to ban armed forces recruiting officers from secondary schools.

The letter from the Trades Council said: "High unemployment and intensive recruitment publicity from the armed forces is placing unfair pressure on young persons in the area.

"To remove this pressure, and help our young people to make a more balanced and objective choice, we ask that the local authority should ban recruitment publicity and recruitment officers from the schools."

But Coun. Jim Doneghan said: "The Army is still an honorable career."

He said the Trades Council were not supporting their allegations with facts. "If I thought pupils were being hoodwinked or brainwashed I would act immediately.'

Coun. Bob Scott added: "If a young lad wants to join the Army, good luck to him."

Education Director, Mr. Geoffrey Denton, said no pressure was put on pupils when forces officers visited schools.

"The visits are only for the purpose of giving opportunity for observation and discussion—not recruitment."

The committee decided to take no action on the letter.

Shields Gazette May 1973

Town councillors were divided on the issue – and the Director of Education claimed, disingeniously, that armed forces' visits to schools were for 'observation and discussion – not recruitment'.

Joint attack on Army recruiting

STUDENTS from Northumberland College of Education and Newcastle University join South Shields Trades Council members tomorrow for a demonstration against the country's biggest Army recruiting drive being held on Newcastle's John Dobson Street car park.

With banners proclaiming "Jobs, not guns" their aim is to picket the display and stop unemployed youngsters joining the Army in a last-ditch effort to get a full-time job.

'It's strange how the Army always pick on the North-East to get their cannon-fodder. They are deliberately exploiting the unemployment situation to drum up recruits," said a Trades Council spokesman.

Newcastle Journal May 1973

Recruiting figures challenge

SOUTH SHIELDS Trades Council today challenged claims made by the town's MP, Mr Arthur Blenkinsop, that unemployment was not a cause of high recruitment to the Army in the North-East.

Mr Blenkinsop said at the weekend that the North-East was not the highest recruitment area for the Forces, according to figures

But today Trades Council president, Mr Malcolm Campbell, said the figures did not support the MP's argument.

"The statistics neither prove nor disprove our contention that percentage recruitment is greater in areas of high unemployment. However, if it is realised the recruitment of young people anticipates the unemployment situation, the figures indicate that, periods of high unemployment to produce high recruitment.

"We would like to know what proportion of recruits in this region are to officer rank and what to other ranks — the real cannon fodder.

The matter, which was first raised when the Trades Council wrote to the town's Director of Education, Mr Geoffrey Denton, about recruitment in schools, will be discussed three times in three days this week.

It will be on the agenda for tonight's Education Committee meeting, for a Trades Council meeting tomorrow, and for the Management Board's meeting on Wednesday morning.

Shields Gazette May 1973

MINISTER OF STATE FOR DEFENCE
WHITEHALL LONDON SW1A 2HB

Telephone 01-930 7022

7 June 1973

Dear Blenkinsop

When I replied on 24 May to your Question about our recruiting figures I was not able to provide you with the figures for 1972/73 nor the breakdown of the figures for the Northern Region by age. I promised to write.

I attach details of the 1972/73 recruiting achievement by regions and a breakdown by age categories for the Northern Region. I am afraid that we could not obtain the comparable age breakdown for earlier years without disproportionate effort. I hope however that this information, together with the information given in my reply, is satisfactory for your purpose.

Yours sincerely

Ian Gilmour

Ian Gilmour

Arthur Blenkinsop Esq MP
House of Commons
London   SW1A 0AA

Parliament at first denied a correlation between recruitment and unemployment – and that the North was targeted in recruitment campaigns.

Social Trends 1972
Government Statistical Office

1972/73 recruiting achievement by regions

Region	Number of Recruits	per Thous %
Northern	3,280	.556
Yorkshire and Humberside	3,851	.442
North Western	5,456	.450
East Midland	2,831	.465
West Midland	3,272	.355
East Anglia	1,117	.373
South Eastern	7,894	.254
South Western	3,020	.445
Wales	1,866	.380
Scotland	4,671	.496
Northern Ireland	962	.344
United Kingdom Total	38,220	

Breakdown by age categories for the
Northern Region in 1972/73

Age	Number
Under 17	1,704
17	633
18	299
19	150
20	134
21	104
22	72
23	66
24	44
25 and over	74
Total	3,280

The official statistics finally proved the accusations of preferential recruitment in the North to be correct – and that 50% of the recruits were only 16.

TUC IS ANGRY AT ANTI-ARMY YOUTH

Bureaucrats at Congress House, headquarters of the TUC, are angry about a campaign by South Shields Trades Union Council to warn young people not to join the British army.

The council recently published pamphlets 'deglamorizing' the role of British troops. They were handed out at labour exchanges in the area.

The message was mainly addressed to school-leavers, students and the unemployed who are subjected to a barrage of propaganda to join the army. The army has set up recruiting centres in all the areas of high unemployment, while other drives are conducted at schools.

The South Shields pamphlet was aimed at dispelling the advertising image of the army. It stated: 'The advertising campaigns for the forces show a life of beer, birds and bingo, but never mention killing—**the main purpose of the forces.**

'You will have to learn to obey orders — any orders. If you are ordered to shoot you will have to shoot—even if it means the death of innocent women and children as has hapened recently in Northern Ireland.

'Could you really do this without question? Do you really know what the war in Ireland, say, is all about? Can you really take sides and kill to order?'

Young people are advised not to be 'conned' by army propaganda about training for

The pamphlet also offers an answer to parental pressure to join the forces. 'Ask them if they really want you to be trained to kill as a profession? Ask them if they really want you to be used in a war that you don't understand, which is only in the interests of capital.

'Remember, the army's interests are not your interests or the interests of the worka trade. They are told life in the forces wil be mainly one of 'boredom, red tape and bull'.

ing class. Let the bosses and the politicians do their own dirty work. Their life is not at risk . . . yours will be!'

The pamphlet concludes by saying: 'If you feel that undue

pressure is being placed on you to join the forces or to take a rotten dead-end job—contact your local Trades Union Council, who will help you to resist pressure and to fight back.'

There is deep concern in the Tory government at present about the level of recruitment into the services. In the first six months of this year, the intake has been almost half the number recruited in the same period in 1972. This is despite a lavish advertising campaign in newspapers, magazines, on television and hoardings

At TUC headquarters officials say that trades councils should not involve themselves in 'international issues'. A trades council is for local issues, a bureaucrat told Workers Press.

He said the South Shields leaflets belonged 'in the incinerator'.

The national TUC's response to the campaign was confused but predictably 'against'. Officials claimed that trades councils 'should not involve themselves in international issues'. (Pacé Marx)

Workers Press 24 August 1973

UNION BRANCH TO QUIT TRADES COUNCIL

Mr Norman Spours

THE South Shields branch of the National Association of Schoolmasters has disaffiliated from the town's Trades Union Council after children in the area had been given anti-Army recruitment leaflets.

Mr Norman Spours, secretary and Press spokesman for the 180-strong branch, said: "It is perfectly true we have decided to disaffiliate, but it is not only over this particular leaflet. We feel that we can no longer keep issuing disclaimers when something like this comes up."

He said the leaflet was something with which the branch entirely disagreed. "We want no part of it at all. We wanted no part of the so-called school-leavers' guide or the election manifesto, particularly the section dealing with education, produced by the trades council."

"I have been instructed by the branch to send a letter informing the trades council of our disaffiliation and I will be sending it off tonight."

Shields Gazette 19 July 1973

Dissociated

The trades council's anti-recruitment leaflet, which was the subject of much controversy at their meeting on Tuesday night, has been issued to thousands of school-children in the area.

The trades council has also received letters from the Post Office engineering workers' union dissociating itself from a possible plan of the council's to picket recruitment offices.

Harton and Westoe Miners' Lodge has also criticised the leaflet and the painters' branch of UCATT has dissociated itself from any action taken with regard to the document.

Several trade union branches disaffiliated from the Trades Union Council over the issue.

12, Oxney House,
Rochester Estate,
Walker,
NEWCASTLE UPON TYNE 6.
Jan. 30th.

Dear Friend,

Could you please assist the Tyneside Anti-Apartheid group by collecting signatures for the enclosed petition at your local ttade union branch, tenants group, political party or church group.

We wpuld also welcome resolutions of solidarity with the majority of the people in Rhodesia being passed at Trades Councils and District Committees.

Yours fraternally,
Norma Manchee.
(on behal f of theTyneside Anti-Apartheid Committee)

The Trades Union Council actively supported the Anti-Apartheid movement which had several active groups in Tyneside, and took part in a massive demonstration against the visiting South African Springboks rugby team in Newcastle on 30th December 1970. This was one of the many such demonstrations which attempted, by direct action, to disrupt segregated games.

the Anti-Apartheid Movement

89 Charlotte Street London WIP 2DQ Tel 580 5311

24 January 1972

Dear friend,

I am writing to call on your Trades Council actively to support the demonstration against the sell-out in Rhodesia on Sunday 13 February.

The demonstration is organised by the Rhodesia Emergency Campaign Committee, which has been set up on the initiative of the Anti-Apartheid Movement. Over 45 organisations are represented on the Committee – from the political parties, trade unions, churches, immigrant and student groups.

The need vigorously to oppose this further racist step by the Tory Government is clear. In Rhodesia massive opposition to the "settlement" terms has taken place under the most difficult and intimidating conditions. Britain is the other partner in this deal and we must not only show our solidarity with the people of Zimbabwe, but also demand an end to British collaboration with the white minority regimes in Southern Africa.

Additional leaflets and information are available from this office.

I hope you will also consider at this time affiliation to the Anti-Apartheid Movement – as part of an ongoing campaign to stop these racist moves. Affiliation costs £2 a year.

I trust you will give these matters your urgent attention.

With best wishes,
Yours sincerely,

Roger Trask

Roger Trask
Field Officer

the Anti-Apartheid Movement

89 Charlotte Street London WIP 2DQ Tel 580 5311

Dear Friend,

Trade Union Conference on Southern Africa

The Anti-Apartheid Movement is holding a conference for trade unionists on Southern Africa.The conference takes place on the weekend March 18/19th at Plaw Hatch Trade Union Country Club,Sharpethorne,Nr.East Grinstead,Sussex. The Conference fee is £6 per delegate,covering accomodation and meals from Saturday lunchtime to Sunday afternoon.

The subjects to be discussed include:-

A political analysis of Southern Africa.
Labour conditions in Portugal's African colonies.
Trade union movement in South Africa
Rhodesia - current situation - British responsibilities.
The Liberation struggle and Western Collaboration with
                              the minority governments.
How trade unionists can oppose these racist links.

The Conference will provide delegates with an opportunity to hear expert speakers,and to fully discuss the situation in Southern Africa and support action trade unionists can take in this country. The links between Britain and South Africa are extensive and growing;and British trade unionists are in a powerful position to strike a blow for the liberation movements in Southern Africa.

There are a limited number of places available so please let me know the names of your delegates (up to 4) as soon as possible, on the form provided.

Further details and background papers will be sent direct to conference delegates.

I sincerely hope that you will be represented at this Conference.

Yours fraternally,

Roger Trask,
National Field Officer.

The trade union movement played a crucial role in ending Apartheid in South Africa.

SOUTH TYNESIDE ANTI-FASCIST COMMITTEE

To All Trade Union And Labour Organisations.

National Front March in South Tyneside

Dear Bro.,

The attention of the South Tyneside Anti-Fascist Committee has recently been drawn to the intentions of the National Front, who are planning a march and rally in South Shields on Good Friday.

The South Shields Trades Union Council has already been contacted, as have other labour organisations. We confidently expect that the STAFC will receive full support for it's opposition to the march.

It is the intention of the STAFC to secure the cancellation of this march, but we need your help if we are to succeed.

On a day of religious observance, when thousands of people turn out to watch processions, the National Front, supported by it's heavies, will seek to spread it's message of blind and fanatical nationalism, race hatred and intolerance. We call for your help to prevent this Nazi organisation from attempting to create the same kinds of division here, which exist in Northern Ireland. The National Front may attempt to use this way in order to display their support for Northern Ireland's extreme, Orange organisations. Good Friday is of particular symbolic importance to them and they feel it may be used to promote religious sectarianism in this area.

Let the people of South Tyneside know of your hostility to the National Front and of your opposition to their proposed march - regardless of their excuse for it. The STAFC calls upon all organisations to state publicly their opposition to this march and, further, should the attempts to call off this march fail, we call upon your organisation to support a peaceful counter-march, details of which may be announced in the next week or so.

KEEP FASCISM OFF THE STREETS

The South Tyneside Anti-Fascist Committee was supported by SSTUC and was active throughout the mid-70s. As a result, the far-right National Front never gained a foot-hold in South Tyneside.

ATTACK ON ANTI-FASCIST

The Secretary of South Shields Trades Council, Bernard Appleton, had his face slashed by a man with a razor in a back lane in South Shields last Sunday night.

This attack follows about 100 phone calls threatening Bernard and his family. The President of South Shields Trades Council, Jim Rowson, has commented:

'This appears to be a disgraceful piece of political thuggery, which makes life in South Shields nastier than before'. He said he believed the attack could be politically motivated.

This attack in South Shields follows the humiliating defeat that the National Front suffered there in the general election, when their vote dropped from almost 2,000 to a pathetic 700. This was mainly due to the activities of the local anti-fascist committee, which the Trades Council supported. The history of the threats to Bro. Appleton goes back to the time of the fight against the Tories' Fair Rent Act.

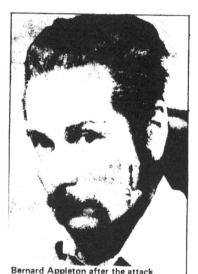

Bernard Appleton after the attack

The Trades Council fought bitterly against the implementation of the Act, but the local Labour council, like all the others in the country except Clay Cross, capitulated and implemented the Act. As a result, relations between the Trades Council and the right wing of the local Labour Party became extremely hostile, with some Trades Council members resigning from the Party.

Red Flag 7 November 1974

Anti-Fascist activity was never without risk.

SOUTH SHIELDS

One of the leading right wingers in the Labour Party was Harry Donkin, a former councillor. Donkin was involved in an incident in the Labour Party rooms with members of the Trades Council, including Appleton, over the use of a duplicator for Trades Council leaflets. Donkin attempted to order the Trades Council members out of the Labour rooms, despite the fact that many of them were Labour Party members.

After statements were made at the next meeting of the Trades Council attacking Donkin's actions, Donkin issued writs against members of the Trades Council, and against the Newcastle *Journal*, which reported the meeting. The writs were never brought to court.

Donkin has since left the Labour Party and found his real political home the National Front. At the count in South Shields on general election night, Appleton was 'leaned on' by members of the Front. Donkin was seen to point out Appleton to members of the Front, and Appleton was warned by a number of people, including Tories and Liberals, to be careful as the Front were planning something against him. Appleton had to leave the count in the company of a number of his friends for protection.

Donkin is a Justice of the Peace and sits on the magistrates bench in South Shields. The local anti-fascist committee

is planning to picket the courts when Donkin is sitting.

They will be demanding his removal because of his membership of a fascist organisation. They will be asking whether black people in South Shields can expect a fair hearing from Donkin when he is a member of an organisation that has a racist policy of re-patriation of coloured immigrants. They will also be asking what sort of hearing fascists who attack trade unionists will enjoy.

Ministry of Housing and Local Government

Whitehall, London S W 1

Telephone 01-930 4300

Minister of State

31 December 1970

Dear Mr Gransby

Mr Howell has asked me to acknowledge
your petition asking him to call for
the cancellation of the proposed
Springbok*s v Northumberland match
on 3 January.

Mr Howell's views on this tour are
very well known and have been
expressed publicly.

Yours sincerely

R S HAUGH
Private Secretary

J Gransby Esq

He meant no! The match went ahead and met a large (and energetic) demonstration.

The Industrial Relations Bill

The 1970 Industrial Relations Bill was seen as the beginning of a systematic government attack on the growing strength and confidence of the trade union movement. The Bill sought to introduce legal controls by the compulsory 'registration' of trade unions and the regulation of union~employer agreements, enforceable by fines or imprisonment.

In a wider context, the Bill could be seen as an early reaction by the state against the growing militancy of community groups prepared to take direct action outside the formal democratic structures.

The reaction of the national TUC's General Council to the Bill revealed a classic dilemma. On one hand they were faced by calls for direct action by their militant grass-root members. On the other hand they felt constrained to play their traditional role within the establishment's rules. They sought to resolve this dilemma by mounting a campaign against the Bill which called for traditional protests (petitions and demonstrations) but which carefully avoided calls for direct action such as strikes or occupations.

It fell to individual trades union branches and Trades Union Councils to act in a more direct manner.

It was perhaps due to this divided opposition that the campaign against the Bill failed. It was passed by parliament largely unamended, and became an Act in 1971.

In July 1972 five dockers were jailed for picketing offences under the Act. They were released when (in an act of unaccustomed militancy) the TUC called a one day general strike. This marked the end of effective implementation of the Act – and reinforced trade union confidence in direct action.

Although the 1971 Act was largely ineffective, trade union fears of future government action proved prescient. The Thatcher government was to enact many repressive measures that the Heath government introduced but failed to make effective. These still remain largely in place although the current Blair government has sought to redress the worker~employer balance by ameliorating some of the more draconian measures.

The political pendulum has not yet stopped swinging..!

South Shields Trades Union Council

SAYS NO!

NO ! TO THE ANTI-TRADE UNION BILL

The government's Bill on Industrial Relations attacks fundamental trade union rights, and traditional workers' freedoms, won after over a century of struggle.

NO ! TO LEGAL INTERFERENCE AT WORK

The Bill, as in Hitler's Fascist Germany, would make many traditional trade union activities unlawful. Even to talk in the canteen about strike action could be illegal. The Bill carries the implications of a Police State with secret agents and informers in the factories, offices and workshops.

NO ! TO GIVING NON-MEMBERS A FREE RIDE

The Bill would make it illegal to induce action to get workers to join a trade union. The Bill is a black-legs charter.

NO ! TO LEGAL CONTRACTS

The Bill would make union-employer agreements legally enforceable. To break an agreement — or even to speak or write against it, would be illegal and the subject of fines or imprisonment.

DECEMBER 8th HAS BEEN CHOSEN AS A DAY OF NATIONAL GENERAL STRIKE ACTION AS THE FIRST BLOW TO KILL THE BILL BEFORE IT BECOMES LAW.

THE SOUTH SHIELDS TRADES UNION COUNCIL OFFERS ITS SERVICES TO ALL TRADE UNIONISTS TAKING STRIKE ACTION ON THAT DAY. FACILITIES WILL BE AVAILABLE AT EDE HOUSE, 143 WESTOE ROAD, ALL DAY ON DECEMBER 8th.

MEETINGS TO BE ATTENDED BY PROMINENT TRADE UNIONISTS ARE TO BE ORGANISED. DETAILS WILL BE ANNOUNCED IN THE PRESS.

Published by S.S. T.U.C.   Printed by F. & A. Tolson, Ltd., Bede Industrial Estate, Jarrow.

The Trades Union Council expressed its opposition to the Bill in its usual moderate manner.

This LEAFLET is ILLEGAL

Under the Industrial Relations Bill—if it becomes law! the Printers, the Officers of the South Shields T.U.C., and the person handing you this leaflet could be sent to prison—and so could you if you passed it on!

```
SOUTH SHIELDS TRADES UNION COUNCIL        Ede .House
                                          143 Weston Rd,
―――――――――――――――――――――――――                 SOUTH SHIELDS.


TO SECRETARIES AND DELEGATES              3rd. Jan.1971
OF ALL AFFILIATED TRADE UNIONS.


Dear Colleague,

                    DEMO-DAY 12th.Jan.

            The T.U.C. has called for all Unions to
make Jan. 12th. a day of protest and demonstration
against the Industrial Relations Bill. It is hoped that
all branches will organis  their own protest meetings
on this day. Information , advice , and assistance on
this matter can be obtained from Ede House on Sat. 9th.
Jan. Leaflets etc. are available for free distribution.

            A combined demonstration for local trade
unionists in South Shields has been organised by the
TradesUnion Council. This will take the form of the
lighting of a BEACON, on the LAWE TOP for the symbolic
burning of the Bill.
            ARTHUR BLENKINSOP M.P. will attend this
demonstration which will take place :-

            on TUES. 12TH. JAN.

            at 8.0 P.M

            on LAWE TOP   Near Beacon Inn )

            A beacon has been chosen as a traditional
form of warning and the Lawe is the historical  place
for resistance to oppression for the people of Shields

            The demonstration will be followed by a
"smoker" in the Beacon Inn at which there will be a
Petition initiated against the Bill.

            It is expected to have a folk group at
the Smoker with appropriate protest songs. It is also
possible that a local drama group will present the
history of the trade union fight for freedom and democratic
rights in dramatic form.

            ALL TRADE UNIONISTS ARE URGED TO ATTEND THIS
IMPORTANT DEMONSTRATION OF LOCAL OPOSITION TO THE BILL.

                    Yours fraternally,

                             Jack Grassby
                             Secretary
```

The national TUC called only for 'a day of protest and demonstrations'.

TRADES UNION CONGRESS

GENERAL SECRETARY: VICTOR FEATHER CBE

CONGRESS HOUSE · GREAT RUSSELL STREET · LONDON WC1B 3LS

Telephone 01-636 4030   *Telegrams* TRADUNIC LONDON WC1

DEPT **Organisation**
OUR REF KG/TF/IO
YOUR REF

December 22, 1970.

Mr. J. Grassby,
Secretary,
South Shields Trades Union Council,
Ede House,
143, Westoe Road,
South Shields.

Dear Mr. Grassby,

Industrial Relations Bill: TUC Campaign

Thank you for your letter of December 11 about the Government's Industrial Relations Bill. I am pleased to note that you have established a campaign committee and that you are going ahead with a number of activities.

You say that at a special meeting arranged by your Trades Council a resolution was carried calling on the General Council to call a national stoppage of work on January 12. As I pointed out in my previous letter the General Council have not included a stoppage of work in their campaign plans. Our campaign is aimed to arouse public opinion and to win support for our case in order to make the Government think again about the legislation. Stoppages of work will not help us to achieve this aim.

Yours sincerely,

Ken Graham

Secretary
Organisation Department

The General Council of the TUC expressed its concern that 'protests' might include strike action.

Lawe beacon as union law protest

Mr Arthur Blenkinsop, South Shields MP, who will be at Tuesday's demonstration against the Industrial Relations Bill.

——— WARNING SYMBOL ———

A BEACON will be lit by trade unionists on the Lawe Top, South Shields, next Tuesday as a symbolic burning of the Government's Industrial Relations Bill.

South Shields Trades Union Council has organised the combined demonstration in response to the TUC's call to make January 12 a day of protest and demonstration against the Bill.

Mr Arthur Blenkinsop, MP for the town, will attend the demonstration, which will be held at 8 p.m. beside the Beacon Inn.

Secretary of the local trades council, Mr Jack Grassby, said: "A beacon has been chosen as a traditional form of warning and the Lawe is the historical place for resistance to oppression for the people of Shields.

"The demonstration will be followed by a smoker in the Beacon Inn at which there will be a petition initiated against the Bill. It is expected to have a folk group at the smoker with appropriate protest songs.

"All trade unionists are urged to attend this important demonstration of local opposition to the Bill, and it is hoped that all branches will organise their own protest meetings on this day."

Information, advice and assistance can be obtained from Ede House, Westoe Road, on Saturday.

Mr Grassby said the South Shields trades council, the local representative of the TUC, is composed of 83 branches which represent over 10,000 members.

Mr Grassby said he had applied to the police for authority to hold the demonstration and as it would not last long he anticipated no objections.

The local M.P. was an ardent supporter of the Trades Councils' campaign – within the constraints of parliamentary opposition.

Mr Arthur Blenkinsop (right), MP for South Shields, and local Labour supporters watch the flames consume a copy of the Government's Industrial Relations Bill on a bonfire at the Lawe Top.

PEACE BILL BURNS—BUT HEAT WILL STILL LINGER

POLITICAL pyromania hit South Shields last night when local trade unionists and the town's MP symbolically burned the Industrial Relations Bill and cast it on to a pyre.

Mr Arthur Blenkinsop, MP for South Shields, standing on the Lawe Top — the high embankment at the mouth of the Tyne — held aloft a copy of the Bill as 50 supporters and spectators watched the secretary of the town's Trades Union Council, Mr Jack Grassby, put match to paper.

Then the blazing Bill was thrown on to the paraffin-soaked bonfire and the flames leapt 8ft. high, lighting up smiles of satisfaction on some of the banner-carrying demonstrators.

But everyone knew that, like the phoenix, the Bill would rise from the ashes and cause a lot of apprehension and vexation in the months to come.

As the flames died, Mr Blenkinsop invited all supporters present to a nearby public house to join in a smoker.

Shields Gazette 13 January 1970

The bonfire, although dramatic, simply served to illuminate the ineffectiveness of this form of protest.

'We'll back strike call' –Tyne yards union chiefs

REPRESENTATIVES of the Tyne's shipyard and engineering workers are supporting the national one-day strike, called for December 8.

At a meeting in Newcastle last night officials of shipyard and works committees throughout Tyneside recommended the Tyne District Committee of the Confederation of Shipbuilding and Engineering Unions to support the token stoppage in protest at the Government's proposed Industrial Relations Bill.

They also endorsed the recommendation of the district committee that there would be meetings in every factory on Tyneside and they supported the committee's call for a mass meeting on January 9 to discuss the Bill.

Shields Gazette 27 November 1970

Mr Don Edwards, the committee secretary, said today: "There was a good discussion at the meeting of what was tactically right. Nobody was against the proposals. Everybody condemned the Bill

TO MEET

Mr Edwards said about the Bill, which the Government says it intends to introduce during the present session of Parliament: "One can't see anything that's good in it. It restricts the freedom, it strikes at the good organisations we have. It's nothing else but a pure attack on the unions. It's intended to strengthen the hands of the employers against them."

The committee will meet next week to decide on the recommendation to support the one-day token stoppage.

And Durham students will have the full backing of their union if they support the strike. Mr Dick Ayre, president of the Durham Students' Union, said that a meeting of the union agreed to this.

Students have called on the executive to propose a teach-in on the proposed laws before December 8.

Support for strike action against the Bill was widespread – this included Durham and Newcastle Students Unions.

'Open house' in Shields for union strikers

SOUTH SHIELDS Trades Union Council will hold "open house" tomorrow for trade unionists taking part in the 24-hour national stoppage to protest at the Government's Industrial RelationsBill.

Members of the trades council will be at Ede House in Westoe Road, all afternoon, with copies of the Bill and leaflets and literature about it. In the evening a special meeting will be held which will be adressed by local unionists — inncluding former miners' leader in South Shields, Mr Paddy Cain.

Secretary of the council, Mr Jack Grassby, said today that he thought the stoppage on Tyneside would be "substantial".

ILLEGAL ACTION

"The Bill, as in Hitler's Fascist Germany, would make many traditional trade union activities unlawful," says the council in leflet being widely distributed today and which, it says, would be illegal under the Industrial Relations Bill.

"The Bill would make it illegal to induce action to get workers to join a trade union. The Bill is a blacklegs' charter."

About 2,000 workers at the North Shields and Wallsend yards of Swan Hunter Shiprepairers will support the stoppage, and it is understood that engineering workers from several large Tyneside firms plan to be off work to morrow.

The Society of Graphical and Allied Trades is holding a meeting in Gateshead Town Hall tomorrow afternoon to "explain" the Bill but this would not affect workers in the newspaper industry, a spokesman said.

SUPPORT TUC

As the strike plans have not had the backing of the TUC many trade union officials at regional and district level were not in a position today to say precisely what the response will be.

The regional secretary of the Transport and General Workers' Union, Mr Mick Chamers, said today: "Our policy is for supporting the TUC. So far as I'm aware none of our membership have indicated support for the stoppage."

The General and Minicipal Workers' Union, which accounts for 108,000 members on Tyneside, has advised its membership not to support the call.

A spokesman for the Amalgamated Union of Engineering and Foundry Workers, which has 28,000 members on Tyneside, said: "Officially our union does not approve of the stoppage to morrow."

Shields Gazette 7 December 1970

The call for a one-day strike failed to get official TUC backing and the action ended in 'protest' demonstrations.

NEWCASTLE AND DISTRICT TRADES COUNCIL

INVITE ALL TRADE UNIONISTS TO JOIN

PROTEST MARCH AGAINST INDUSTRIAL RELATIONS BILL

Newcastle
Saturday, 13th February, 1971
12.30 p.m.

FOLLOWED BY

Public Meeting
CITY HALL, NEWCASTLE
2.0 p.m.

WATCH PRESS FOR DETAILS

TRADES UNION CONGRESS

GENERAL SECRETARY: VICTOR FEATHER CBE

CONGRESS HOUSE · GREAT RUSSELL STREET · LONDON WC1

Telephone 01-636 4030   *Telegrams* TRADUNIC LONDON WC1

DEPT   Organisation
OUR REF   KG/TF/EB/129
YOUR REF

Mr. Jack Grassby,
Secretary,
South Shields Trades Union Council,
Ede House,
143, Westoe Road,
South Shields.

November 24, 1970.

Dear Mr. Grassby,

Industrial Relations Bill: TUC Campaign

Thank you for your letter of November 19 about the Government's proposed industrial relations legislation.

You say that a resolution criticising the leadership given by the General Council was passed at a recent delegate meeting of South Shields Trades Council. You also mention that you consider that Congress should be recalled as a matter of urgency.

The start of the TUC's campaign against the proposed legislation will not be linked in any way to Congress. The campaign will indeed be well on its way by the time that Congress is held. Many events, meetings, conferences and demonstrations will be taking place before Congress is held. The General Council have not included a stoppage of work in their campaign plans, and indeed do not want trades councils to encourage this type of action.

You do not refer to any local activity that you have planned. I hope that you will give full consideration to the notes that we have recently circulated and that you will play an active part in the TUC's campaign.

Yours sincerely,

Ken Graham

Secretary,
Organisation Department.

*See reply
proposed by action committee*

The Trades Union Congress had sought to dampen down the many trade union calls for strike action. They succeeded – and so did the Bill.

Letter to A.B.

Agreed

OPPOSITION WHIPS' OFFICE

March, 1971.

Dear Colleague,

Having now completed the Committee Stage of the Industrial Relations Bill I wish to thank you for your splendid support during the arduous hours spent discussing it.

There were 147 Divisions on this Bill and you voted in ...*147*... of them.

Again thanking you for your support.

Yours sincerely,

Bob Mellish

The local M.P., Arthur Blenkinsop, fought a vigorous, but futile, parliamentary battle against the Bill.

An innovative, but ineffective, gesture by the Trades Union Congress.
(This is what used to be called a 33⅓ rpm record)

TRADES UNION CONGRESS

GENERAL SECRETARY: VICTOR FEATHER CBE

CONGRESS HOUSE · GREAT RUSSELL STREET · LONDON WC1B 3LS

Telephone 01-636 4030   *Telegrams* TRADUNIC LONDON WC1

IN REPLY PLEASE QUOTE
CIRCULAR NO. 15 (1972-73)

DEPT Organisation
OUR REF VF/KG/MK
YOUR REF

September 28, 1972

TO THE GENERAL SECRETARIES OF ALL
AFFILIATED ORGANISATIONS,
RAC SECRETARIES, REGIONAL EDUCATION
OFFICERS, AND THE SECRETARIES OF
ALL TRADES COUNCILS AND FEDERATIONS
OF TRADES COUNCILS

Dear Colleague,

Industrial Relations Act:
Suspension of Certain Unions

You will be aware that the Brighton Congress
decided that each of the affiliated unions continuing
registration under the 1971 Industrial Relations Act
shall continue to be suspended from membership of
Congress, and authorised the General Council to remove
the suspension of those unions which comply before
December 31, 1972 with Congress policy of non-
registration. If a union remains registered after
December 31, 1972 and thus continues to be suspended
until the 1973 Congress it will have the right to
appeal to that Congress provided it has continued
in membership of the TUC by complying with the Rules.

The attached appendix gives a complete list of
the unions which are currently suspended.

The consequences of suspension are that all the
TUC's facilities and services to suspended unions are
withdrawn.

Following the passing of the Bill the TUC 'instructed' unions 'not to register' under the Act, and suspended those who did. Action at last – but too late and too little.

Secretary,   9th.Nov.1972
Health Service Branch 130 SS
C.O.H.S.E.,

  Secretary,
  Corporation Branch
  C.O.H.S.E.

Dear Colleague,

      I have to inform you that at its last Council meeting
the South Shields Trades Union Council carried a motion to suspend
your branch from membership because of your Unions continued
registration under the 1971 Industrial Relations Act in contra-
diction of the declared principles of Congress.

      Regret at the necessity of this action was expressed
by delegates together with the hope that your Union will find a way
of meeting TUC policy on this matter at which time we would be pleased
to welcome your branch back into membership.

      We are grateful for the part played by your delegates
in the work of the Trades Union Council and hope we shall be able
welcome them back to our Council , to work again alongside their
fellow trade unionists in the near future.

                              Yours fraternally,

                              Jack Grassby
                              Secretary.

The SSTUC was the first local trades union organisation to take action against those unions which 'registered' under the Act. Some score of unions were expelled from the Trades Union Congress and were subsequently barred from joint trades union activities

Trades unionists decide to expel seamen's branch

Shields Gazette 17 May 1972

SOUTH SHIELDS Trades Union Council, has become the first trades council in the country to expel one of its member branches for remaining registered under the Industrial Relations Act. Last night's meeting of the trades council decided to "disaffiliate" the National Union of Seamen, and today a senior spokesman for the NUS said he was "upset and disgusted" by the decision.

The motion to disaffiliate the NUS came from the North Durham TASS branch of the AEUW, and an amendment to refer the matter to the Trades Union Congress general council was defeated on the casting vote of the trades council chairman, Mr Joe McAlroy. No delegate from the NUS was present at the meeting.

Mr Mattie Magrs, senior secretary of the South Shields branch of the NUS, said he was "very surprised" when told of the council's decision by the Shields Gazette today.

He said the decision had reversed a previous one taken by the council, and he had not attended last night's meeting because of "pressure of work" and because he had not received notice of the meeting.

"I am upset and disgusted by the decision, and I wish I had been there last night. There have always been close links between the NUS and the trades council, and I think it was very wrong just to turf us out like that in our absence.

"We are all trade unionists together, and there should be links between us," said Mr Magrs.

The NUS has five delegates on the trades council, and Mr Magr himself has been associated with it for over 20 years.

When official notice of the disaffiliation is received, said Mr Magrs, the NUS branch would probably appeal against it. He said he assumed he would be resigning his official positions on the council.

A spokesman for the council said today that he hoped other trades councils would follow the lead given by South Shields, without waiting for instructions from the Trades Union Congress.

"The decision demonstrates that ordinary trade unionists can take matters into their own hands and throw out trade unions which cooperate with the Industrial Relations Act," he said.

The National Union of Seamen was soon to take a different direction under its new South Shields born General Secretary, Jim Slater.

UNION MEN MAY RISK JAIL

TRADE unionists in South Shields may be among the first in the country to risk imprisonment when the Industrial Relations Bill is made law.

"There are local trade unionists who are prepared to take steps which under the Act would be illegal, and to challenge the law to take a case against them," said Mr Jack Grassby, secretary of South Shields Trades Union Council today.

Mr Grassby said the local trades union council was arranging a meeting of trade union officers and shop stewards to hear legal advice on the implications of such action.

"Further action along these lines would then be considered," he said.

QUESTIONS ASKED

"This Bill is moving the country towards a crisis of democracy. Parliament is now trying to dictate not only how the wealth produced by workers should be distributed, but also how workers should conduct themselves while producing it," he said.

Trade unionists are beginning to question the over-riding authority of Parliament, in particular on the right of Parliament to overrule other forms of industrial democracy, Mr Grassby said.

Last night, the trades union council reaffirmed its opposition to the Bill and repeated its call for compulsory non-registration of trade unions by the Trades Union Congress and the use of strategic strike action.

Shields Gazette 21 August 1973

Action by trade unionists in support of strikes in which they were 'not directly concerned' became illegal under the Act. Much of the work of the Trades Union Council was consequently placed outside the law. This did not stop their traditional fraternal support in industrial actions – although by then technically illegal.

Trades Council will continue 'illegal' support

SOUTH SHIELDS Trades Union Council is to continue its support for industrial action by the railwaymen, despite warnings from officials that such support may be illegal.

Secretary, Mr Jack Grassby, told delegates at a special meeting of the TUC that, since the council's decision to support the rail-waymen had been taken last week, the situation had changed.

He said: "When the resolution was passed the railwaymen were taking official action; it was official support for official action.

"After that time the Industrial Relations Court ordered a cooling-off period and officials of the National Union of Railwaymen have instructed their members to conform.

"If we now support industrial action we are supporting action which is unofficial and illegal under the Act."

IN CONTEMPT

Mr Grassby said it was not his personal feeling that the TUC should withdraw its support for the railwaymen, but he felt he had to make the legal position clear.

President, Mr Joe McAlroy, said the TUC's support "could be held to be in contempt of court. The TUC could be fined, and it is your money that could be taken."

There was, however, no motion to rescind last week's decision and Mr Grassby said he hoped that that decision had not been merely "a pious resolution."

"I hope that when this Council says that it supports the railwaymen, it means it will support these workers in the same way as it supported the miners — by giving moral, organisational and financial support, even though I feel that this is illegal."

TRADES UNION CONGRESS

GENERAL SECRETARY: VICTOR FEATHER CBE

CONGRESS HOUSE · GREAT RUSSELL STREET · LONDON WC1B 3LS

Telephone 01-636 4030   *Telegrams* TRADUNIC LONDON WC1

IN REPLY PLEASE QUOTE
CIRCULAR NO. 208 (1971-72)

DEPT Organisation
OUR REF VF/KG/MK
YOUR REF

July 27, 1972

TO THE GENERAL SECRETARIES OF
ALL AFFILIATED ORGANISATIONS
RAC SECRETARIES AND THE
SECRETARIES OF ALL TRADES COUNCILS
AND FEDERATIONS OF TRADES COUNCILS

Dear Colleague,

Cancellation of Protest Stoppage of Work

I informed you yesterday (Circular No. 206) of
the General Council's decision to call on all
affiliated unions to organise a one-day stoppage of
work and demonstrations on Monday next for the release
of the five dockers imprisoned by the National
Industrial Relations Court.

As you will know, the men were freed yesterday
as a result of intervention by the Official Solicitor
and following widespread protests and indications of
support for the action decided upon by the General
Council.

The call for the one-day stoppage of work and
demonstrations on Monday next is therefore cancelled.
Affiliated unions and Trades Councils are requested
to take note of this information.

Yours sincerely,

VICTOR FEATHER

General Secretary

*The threat of a one-day strike stopped the jailing of trade unionists under the Act, and
saw off its effective implementation. A revealing moment of what might have been!*

Unemployment, Strikes
& Occupations

The fight to preserve traditional industries such as mining and ship-building was expressed by calls to union branches for direct action in the form of strikes and occupations. The call for a Tyneside general strike to save Palmers shipyard was typical of these events.

What all these actions had in common was that, for the most part, they were carried out without official national support and often in the face of establishment opposition. What they also had in common was that, at least in the long term, they failed.

What they might have achieved with the active support of the official Labour movement remains problematic. We would have to wait until the 1974 Miners' Strike when direct action by the miners, supported by virtually the whole Labour movement, showed it could change governments – if not the fate of the mining industry.

An important campaign by the South Shields Trades Union Council was its fight for alternatives to unemployment in the form of paid training and/or education. The SSTUC won the right of claimants of unemployment and/or social security supplementary benefits to attend college.

Colleges soon learned to develop courses, especially designed for unemployed young people on benefit, and in these can be seen the genesis of the government's Youth Opportunity Programme Scheme (YOPS) followed by the Youth Training Scheme (YTS), *(see 'Students and School Leavers)*.

The arguments deployed by the SSTUC at that time concerning the treatment of the unemployed continues to affect the political agenda and are manifest in the current government's 'New Deal' scheme for the young unemployed.

The South Shields Trades Union Council supported many local and national strikes, official and unofficial. They used the conventional means – demonstrations, petitions, and expressions of solidarity – but also took some more direct action. This included the establishment of joint SSTUC~trade union strike committees – the 'Strike Liaison Committees'; and the establishment of 'Strikes Claims Committees' in conjunction with the Claimants' Union.

These actions involved the SSTUC in some unexpected situations.

In November 1972 women workers at Barbours clothing factory took strike action for a pay rise and union recognition. Strikers were encouraged by the SSTUC to make a claim for social security payments under the 'urgent need' provision of the 1966 Act.

In the event the women were refused claim forms by the Department of Health and Social Security clerks at Wouldhave House, the local DHSS offices. The strikers refused to leave the offices until their right to make a claim was recognised and in the ensuing mêlée the DHSS manager called in the police. The Claimants Union invited the police to arrest the DHSS manager for breaching the 1966 Social Security Act. They didn't.

Subsequently the DHSS was to admit that it was wrong not to have allowed a claim to be made. The SSTUC accused the police of aiding and abetting a breach of the law – a nice legal point, still unresolved.

The Barbour workers finally won both their pay rise and union recognition (TGWU).

The 1970 Council cleaners strike was supported by the SSTUC by the novel tactic of urging the public to withhold that part of their rates accountable to public cleaning.

The SSTUC sought legal redress from the town council for 'breach of contract' in failing to provide cleaning services and the action ended up in Durham Court of Quarters Sessions under the reputed hard man Judge Alastair Sharp. The legal action failed (as could be expected) but the learned judge alarmed the SSTUC members by calling them 'village Hampdens' (in a reference to Gray's Elegy):–

'The court means no disrespect to these men in calling them 'village Hampdens'. They are standing up for the rights of the citizen. They have the courage to come to the Court of Quarter Sessions with their grievances.'

It was not clear who was the more confused – the SSTUC or the judge – or who the 'little tyrants' would have been!

An application for expenses by the local authority was rejected by the judge – and the SSTUC members were charged 35p by the Clark of Court for the hearing. It was worth it, but it left the SSTUC in dismay as to how the judge could have praised their revolutionary action.

The national Dockers Strike in July 1972 caused a declaration of a National State of Emergency – the 4th such declaration in two years. The issue was the jailing of five dockers by the newly formed Industrial Relations Court. A national one-day strike was called by the TUC.

The SSTUC prepared well for this strike and some members were disappointed when the dockers were freed and the strike aborted.

In June 1973, twenty four Shewsbury building workers were charged with conspiracy arising from picketing action during their recent strike. In an expression of solidarity, and in line with their policy to seek direct action, the SSTUC called for a picketing of South Shields Court and police station at the same time as the building workers were to be brought to trial. The members of this demonstration were photographed by the police and a lengthy argument developed, involving the local MP, regarding the rights of the police in this context.

In December 1974 the workers of Jarrow Tube Investments, threatened with redundancy, occupied their factory and, in an imaginative gesture, welded the gates closed. The workers ultimately lost the fight and the factory shut-down. They did however win much improved redundancy benefits – including some office equipment – and many subsequent SSTUC and CU leaflets were typed on Jarrow Tube equipment.

PALMERS — HEBBURN
───────────────

Copy of notes taken at a meeting with the
Minister of Technology, Wednesday, 2nd
September, 1970

─────────

Mr. E. Fernyhough, Member of Parliament for Jarrow, introduced the deputation.

Councillor H. Downey, Chairman of Hebburn Urban District Council, referred to the statement which had been sent to the Minister that is to say, Mr. Kinghorn's letter of the 25th August, 1970. The points made in that letter he said were the main points the deputation wanted to discuss with the Minister. The Minister said that he hoped that the members of the deputation would bring out the main points in discussion.

In the general discussion that followed, various members of the delegation made reference to the following points :-

1.   The unemployment situation in the Mid-Tyne area.

2.   The bridging operation agreed by the previous Government.

3.   The feeling locally that Vickers had made no attempt to keep faith with the agreement reached with the previous Government.

4.   The view that the Yard could be made efficient and profitable without constant shoring up from the public purse.

In making these points, members of the deputation amplified what was said in the Clerk's letter of the 25th August, 1970. The deputation also asked for the report of the Shipbuilding and Ship Repair Council on the Ship Repair Industry to be published and asked that a Joint Working Party including representatives of the Government and the local authorities and other interested bodies should be set up in order to try to find some viable use for the Yard.

The Minister emphasised that he and the Department were very conscious of the real problem that the closure of Palmers Yard created for the local authorities. The Department wished to play as full a part as possible in bringing about an improvement in the situation. He thought this would result from a properly developed regional policy and not by stop-gap measures which involved propping up unprofitable facilities. After a very full consideration of the report of the Ship Repair Industry, the Minister was convinced that the outlook for Ship Repair at Palmers was not very bright and did not justify any further financial support.

The Minister emphasised that he and his Department would be ready to talk to anyone who had proposals to make about the ways in which the Yard could be maintained as a source of employment but did not wish to mis-lead the deputation into thinking that further Government money would be forthcoming to support the Yard as things were. He pointed out that even the £200,000 which was involved in the bridging operation would only be paid if Vickers could demonstrate the losses that had been incurred. He himself was in favour of publication of the Report on Ship Repairing as the deputation had proposed but it was not for him to decide on this question.

There was then much discussion about Mr. McGarvey's proposal that there should be a Working Party to examine the future of the Yard. The Minister and Mr. Ridley stressed their readiness to help in any way possible but did not see the need for a formal Working Party and could not promise further financial support.

A report which must echo many reports over the years.

HEBBURN   URBAN   DISTRICT   COUNCIL

R. W. KINGHORN
CLERK & SOLICITOR

COUNCIL OFFICES
CIVIC CENTRE
HEBBURN
CO. DURHAM
TEL:-HEBBURN 83-2361

Our Ref.FC/MP.

3rd September, 1970.

Dear Sir,

Palmers (Hebburn) Ship Repair Yard

Following the result of the meeting between the Minister of Technology and the appointed deputation. I am to inform you that an Emergency Meeting of all interested bodies is to be held on Saturday, 5th September, 1970. in the Council Chamber Hebburn commencing at 11.0am.

I shall be pleased if you would make every effort to attend this meeting.

Yours faithfully,

W. Kinghorn

Clerk of the Council

J. Grassby, Esq.,
Secretary.
South Shields Trades Council,
C/O Ede House,
143, Westoe Road,
South Shields.

The campaign to save Palmers can be seen as a bureaucratic failure with perceived impotence in the face of economic forces.

H E B B U R N   U R B A N   D I S T R I C T   C O U N C I L

RESOLUTION Passed unanimously at special emergency meeting held on Monday, 17th August, 1970.

RESOLVED: That this Council expresses the gravest concern at the announcement that Palmers Hebburn Shipyard of Vickers Armstrong is to close with consequent loss of hundreds of jobs in an area where unemployment is already a major problem. The Council calls upon the Minister of Technology to receive a deputation of representatives of local authorities, trade unions and members of Parliament for this division to make representations to keep this establishment open and active at all costs.

We further ask that the Ministry of Technology demand that Vickers Ltd. keep this establishment open and active until the report of the Committee investigating Ship Repair Industry has been presented to and debated by Parliament.

The Council further instruct the Chairman of the Council to convene a meeting of representatives of local authorities, trade unions and the North Eastern Development Council and the Northern Group of Labour M.P.'s and any other interested body on Friday, 21st August, 1970, at 7 p.m. to mount a concerted campaign to keep the Yard open.

The Council further instruct the Chairman of the Council to call any meeting at any time with any organisation he thinks fit and hereby empower him to call upon any member or members of the Council - elected or staff - whom he desires to assist him in this Council's efforts to keep this Yard open as a viable Ship Repair Establishment.

The Council further resolve to back any effort the Confederation of Ship Building and Engineering Trade Unions, the Northern Group of Labour M.P.'s and the North Eastern Development Council may take to keep this Yard open.

Hebburn District Council gave the classic establishment response; unable to call for direct action they called for 'meetings' and unspecified 'campaigns'.

14—Shields Gazette, Friday, September 18, 1970

Top talks fail to raise hopes of saving Palmers

By Noel Howell, Our Industrial Correspondent

HOPES of saving Palmers Hebburn yard are still dim after top-level talks between TUC chief, Mr Vic Feather, and Technology Minister Mr John Davies. Mr Davies hinted, during the talks, that the Government might extend its £200,000 bridging operation to keep the yard open if a firm buyer was in the offing.

But a buyer would have only eight days in which to make a viable offer to Vickers, who own the yard. Palmers is due to close next Friday, and the bridging operation will end.

"I am not very optimistic," said Mr Feather after his talks in London with the Technology Minister.

Vickers has confirmed that so far no firm offer has been made for Palmers shiprepair yard, which has been losing money for some time.

Seven hundred and fifty men face redundancy and some have already been given notice.

Whole industries

" I think the outlook for Jarrow and Hebburn is very bleak," said Mr Feather.

'Worse ahead'

THE secretary of South Shields Trades Council. Mr Jack Grassby, said today: "This is terrible news, but worse is to come. It is now clear that the Government intends to withdraw help from the shipbuilding and shiprepairing industry as a whole. Tyneside will have to fight for survival."

Plans to gather support for the one-day "general strike" in protest against Palmers closure were going ahead, Mr Grassby said. "Appeals have been sent to all Tyneside Trades Councils and already individual messages of support are coming in.

"Trade union branches will be considering this action at their local branch meetings during the next few weeks. It remains to be seen whether the people of Tyneside will react to this threat to their future by taking the only protest action left open to them."

SOUTH SHIELDS TRADES UNION COUNCIL

EDE HOUSE, 143 WESTOE ROAD, SOUTH SHIELDS.   Tel : South Shields 60762

Vic. Feather,
General Secretary T.U.C.,
Congress House,
Great Russell St.,
LONDON WC1.   25th Sept. '70.

Dear Mr Feather,

        The South Shields Trades Union Council
would be pleased to receive your advice as to whether
a Trades Council, or a Federation of Trades Councils,
acting in accordance with its rules and standing orders,
would be in order to :-

        1. "promote" a token strike amongst its
consituent trade union branches - by this we mean
to recommend them to consider such action in accordance
with their own rules and constitution,

and/or   2. " organise" such a strike - by this we mean
co-ordinate action on such matters as timing etc.

        We are concerned here not with the
advisability or propriety of such action but simply
whether it is constitutionally permissible.

                          Yours fraternally,

                          Jack Grassby
                          Secretary.

---

*The South Shields TUC sought the approval of the Trades Union Congress to
'promote' and 'organise' strike action on Tyneside.*

TRADES UNION CONGRESS

GENERAL SECRETARY: VICTOR FEATHER CBE

CONGRESS HOUSE · GREAT RUSSELL STREET · LONDON WC1B 3LS

Telephone 01-636 4030   *Telegrams* TRADUNIC LONDON WC1

DEPT ORGANISATION
OUR REF KG/MG/MW
YOUR REF

September   30   1970

Mr   J   Grassby
South Shields Trades Union Council
Ede House
143 Westoe Road
South Shields

Dear   Mr   Grassby

Thank you for your letter of September 25 in which you ask whether it is constitutionally permissible for a Trades Council or Federation of Trades Councils to promote a token strike.

As stated in my earlier letter concerning Palmer's Shipyard, Hebburn, it is not within a Trades Council's terms of reference to call for a stoppage of work. Decisions about such matters are for the national executives of unions with branches in the area. As a result of several unfortunate experiences and as a safeguard for Trades Councils, Congress has decided that Trades Councils must not intervene in any way in any industrial dispute without the written consent of the national executive of an affiliated union actually concerned.

Yours sincerely

Ken Graham

Secretary
Organisation Department

This reply from the TUC did not actually say 'no' and the call for a one-day strike on Tyneside went ahead.

SOUTH SHIELDS TRADES UNION COUNCIL

EDE HOUSE

143 WESTOE RD

SOUTH SHIELDS

TO SECRETARIES OF LOCAL
TRADE UNIONS :

18TH SEPT.'70

TYNESIDE GENERAL STRIKE

Dear Colleague,

      The South Shields Trades Union Council is
calling for a one day general strike on Tyneside in
protest against the closure of Palmers shipyard and the
absence of any government plans to alleviate the entirely
unacceptable level of unemployment in the region.

      Following a meeting by Vic Feather, General
Secretary of the T.U.C., with the Minister of Technology
it is clear that the government now intends to follow a
general policy of withdrawal of aid from industry in the
region. The future of the whole shipbuilding and ship-
repair industry has been placed in jeopardy and the future
of other local industries placed at risk.

      Vic Feather has described the future for
Tyneside as "bleak".

      The level of male unemployment on Tyneside has
already reached an average figure of 7.5% , and in some
parts is as high as 13%.

      The South Shields Trades Union Council has
proposed this one day general strike as a protest and a
warning that this situation is not acceptable and that
trade unionists will not stand by and watch the progressive
run down of the region.

      We invite the fraternal support of your
branch for this action and ask that you

      1. make public or let the South Shields Trades
Union Council know of your support,

    and   2. instruct your regional officers to co-
operate with the N.E. Federation of Trades Councils in
co-ordinating action.

Yours fraternally,

JACK GRASSBY
Secretary

Palmers: they see TUC chief

By John Landells, Our Shipping Reporter

IN THE fight to save Palmers Hebburn ship-repair yard, two members of the Tyneside Action Committee are setting off tonight on a special trip to London, to see Mr Vic Feather, the TUC general secretary.

Coun. Hugh Downey,

chairman of Hebburn Council, who is leading the action committee, and Coun. John Evans, will see the TUC chief at his headquarters tomorrow morning.

They will brief Mr Feather on the Palmers situation before he meets Mr John Davies, the Minister of Technology, in the afternoon, to make what seems likely to be

the final appeal to the Government to provide aid to keep the yard open after September 27

Every help

"We would very much like to have gone into the meeting between Mr Feather and the Minister," said Coun. Downey today. "This, however, is a TUC delegation to Mr Davies and it is felt that it should remain as such.

"We will, however, give all possible help and information to Mr Feather and his colleagues before they go to the Ministry and we expect to stand by afterwards to see what results are achieved."

Accompanying Mr Feather tomorrow afternoon will be Mr George Smith, secretary of the Woodworkers' Society, who is a member of the TUC General Council and chairman of the TUC Production Committee. Also there will be Mr Pat Fisher, who is in charge of the TUC's production department.

After the firm 'No' which Mr Davies gave to the action committee a fortnight ago when it pleaded for help for Palmers, it seems unlikely that the TUC delegation will have any success with its bid.

Close touch

Concern at the closure of Palmers was voiced by members of the Tyne district committee of the Confederation of Shipbuilding and Engineering Unions at their monthly meeting last night at Newcastle.

"Even at this late stage, the committee will try and do everything possible to prevent the closure," Mr George Arnold, the chairman, said today. "We are working in close liaison with the action committee and are now waiting to see what Mr Feather might achieve."

Mr Arnold gave his personal support to the call of South Shields Trades Union Council for a one-day strike in the area to protest against the closing of the Hebburn yard.

"This is in line with views I have already expressed," he said. "Many of our members are worked up by the Palmers situation and it is very possible that some industrial action will be taken as a form of protest."

MR JACK GRASSBY
No Government effort.

Shields calls for strike on Palmers

TRADE unionists in South Shields have called for a one-day token strike of all Tyneside workers to protest about the closure of Palmers Hebburn shiprepair yard and the lack of Government measures to bring jobs to the region.

The "general" strike call was made by the South Shields Trades Union Council, and will be sent to other trade unions on Tyneside. The strike motion was passed without any votes against.

The motion will be sent to the North-East Federation of Trades Councils, who will discuss the proposal, probably at its next meeting on October 3.

And copies of the motion will be sent to branch secretaries of all local trade unions asking for support for the strike plan, and asking for cooperation with the North-East Federation.

LACK OF RESPONSE

South Shields council secretary, Mr Jack Grassby, said today: "This is an expression of frustration by local trade unionists in the face of a complete lack of response from Government Ministers and local employers.

"The Labour Government did take action to help the region and we succeeded only in standing still. The Tory Government appears prepared to take no action at all."

No date for the proposed strike has been suggested. Mr Grassby said details of the strike would have to be arranged by the North-East Federation.

Shields Gazette 16 September 1970

Strike backing

Gateshead Trades Council announced today that it will back South Shields Trades Union Council's call for a Tyneside strike to spotlight the area's growing unemployment problems, intensified by the shutdown at Palmers.

Shields Gazette 26 September 1972

The call for a Tyneside general strike shocked the local government establishment and the trade union bureaucrats. 'Opposition' to the closure was one thing, but action..!

Tyneside may strike over yard closure

Trade unionists are calling for a one-day general strike on Tyneside, in protest at the closure of a ship repair yard in an area of high unemployment.

The Trades Union Council at South Shields, County Durham, is pressing for the strike to show the Government that the North is not prepared to remain a "poor relation."

Hostility has been growing since it was announced that the Palmer ship repair yard at Hebburn-on-Tyne would close at the end of the month, putting 750 men out of work. Appeals to the Government to keep it going have failed.

By our Correspondent

Trade unionists feel that the area is suffering for its political allegiance, and the council is calling for the North-east Federation of Trades Councils to promote the strike.

Delegates from 83 unions, representing 10,000 people in South Shields, have unanimously supported the idea. The council secretary, Mr Jack Grassby, said: "This would be a protest against the closure, and the absence of any Government plans to alleviate the entirely unacceptable level of unemployment in the region."

On Tyneside, the unemploy-ment rate is 5 per cent, compared with the national figure of 2.5 per cent. The figure for the North-east as a whole is 4.5 per cent.

Mr Grassby added: "I am sure this strike will succeed because feelings are very high. It would show that unless the Government are prepared to try and improve the unemployment situation in the area, which at present they are not, there could be more action.

"This is the result of the sheer frustration of delegations which have seen the Government and the shipyard owners. Vickers, to try and get a reprieve, but without success."

The Guardian 17 September 1970

The call for strike action caught the attention of the national press – perhaps recalling the impact of the 1968 general strike in France.

Registered at

Sunderland & TUC *Trades Council*

Secretary

Mr. H. Mitchell,
23 Swinden Road,
Springwell Estate,
SUNDERLAND,
4,10.70.

Dear Secretary,

<u>Proposed One Day General Strike, Tyneside</u>

Your letter of the 22.9.70. with reference
to the above was placed before the delegates
and received unanimous support.

Wishing you success in your efforts,

Yours Sincerely

Secretary,

J.Mitchell

Mr. J,Grassby,
Ede House,
143 Westoe Road,
South Shields,

The call for strike action received the support of many trades unions at grass-root level, together with political and student organisations.

106 Holly Ave,
Newcastle 2.
811728.
19.10.70

Dear Comrade Grassby,

      The Left-Wing Society of Newcastle Polytechnic today passed a resolution of support for the S.Shields Trades Council's call for a one day strike against unemployment in the North East. We intend to initiate a campaign to win the student's union to support and participate in the strike, and our members who are teachers will press for similar action by their union. It would be a great help if you could send me a copy of the original resolution passed by the Trades Council, together with any other statements on the aims of the campaign and on what progress has been made in winning support for it so far.

      As part of the campaign within the poly we hope to persuade the union to hold a general meeting on unemployment to be addressed by a representative of S.Shields Trades Council or of some other trade union organisation which is supporting the stoppage. The meeting will have to be held during daytime - most probably at either 1pm or 5pm. I would appreciate it if you could give me the names of people who might be prepared to speak at it.

      Yours Fraternally,

Sandra Peers.

Mrs. S.L.Peers.
On behalf of the Left-Wing
Society.

WEAR JOINS CALL FOR AREA STRIKE

SUNDERLAND trade unionists have joined South Shields Trades Union Council in a call for a one-day general strike in protest at the closure of Palmers Hebburn shiprepair yard and the Government's policies for the North-East.

The Sunderland council agreed unanimously to support the South Shields plan, Mr Jack Grassby, the South Shields secretary, said today.

"We welcome this support from Sunderland Trades Council. It shows the strike is gaining support, and it shows trade unionists are not prepared to stand idly by and watch the introduction of a Government policy which withdraws aid from the region," Mr Grassby said.

He said the policy had already caused the closure of Palmers and now threatens the whole shiprepair, shipbuilding and other traditional industries in the North-East.

The support from Sunderland emphasises the general nature of the protest, Mr Grassby said.

Gateshead Trades Council supported the call for a strike when it met last week. "A one-day general strike in the Tyne and Wear area is now a very real possibility," Mr Grassby said.

Shields Gazette 30 September 1973

One-day strike demand attacked

By STUART GARNER

Our Industrial Reporter

THE call for a general strike to protest at the closure of Palmers' shipyard was condemned last night by a leading North-East trade unionist.

Trade union men in the region would be seen as "firebrands" and the move would not help attract new jobs, said Mr. Harry Luxton.

Mr. Luxton, general secretary of the North-East Federation of Trades Councils, was commenting on motions calling for strike action from Gateshead and South Shields trades councils.

The Gateshead motion said: "This trades council calls upon the North-East federation to promote a one-day general strike on Tyneside as a protest against the closure of Palmers shipyard and the absence of Government plans to alleviate the entirely unacceptable level of unemployment in the region."

Mr. Luxton said: "This motion is almost identical to that of South Shields. The fact is that the federation is not supposed to deal with disputes either on one side or the other.

Abortive

"Each trade union is autonomous and must decide its own point of view. I shall suggest that these motions are passed straight over to the Confederation of Shipbuilding and Engineering Unions.

"These trades councils are being a bit abortive in suggesting this action over a shipyard which is about to close.

"The NEFTC would not allow itself to be used as an instrument of industrial unrest. It is getting too ridiculous for words.

"This sort of thing does not help the image of the North-East at all. We shall be seen as firebrands and it would not help bring employment to the region."

Action

The federation, he said, was already planning positive action on the jobless problem. A conference was being organised and only the date remains to be fixed.

Coun. Fred Johnson, chairman of the Gateshead Trades Council, had said yesterday that he expected almost 100 per cent. support for the strike call from other councils on Tyneside.

The action would be a demonstration to the Government of the strength of feelings about unemployment.

Newcastle Journal 25 September 1970

The TUC establishment not only failed to support the call for strike action but actively opposed it.

TRADES UNION CONGRESS

GENERAL SECRETARY: VICTOR FEATHER CBE

CONGRESS HOUSE · GREAT RUSSELL STREET · LONDON WC1

Telephone 01-636 4030   *Telegrams* TRADUNIC LONDON WC1

DEPT **Organisation**
OUR REF **KG/TF/LD/448**
YOUR REF

September 28, 1970.

Mr. J. Grassby,
South Shields Trades Union Council,
Ede House,
143, Westoe Road,
SOUTH SHIELDS.

Dear Mr. Grassby,

Palmer's Shipyard, Hebburn

Thank you for your letter of September 22 which has been referred to me by our Production Department. You say that you are gravely concerned about the closure of Palmer's Shipyard and the threat to the shipbuilding and ship-repairing industry in your area and that as a protest your Council has decided to support a one-day token Stoppage of work.

We understand the anxiety that is felt about this problem locally and I am pleased that your trades council is playing an active part in the campaign against the closure. However, it is not within a trades council's terms of reference to call for a Stoppage of work. Decisions about such matters are for the national executives of unions with branches in the area. I would strongly advise your council not to take the action proposed.

Yours sincerely,

Ken Graham

Secretary
Organisation Department

The Trades Union Congress became alarmed at grass-root trade union support for strike action – what they euphemistically called a 'stoppage of work'.

Tyneside call for strike yard closure

By ROSALIND MORRIS

Mr Harold Wilson's attack on the Government's policy towards Palmer's ship repairing yard at Hebburn-on-Tyne during his speech to the Labour Party conference yesterday, was given a mixed reception on Tyneside. where a local trades council has called for a one-day general strike in the region to protest at the closure of the yard last weekend.

Mr A. White, managing director of Palmer's, which is owned by Vickers, said : " Several politicians have referred to our problems during the last few months, but there has been no result. I don't think any remarks by Mr Wilson at the Labour Party conference wil help.

" The loan given to us by the Labour Government in May was merely a bridging operation until a policy was worked out for the whole ship repairing industry.

" No policy was produced by either the Labour or Conservative Governments and so it was not altogether a surprise to us when the present Government refused to give us a further loan. Until a policy is devised for the whole industry there can be no real solution to its problems."

Mr White said Mr Wilson's use of the words " Palmer's Hebburn closed last weekend with all the phrase ' Palmer's Yard ' meant " was not relevant to present problems. " This is the spectre of the Jarrow hunger march which has arisen and is rattling its chains," he added.

Mr J Crassby, secretary of the South Shields Trades Council. who called for a one-day general strike on Tyneside in protest at the closure of the yard, said he was encouraged by Mr Wilson's speech.

" He is underlining the basic frustration and desperation of people who have been subject to an unemployment level of 10 per cent for males for many years," he said. " The call for a strike is not simply a protest about Palmer's. It is a protest against the Government's policy of withdrawing aid to what they call 'ailing industries'."

The strike call is to be discussed by the North-east Federation of Trades Councils on October 10.

Mr G. Arnold, chairman of the Confederation of Shipbuilding and Engineering Workers. said he was in favour of the strike because it would show the complete dissatisfaction of all the trade unions with the Government's policy.

Unemployment figures in Hebburn and Jarrow do not yet show the impact of the closure. Mr H. Townsend, manager of the Hebburn and Jarrow employment exchange. said yesterday that about 400 of the 750 men and women made redundant by the closure had registered at the exchange, but the full effects of the closure would not appear until next month.

Shields Gazette 30 September 1970

Harold Wilson, then opposition leader, sought political advantage – without political commitment.

HOUSE OF COMMONS
LONDON, SW1   13th. Oct.1970.

Dear Bro. Grassby,

        Thank you for your letter dated 22nd. Sept. 1970, regarding Palmers Yard closure and the possibility of a one day strike in protest being called by your council.

        There are certain difficulties in acceeding to your request for a public expression of support from the 'Labour group of M.Ps' as such.

        Firstly, the group will not be meeting until after the House resumes on Oct. 27th, and secondly it is by no means certain that it would be agreed that in a tactical sense, this would be the best action to take from the groups point of view.

        I am sure you will agree that the two M.P.s most closely involved, Arther Blenkinsop & Ernest Fernyhough have done their utmost to avert the tragic closure, and in their efforts they have had the full backing of the Northern Group, and your council can be assured that when parliament resumes the matter will not be allowed to die. Every political pressure will be applied as long as the present high level of unemployment persists in the region.

        It is therefore my personal view however that Industrial action and Political action should be pursued seperately, and there are certain tactical advantages in doing so, although I do appreciate this is a matter of opinion.

        I shall place this correspondence before the Group at our first meeting, but in the meantime your members can be assured that there will be no relaxation in the fight for justice in the North-East, a fight which is becoming increasingly obvious, will be a tough one under the present Tory Government.

        My best wishes to you and your members,

                Yours Sincerely,

J.Grassby Esq.,
Secty.S.Shields T.U.C.,
Ede House,
143, Westoe Road,
South Shields.

             (Gordon A.T.Bagier M.P.)
             Secty.Nth.Group M.Ps.

The parliamentry Labour party distanced itself from the action – without actually opposing it.

Strike call lacks support

By Journal Reporter

A ONE-DAY Tyneside strike may be called off because of lack of support from trade union regional offices.

The call comes from South Shields Trades Council which is protesting at the closure of Palmers ship repair yard at Hebburn.

So far not one trade union regional office has supported the strike call. Several trade union officials have condemned it.

The fate of the proposed strike now depends on a meeting of the North-East Federation of Trades Councils on October 10. Unless the Federation backs the strike it will be called off.

Mr. Jack Grassby, secretary of South Shields Trades Council, said: "We have had several messages for individual support from branches. Many will not be discussing it until their next meeting."

He added: "A lot of trade unionists have said that they will not support the call, but others will back it. We will not really know what will be happening until October 10."

Newcaslte Journal 30 September 1970

The North East Federation of Trades Councils conspiciously failed to support the call for action and the strike was called off.

Only 50 men see Tyne yard close

Only about 50 of the 750 men at Palmer's ship-repair yard in Hebburn-on-Tyne were at work yesterday to see the yard—once home of the world's largest ship-builder—close for the last time, after 118 years.

Most of the men had already taken their pay and redundancy money, and left. Mr John Gillespie, the area exchange manager, said that at present there are 1,514 people out of work in Hebburn and neighbouring Jarrow, 991 of them men. The full effect of the closure would not be known for at least a week.

Unions on Tyneside are giving support to a call by the trades council at South Shields for a one-day general strike in protest at the closure. M Jack Grassby, the secretary of the council, said: "This closure is threatening the whole ship-building industry, and the trade unions do not intend to stand idly by and watch the progressive rundown of the region."

Many of the redundant men at the yard believe it will be taken over, but the owners, Vickers, report that there have been no firm offers for it.

Shields Gazette 26 September 1970

The South Shields Trades Union Council (and others) would have to wait until 1972 and 1974 when the miners' strikes would provide the opportunity for successful involvement in wide-spread industrial action.

A THREAT TO OUR LIVELIHOOD AND OUR FUTURE . .

AN AFFRONT TO OUR DIGNITY

AN INSULT TO EVERY SHIELDS WORKER —

November 1971 - - Unemployment Figures

SOUTH SHIELDS AREA

MEN	5,101
BOYS	394
WOMEN	892
GIRLS	306
Total	6,693 Unemployed

JOIN

The South Shields Trades Union Council's

PUBLIC PROTEST
AND   DEMONSTRATION

SATURDAY, 27th NOVEMBER 1971
at II a.m.

Employment Exchange, Ocean Road

**An Address will be given by Delegates from
Upper Clyde Shipbuilders Shop Stewards Committee**

FOLLOWED BY THE LOBBYING OF OUR M.P.
ARTHUR BLENKINSOP IN THE TOWN HALL

FIGHT for the RIGHT to WORK !

Issued by South Shields Trades Union Council, 143 Westoe Road, South Shields and Printed by F. & A. Tolson, Jarrow.

The trades unions did not neglect the traditional (ineffectual) gestures of protest.

Shields Gazette

and Shipping Telegraph

No. 33195 (Established 1849)   Saturday, November 27, 1971

HOME

2½p.

JOB LIST GOES IN

MP given work rally action call

ABOUT 80 banner-carrying trade unionists and un-employed people marched from South Shields Em-ployment Office to the Town Hall today in a demon-stration against unemployment.

With police in attendance, they marched along Ocean Road and up Fowler Street in fairly dense traffic. Once at the Town Hall they assembled then filed into the reception rooms upstairs, where they discarded the banners.

Upper Clyde Shipbuilders,
Joint Shop Stewards' Committee,
Clydebank Division,
Clydebank,
Dunbartonshire.

1st December, 1971.

Mr. J. Grassby,
South Shields Trades Union Council,
Ede House,
143 Westoe Road,
South Shields.

Dear Brother Grassby,

On behalf of the above Committee I would
like to take this opportunity to thank you for
inviting us to your demonstration and lobby on
Saturday, 27th November, 1971, and for the
colledtion taken up at the meeting which
amounted to £12.67½ for which I enclose receipt
herewith.

May I personally take this opportunity to
thank you and your Committee for the hospitality
extended to myself and Brother McComish on that
day.   My warmest thanks to yourself and
Brothers Florence, Campbell and McIlroy for
their assistance in making this a most
memorable occasion for me.

Yours fraternally,

Con O'Neill

C. O'Neill,
Secretary.

Photo: Shields Gazette

A very motly throng of councillors, trade unionists, strikers and unemployed, demonstrated on the steps of South Shields' Town Hall.

Workers Press, Thursday November 16, 1972 PAGE 3

Rainwear workers want union of choice

WOMEN AND GIRLS on strike for over three weeks at the Barbours' rainwear factory, South Shields, have been given an apology by a local head of the Department of Health and Social Security after their recent eviction from the premises, by police.

Above: Three of the pickets Margaret Clark, Jean Banko and Alwyn Yeoman — Margaret and Alwyn were at the Social Security office when the police were called.
Below: The picket line outside Barbours' factory.

The women who went along with a delegation from the local Trades Council to meet DHSS heads were promised an investigation into the incidents. They were given an assurance 'that on no future occasion would police be used to prevent or inhibit members of the public from making legitimate claims for benefit'.

The apology came after the department concerned was accused of 'intimidation' and an 'unprovoked' attack on seven peaceable girls, when they used police to evict them.

Trades Council secretary Jack Grasby told Workers Press:

'At the meeting we are told these girls had every right to make an application for emergency payments. When the office refused, they continued to press for their rights and police were called to evict them.'

Women on the picket line spoke to Workers Press about the strike. Said Mrs. Elizabeth Jowsey, strike committee treasurer:

'Barbours are trying to dictate to us—they don't want the union we want in here. They want a small union in that they can manipulate.

'We are more determined than ever. We will stay out and get in our own union, the Transport and General Workers'. If they try to bring in non-union labour or new-starters from the dole queues, the pickets will stop them. We have already been pledged support from other workers who will join out picket line.

'This is a fight to the finish as far as we are concerned—we must establish our basic trade union rights. Somebody asked "What if the Tories order us back?" Well, let them try. We would still stand firm.'

Said picket Mrs. Margaret Turnbull: 'We think we have every right to join a trade union of our choice.

'Without a union they just ignored any demands we made. We want a united work force with our own representatives.

'With a trade union we can demand a living wage. If you like we are getting ready for the Common Market and more Tory inflation.'

Margaret Clark (18), a member of the strike committee, was one of the seven evicted by police from the Social Security office.

'We will stay out indefinitely,' she told us. 'If we go back without a union, it would not be worth working there any more.

Women workers at Barbours' rainwear factory on strike for a pay rise and union recognition.

Workers Press. Thursday November 16, 1972 PAGE 3

Strikers get an apology

I was at the Social Security office to make a fresh claim for hardship.

'I nearly died when the police came in—we only wanted to put a hardship claim in because of changed circumstance since we were refused four days earlier.

'When they refused to even listen to our claim we refused to move. That's when the police came in and forcibly evicted us. We were not causing trouble or demonstrating or even arguing—the officials of the Social Security refused to talk to us.'

Alwyn Yeoman (20) is another single member of the strike committee evicted from the Social Security office when making her hardship claim.

She said: "There is no question of going back without a union. That's why it was a unanimous vote to stay out at our last meeting.'

Margaret Turnbull and Elizabeth Jowsey, two of the women who are demanding the Transport and General Workers' Union is allowed to represent them.

Barbours' profits and Dividends		
Year ending	31/8/70	31/8/71
Turnover	£255,131	£347,386
Directors' pay	£28,433	£39,667 (3 directors)
Net profit before tax	£31,676	£65,057
Taxation	£20,457	£32,100
Earned for Dividends	£11,219	£32,957

EMPLOYEES		
Year ending	Average no.	Aggregate remuneration
31/8/71	119	£62,995

Sorry we brought in police says Social Security

The police were called to Wouldhave House, (the local DHSS office) when striking Barbours' workers were refused the right to claim benefits. The DHSS were to apologise later and the role of the police in evicting legitimate claimants was questioned.

Chief Constable,
Durham Constabulary,
Aykley Heads,
DURHAM.   15th Nov. 1972

Dear Sir,

    We wish to draw your attention to an incident which occurred
on Friday 10th Nov 1972, in which seven women were removed from the
offices of the Department of Health & Social Security, Wouldhave House,
South Shields, by members of your constabulary, involving, atc least in one
instance, the use of physical force.

    It has been established that these women, on an official strike ,
were making a proper and peaceful application for Social Security
benefits with the rightful assistance of Claimants Union advisers.

    We are aware that the police were called in by Officials of the
DHSS, but we would point out that it has been accepted by their Regional
Office that these local Officials were acting improperly in refusing to
accept applications for benefits and in seeking to have the claimants
removed.

    As a consequnce of this action members of your force have been
instrumental in physically preventing a legal application for benefits
being made and have collaborated in an illegal action to refuse proper
access to the Department of Health & Social Security by members of the
public.

    We would point out the dangers implicit in a situation where the
police are seen to be the implementers of arbitrary decisions of the
officials of any government department rather than the impartial
custidians of the law and servants of the public.

    We should be grateful to have your comments on this incident and
would be pleased to have your assurance that in future members of your
constabulary will not seek to prevent or inhibit members of the public
making a rightful application for benefits.

                        Yours faithfully,

                             Jack Grassby
            Secretary, Strike Liaison Committee.

Ultimately the police, and the DHSS, were to accept this right to claim benefits.

By Appointment to
H.R.H. The Duke of Edinburgh
Manufacturers of Waterproof & Protective Clothing
J. Barbour & Sons Ltd · Simonside · South Shields

J. Barbour & Sons Ltd

Simonside, South Shields, County Durham NE34 9PD. Telephone (08943) 2233

We are enclosing a statement which the Company is issuing to the Press, which we feel may clarify some of the issues in the present dispute.

You will see that the main point in this statement is the offer to all of the past members of our staff to bring in a new wage structure immediately, provided that there is also an immediate return to work.

This offer would give a basic minimum time rate of 32p per hour and a piece rate of 40p.

We think that there is a very good chance of our being able to obtain Government consent to these new rates in view of the fact that the Wages Council met before the freeze last week but there is little doubt that so long as we are not actually paying the new rates to our staff, due to the dispute, this weakens our claim.

Obviously we would have to continue paying at our old rates until such time as we receive official permission but we undertake to do everything possible to try and obtain permission, as this is in your interests and our own.

We do hope that you will appreciate that we are making a sincere attempt to break the present deadlock and that this offer will now enable you to re-commence work with us.

Yours faithfully,
J. BARBOUR & SONS LTD.

K. Charlton. F.C.A.
Managing Director.

7 November 1972

/ja

Manufacturers of 'Beacon', Thermproof and 'Beaconoid' P.V.C. Waterproof Clothing
Protective Clothing for Industry · Fishing · Shooting · Motorcycling · Agriculture · General Wear
Contractors to Nationalised Boards, Public Utilities and Local Government Authorities

Barbours management conceded defeat – but tried to mask it with a reference to "Government consent."

Barbours' workers sought public support for their strike for a pay rise and trade union recognition. Their persistent picketing of their factory, aided by SSTUC and workers from adjacent factories, prevented it from opening.

Shields Gazette

and Shipping Telegraph

No. 33491 (Established 1849)   Monday, December 11, 1972   HOME   3p.

IT'S STRIKE V-DAY

Shields girls win union recognition

THE 70 women strikers at the South Shields factory of J. Barbour Ltd. have won their seven-week battle for union recognition and a £2-a-week pay rise.

The managing director, Coun. Ken Charlton, agreed to talk to union officials after stormy scenes early today when more than 150 workers and trade unionists stopped him from opening up the Simonside factory.

A dozen policemen and two policewomen asked the pickets — including 70 men from the nearby Elsy and Gibbons factory — to move. When they refused, Coun Charlton agreed to meet the women's strike committee and Transport and General workers' Union group secretary, Mr Joe Mills.

After more than 30 minutes of negotiations, Mr Mills came out of the factory and told the waiting strikers that Coun. Charlton had agreed to recognise the union and pay a Wages Council award of £2 a week. Mr Mills told the Shields Gazette: "This is a magnificent victory. I will be starting negotiations on Wednesday morning for a new deal to come into force after the wage freeze."

After early-morning picketing at the factory of J. Barbour and Sons, South Shields, striking employees march with their branch banner after the management recognised their union. Another picture Page 7.

By Appointment to
H.R.H. The Duke of Edinburgh
Manufacturers of Waterproof & Protective Clothing
J. Barbour & Sons Ltd   Simonside   South Shields

J. Barbour & Sons Ltd

Simonside, South Shields, County Durham NE34 9PD. Telephone (08943) 2251

Following our letter and statement yesterday, we have today been officially informed that the Wage freeze does not apply to this firm in view of the fact that we undertook in advance to bring in the new wage rates from Monday, 6th November, 1972.

We are therefore able immediately to pay the rates previously mentioned – a time rate of 32p per hour for 18 years of age and over and 40p for piece work – and all workers starting work with us from now will be paid these rates.

Yours faithfully,
J. BARBOUR & SONS LTD

K. Charlton F.C.A.
Managing Director

8 November 1972

/lh

Manufacturers of 'Beacon', Thornproof and 'Beaconoid' P.V.C. Waterproof Clothing
Protective Clothing for Industry · Fishing · Shooting · Motorcycling · Agriculture · General Wear
Contractors to Nationalised Boards, Public Utilities and Local Government Authorities

Following their recognition of the Transport & General Workers Union Barbours' management personnel was changed, and wages, conditions and union~employer relations improved.

Barbours' women win!

A GREAT victory for trade unionism has been won by the 70 women strikers at Barbours' Rainwear, South Shields. After eight weeks of determined struggle they have defeated the management and forced complete recognition of the union of their choice—the Transport and General Workers' Union.

Crunch-time came yesterday morning when the women were joined on the picket line by miners, engineers and Trades Council delegates from South Shields and Jarrow.

At 8.30 a.m. when the police were preparing to break through the picket line, 80 sheet metal workers rushed from their factory next door and defended the Barbours women and girls.

Barbours were understood to be hoping to bring in new labour, but all entrances were blocked by pickets and no one got in, not even the staff workers and non-union supervisors who had previously worked.

And, as police arrived, manager Ken Charlton was prevented from opening the door.

Police reinforcements were rushed in, only to find that workers at the factory next door—Elsie and Gibbons—were joining the strike.

Police made no attempt to break the picket and eventually the manager asked to meet the union representatives.

At this meeting he capitulated. The victorious strikers returned to work today with full recognition for the T&GWU, an immediate £2-a-week increase, and the management committed to further negotiations with the stewards.

After seeing the management, strikers and their supporters marched through South Shields shouting 'Barbours have won'.

Jack Grassby, secretary of the South Shields Trades Union Council commented:

'We all want to pay tribute to the Barbours girls. They have fought the battle of their lives and have won. It is a victory for the whole working class and the trade union movement. It will long be remembered in South Shields.'

Despite their tight financial circumstances after eight weeks on strike, a meeting of the girls raised £2.50 for the Workers Press Appeal Fund.

● See photographs p.11

Shields Gazette, Monday, November 2, 1970—9

'Dock rates' to back council strikers

APPEAL BY TRADE UNION SECRETARY

AN APPEAL to the ratepayers of South Shields to withhold **p**art of their rates to the town council to show their sympathy with the council workers in their effort to get a "living wage," was made today by Mr Jack Grassby, secretary of South Shields Trades Union Council.

But the chairman of the Finance Committee, Ald. Edmund Hill, thought this was a foolish attitude to take, and another way of applying union pressure.

Mr Grassby said: "Preliminary legal advice has shown there is a prima facie case to be made out against the local council for a breach of contract which is entered into when the rates are paid for certain services to be carried out, and which are not, in fact, being provided. There may, therefore, be a legal case to be made for the withholding of a related proportion of rates — or a demand for repayment.

"A first rough calculation shows that the amount involved in South Shields is something like 2s. 6d. per week per household. For the period of the strike to date, this is about 10s. per household," he said.

Another way

Mr Grassby makes a personal call for the ratepayers in the town to withhold that amount until the legal aspects have been clarified, as a protest against the council, and in sympathy with the council workers.

He advised that council tenants should knock the amount off their current weekly rent, and private house-owners should withhold the money from their current monthly rate.

"Whatever the outcome may be of legal investigations being carried out, this action will at least have the effect of putting economic pressure where the blame belongs — on the local town council. Financial pressure might thus prevail to end the strike where reason, social justice and democratic opinion have failed," said Mr Grassby.

Ald. Hill commented: "It is foolish to take an attitude like this. It is the same argument as people saying they have no children so should not contribute towards education. It is just another way of the Trades Union Council trying to put pressure on the council."

On the legal position, Ald. Hill said: "Nothing has come before the council about this to my knowledge."

A little late

He said he had spoken to the Borough Treasurer, but as no copy of Mr Grassby's statement had been seen at the town hall, he could make no further comment.

A spokesman for the General and Municipal Workers' Union said today the advice could have come too late, because he was hoping for a settlement this week.

"It would obviously help our case if people did noy pay, but it is a little late now to put on this pressure," he said.

The spokesman said it would give them food for thought in the future, but it would be up to the individual whether or not he paid the full rate or not.

The deputy divisional officer for the National Union of Public Employees, Mr Ron Curran, said: "Anything that would assist to bring about a settlement is something I would welcome. If this can be done legally, I would support it."

The South Shields TUC sought to support a town council cleaning workers' strike by taking legal action against the council for 'breach of contract'.

T. D. MARSHALL, HALL & LEVY

INCORPORATING CROFTON & HAMILTON

SOLICITORS

H. J. TAVROGES
T. W. MAY, LL.B.

CONSULTANT
MONTAGUE LEVY

OUR REFERENCE

YOUR REFERENCE

COMMISSIONERS FOR OATHS

SAVILLE CHAMBERS,
SAVILLE STREET,
SOUTH SHIELDS
AND AT THE GREEN, EASINGTON

TELEPHONE
NUMBERS
SOUTH SHIELDS
3181 (3 LINES)
EASINGTON 487

HT/JG/P

10th November, 1970.

Mr. J. Grassby,
Red House,
Westoe Village,
SOUTH SHIELDS.

Dear Jack,

re: PROPOSED APPEAL

Further to our conversation at the telephone the other day I have not been able to find any precedent in respect of your proposed appeal but I think that I am right in saying that there is no prescribed form and accordingly I have drafted one which I think is appropriate.

This will have to be completed by each person who is appealing and of course in addition to the original being sent to the Clerk of the Court of Quarter Sessions, County Hall, Durham, a copy should also be sent to the Town Clerk at the Town Hall.

Yours sincerely,

Enc:

Friendly solicitors gave free legal advice.

COUNTY OF DURHAM

J . T . B R O C K B A N K
CLERK OF THE PEACE

TELEPHONE : 4411

C O U N T Y H A L L
D U R H A M

MY REF.

YOUR REF.

TGH/JER

11th March, 1971

Dear Sirs,

Appeal to Quarter Sessions
John Grasby v. South Shields County Borough Council

I shall be glad if you will let me have 35p being my fee for the hearing of the above Appeal (s) which was/were dealt with by Quarter Sessions on 5th March, 1971.

Yours faithfully,

J.Y. Brockbank

J. Grasby, Esq.,
4 Weston Village,
SOUTH SHIELDS,
Co. Durham.

Form QS/20

The Appeal was rejected – but the 35p hearings cost was reckoned to be good value.

County Palatine of Durham

DURHAM COUNTY QUARTER SESSIONS

IN THE MATTER of an appeal by

	JAMES FLORENCE	
	ROBERT FREDERICK GROWCOTT	(Appellant)
AND	JOHN GRASSBY	

and

SOUTH SHIELDS COUNTY BOROUGH COUNCIL (Respondent)

To :— J. Grassby, Esq.,
4 Westoe Village,
South Shields,
Co. Durham.

NOTICE IS HEREBY GIVEN that the Quarter Sessions, will be held at the Assize Courts, Old Elvet, in the City of Durham, on **Friday** the **5th** day of **March** 19 **71** at 10-30 o'clock in the forenoon, for the purpose of hearing the above Appeal.

DATED this **8th** day of **February** 19 **71**

J. J. Brockbank

Clerk of the Peace of the County Palatine of Durham.

County Hall,
Durham.

Shields Gazette

and Shipping Telegraph

HOME

No. 33003 (Established 1849)   Friday, March 5, 1971

RATES REBATE FOR STRIKE DISMISSED

AN APPEAL by three South Shields ratepayers against the rates which were levied on them during the period of the dustmen's strike last year, was dismissed at Durham Sessions today, the chairman, Judge Alastair Sharp, commenting: "The court means no disrespect to the three men in calling them 'village Hampdens.'

"They are standing up for the rights of the citizen. They have had the courage to come to bring to the Court of Quarter Sessions their grievances. I am bound to say, however, that their appeal is misconceived in law. They were submitting their case on the basis that rates are levied as a matter of contract between the local authority and the ratepayer.

"That is not so. Rates are levied as a result of a power granted to a local authority by Parliament."

Judge Sharp said that rates were levied as a result of an estimate. For instance, provision was made for snow-clearing in the winter.

"This year, touch wood, we have had a mild winter and it may well be that a local authority will show a saving. They will carry this forward. They don't hand it back to the rate-payers."

FOUR WEEKS

The three appellants were Mr James Florence, of Mowbray Road, a former town councillor; Mr Robert Growcott, of Devonshire Street, and Mr Jack Grasby, of Westoe Village, representing council and private tenants.

The three claimed rebates of the proportion of the rate levied for services not provided during the strike, from October 12 until November 9, a period of four weeks.

Mr Grasby is secretary of South Shields Trade Union Council.

Mr Florence said that the services involved in the strike were those covered by the council's town improvement committee which were controlled by the cleansing department.

The services included refuse collection, refuse disposal, gully-cleansing, sewage-flushing, street-cleaning and public lavatories.

A SAVING

Mr Florence said that on one day during the strike no manual worker was available and therefore services not provided.

He said he had estimated that through the strike, the council saved £15,100 for non-payment of wages and non-provision of services. He said that on the day when all manual workers were on strike, there was a saving in wages of £5,400, making a total saving of £20,500.

"In my case, the amount involved during the strike was 10p. This is a very modest amount, but I claim it as a rebate. I believe that this appeal raises a matter of a fundamental principle."

SPENT MONEY

Cross-examined by Mr Dennis Orde, for South Shields Town Council, Mr Florence agreed that the council would have spent money trying to help rate-payers during the strike.

He agreed that he had not made provision of this in his estimates of the rebate.

Mr Growcott said he wished to be associated with Mr Florence's remarks and the cost of the saving in his case was 6p.

Mr Grossby, who said he owned three properties which included his own house and another house and a hostel, said the saving in his case was 14p. He also said that he had to pay 50p to have rubbish removed privately from the hostel when the strike was on.

PLASTIC BAGS

Mr Ellwood Potts, general accountant with South Shields Corporation, said in evidence that the cost to each ratepayer for property with a rateable value of £56 was 1½p per week to carry out the services previously listed by Mr Florence.

After taking into account the cost of overtime, the provision of plastic bags for rubbish removal during the strike, the net saving to the council was just over £3,000.

This represented a saving of one-tenth of a new pence for each owner with property with a rateable value of £56.

● **John Hampden (1595-1643): famous for his refusal to pay ship money.**

Actually, Hampden, a land-locked farming land-owner and parliamentarian refused to pay a shipping tax. He was prosecuted under Charles I in 1637. He also lost.

BRUX ...JARROW ...FACTORY OCCUPATION .. URGENT ! !

TUBE INVESTMENTS... the Multi-National company that boast's "We bring jobs to Jarrow" ..can now claim sole responsibility for the loss of over 300 jobs in the Jarrow area.

On Dec. 20th 1974 Tube Investments closed down the Jarrow Tube Works affecting 280 men and their families...BUT with the promise of another firm moving onto the site.

On Jan. 10th 1975 they announced that the Jarrow site was to expand and ALL of their operations were to be centred here employing over 165 men by the end of 1975.

On March 28th 1975 Tube Investments decided to close down completely and move out of Jarrow.

The men were told at 12 noom that day that they were no longer needed and that the site was closing down completely.

The men involved on this site Occupation took the decision of Tube Investment's in January to EXPAND the site seriously and they took on committments and responsibility that affected their WIVES and CHILDREN !

Tube Investment's now about face and "change their minds" This is NOT the 1930 'S ....there will be no JARROW MARCH.

We have OCCUPIED the factory to prevent Tube Investment from moving any Machines or equipment out of Jarrow.

WE DEMAND the RIGHT to WORK

This fight canot be left to the men at Brux...This is YOUR fight.

Already the Jarrow and Hebburn and South Shields T.U.C. have realised the importance of this stand and have plegded their support.

Much more is needed ..YOU can assist by giving YOUR support.

FINANCE is urgently needed to run this OCCUPATION

RUSH DONATIONS and messages of support to....

"Occupation Fund"
92 Northbourne Rd.
Jarrow. Tyne & Wear.

The occupation of Jarrow Tube Works was led by a staunch member of SSTUC, Hughie Nicol.

BRUX OCCUPATION COMMITTEE WITH JARROW & HEBBURN AND SOUTH
SHIELDS TRADES COUNCILS ARE ORGANISING THIS CONFERENCE

THE RIGHT TO WORK

SPECIAL CONFERENCE
Saturday May 10th
The Labour Club, Park Road, Jarrow
11.00 a.m. - 4.00 p.m.

RECESSION, slump . . . factory closures and short-time working . . . This is 1975 in Britain. The crisis of the whole capitalist world coupled with rampant inflation.

To the working class, this means unemployment and savage attacks on our standards of living. One factory in Jarrow last month fought desperately to stop the closure at Brux.

This message remains with us today:

- *No more Jarrow marches*
- *Demand the Right-to-Work*
- *Occupy factories threatened with closure*
- *No short-time and no wage cuts*
- *Open up the company books*
- *Demand nationalization without compensation and under workers control*

PTO

Engineers weld gates at north-east sit-in

On duty at the Brux (Tube Investments) plant.

BY OUR OWN REPORTER

JARROW—Engineering workers have welded the gates of their factory to stage an occupation in defence of the basic right to work.

The 30 workers took the lead in the fight against unemployment within an hour of being told that the factory was closing and they were all being made redundant.

STATEMENT

At midday on Friday the management of Brux Ltd, a subsidiary of the giant multinational Tube Investments, told the work force that they were closing down immediately and they wanted everyone off the site by 4 o'clock.

The shop stewards called a meeting and a demand from the floor to occupy the factory was carried unanimously. All the gates

Workers Press 19 March 1975

After 6 weeks of bitter fighting with Tube Investments at Jarrow, these men have important lessons to discuss with the whole trade union movement, both on Tyneside and throughout the country.

This is why a CONFERENCE on the RIGHT-TO-WORK has been called in Jarrow on Saturday May 10.

The Brux men today . . . you tomorrow. This is the meaning of slump. Prepare to defend your jobs. Attend this conference.

The old concept of redundancy pay for leaving your job is bankrupt. With one million unemployed, massive short-time working, recession and factory closures are here with us today.

Every shop steward, militant and trade unionist is now obliged to warn the working class and prepare them for the coming struggles.

This is the purpose of the conference in Jarrow on May 10. Defend the Right-to-Work.

The whole trade union movement, every shop stewards committee in the factories must be prepared to stand up and fight.

Jarrow & Hebburn, and South Shields Trades Councils are assisting the Brux Occupation Committee.

Brux Occupation Committee, with the assistance of Jarrow & Hebburn, and South Shields Trades Councils as joint sponsors, are organising this conference and urge all trade unionists to attend.

Make sure your shop steward or factory committee is represented. Make sure YOU attend. Credentials 15p

Please send me Credentials / Agenda for the conference:

Name ....

Address..

....

Trade Union / Factory..

Amount enclosed ....

Complete form and post to: H. Nicol, Peoples Place, Derby Terrace, South Shields

Published by H. Nicol. Peoples Place, Derby Terrace, South Shields
Printed by New Press (TU). 186a Clapham High Street, London SW4 7UG.

The occupation failed and Jarrow Tube Works closed.

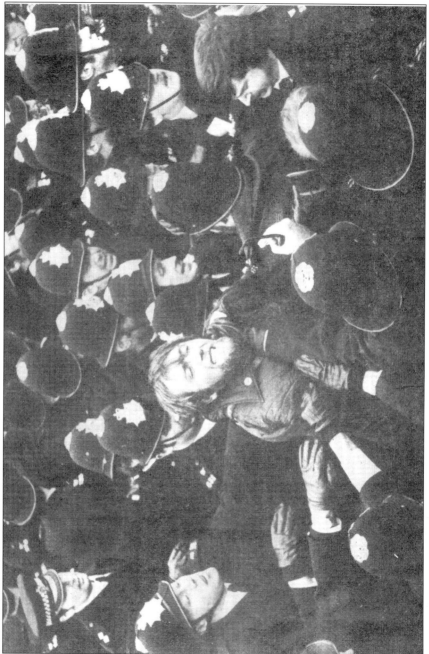

An image of the times–a picket mobs the police.

The Unfinished Revolution

SOUTH SHIELDS (outdoor) BRANCH
20 TUNSTALL AVE.,
SOUTH SHIELDS.   FEB. 20TH. 1971

POST OFFICE WORKERS STRIKE

Dear Colleague,

We are now entering the fifth week of our struggle.
Initially our strike commenced over the refusal of our employer,
the Post Office , to grant our claim for a wage increase of £3 or
15%. on our maximum rate of pay, coupled with a claim for the reduction in Incremental Scales — a reasonable claim.

During the strike our employer has refused to
negotiate with us , despite the loss to them of £500,000 a day
a figure which has increased to £700,000 a day since the 15th.Feb.
This attitude of our employer has changed the complexion of the
strike from a wage claim to that of a struggle for the very existance
of our Union and the subsequent working conditions of our members.

If we lose this struggle we lose our freedom. The Post
Office will realy go to town on us — we can't afford to lose.

The attitude of the Post Office during the strike has
turned the feeling of goodwill that has existed amongst us for
many years to one of bitterness and it will take many many years
before things are back to normal in this respect.

It is felt that at this stage that the Post Office is
under pressure from the Government not to raise their offer above the
8%-9% . That being the case we have to win not only for ourselves
but for the rest of the lower paid workers in the Trade Union
movement.   During the past weeks the generosity of our friends
in the trade union movement has been amazing and has overwhelmed us.
There is no doubt that the financial help and messages of support
that we have had have helped us greatly to overcome the hardships
of the past month — this help is still needed.

To-date we have received help from the following :—
Middle Docks, Reyrolles, P.O. Management, South Shields Trades
Union Council. Staff and students of the Marine & Technical College
are having collections .

Any further offer of help would be most welcome
and these may be sent to me at the above address or at 110 Imeary
Street.   Yours fraternally,

                                    S. Hyde
                                    Secretary.

THIS APPEAL HAS THE SUPPORT OF THE SOUTH SHIELDS TRADES UNION COUNCIL
AND ALL TRADE UNIONISTS ARE EARNESTLY ASKED TO HELP THE P.O. WORKERS
IN THIS FIGHT FOR ALL LOWER PAID WORKERS AND PUBLIC EMPLOYEES.
                                    JACK GRASSBY.

Another of the many strikes supported by the SSTUC.

UNION OF POST OFFICE WORKERS
SOUTH SHIELDS (Outdoor) BRANCH

Secretary: ....

Treasurer: ....

Ref. No........................

1 Watson Ave,
South Shields.

Tel SS 60463.
3 March

19 71

Mr. J. Grassby,
Secretary,
SS Trades Council,

Dear Colleague,

Further to my visit to
Ede House on Saturday last, and our discussion on the distribution
of leaflets for the T.U.C.

Our local committee of the
U.P.W. at a meeting held on 2 March '71, have agreed to give you and
your Council support in the distribution of these leaflets. The degree
of help would in the main be restricted to advice on how you could
set about the problem of distributing these leaflets.

Perhaps you could contact
me, when it would be convenient for one of our Branch Officials to
discuss further details with you and your committee.

Yours Fraternally,

Branch Chairman.

*The Post Office worker repaid their debt to the SSTUC by agreeing to
distribute leaflets free.*

A STATE OF EMERGENCY

A NATIONAL STATE OF EMERGENCY WAS PROCLAIMED TODAY BY THE PRIVY COUNCIL AFTER IT MET ON BOARD THE ROYAL YACHT BRITANNIA.

Ministers were flown in an aircraft of the Queen's Flight to the windswept airstrip on the lonely Island of Islay off Western Scotland. They were then taken by barge to the Royal Yacht anchored just off the island.

The state of emergency, signed by the Queen, comes into effect from midnight tonight. It will give the Government control and emergency powers over the docks. It is forced by the week-long strike of dockers which seems certain to continue for at least a few more days.

This is the fourth state of emergency to be proclaimed by the Conservative Government since it took office in June, 1970—a record for any Government in recent history.

The Home Secretary, Mr Robert Carr, was among the Privy Ministers at the Privy Council. He was reporting to the Commons after returning to London in one of the Queen's aircraft.

He will announce the state of emergency.

COMMONS DEBATE

A debate in the Commons will be held early next week before MPs begin their summer holiday.

It is not expected that many of the powers authorised by the state of emergency will be used immediately, although it is anticipated that port emergency committees will be set up in all docks to establish which essential supplies may need to be moved.

The decision to seek a state of emergency was taken after a Ministerial meeting last night, after consultations between the Minister of Agriculture, Mr James Prior and representatives of animal feed suppliers and the National Farmers' Union.

MINERS' STRIKE

This is the second state of emergency to be proclaimed by the Government because of a dock strike. The earlier occasion was in July, 1970, only weeks after Mr Heath had formed his administration.

Since then, there have been national emergencies created by the power workers' dispute in December 1970, and the miners' strike in February this year.

Mr Robert Carr

Shields Gazette 3 August 1972

The 1972 national dockers strike caused the fourth state of emergency to be declared in two years.

Shields men angry with colleagues

BY OUR SHIPPING REPORTER

THE 130 dockers at Tyne Dock are angry over the reluctance of their 130 fellow dockers at North Shields to take part in the national dock strike. They have unanimously passed a resolution "dissociating" themselves from the remarks made on behalf of the North Shields men.

MR YOUNG

"We are not reluctant strikers," declared Mr Alan Young, union branch chairman of the Tyne Dock men.

"Nobody wants a strike but the majority decision was taken to hold one and you have got to stand by it,

"We dissociate ourselves from the comments of the North Shields dockers and stand 100 per cent behind the national delegate conference decision."

Mr Young was attacking the remarks of Mr John Bell, secretary of the North Shields dockers, that his men did not want to strike because they thought the docks industry was "the

Shields Gazette 3 August 1972

Bid to recall dockers' meeting

AN all-important decision to recall a dockers' delegates' conference to consider ending the national port stoppage is expected to be taken early next week, **writes Our Industrial Correspondent.**

It is believed it will follow the next meeting of the Aldington-Jones Committee, which is planned for either Monday or Tuesday. If the transport workers' **leader** Mr Jack Jones makes the decision after the meeting, the conference could be held a day or so later.

Mr Jones and the Port of London Authority Chairman, Lord Aldington — joint heads of the committee whose interim report on the manpower problems of the docks was rejected by the delegates — today continued their efforts to secure more guarantees of job security.

MAIN POINT

They are concentrating on trying to gain assurances of work for dockers at inland container and cold store depots.

Dockers' leaders rejected the report because they said they wanted results, **not** promises, on the issue.

Mr Jones reported progress towards "tangible results" and it is hoped that it will not be long before recalling the conference.

TYNE-DOCK DOCKERS

STRIKE BULLETIN   NO.1

THIS BULLETIN IS ISSUED TO THE PEOPLE OF SOUTH SHIELDS
BECAUSE WE, THE DOCKERS, DO NOT FEEL THAT OUR CASE HAS BEEN
ADEQUATELY REPORTED IN THE PRESS.

First this strike is NOT about higher wages - it is a fight
against redundancies , against unemployment , and for security
of livlihood for our families.

Three years ago the Danish butter-boat Magnolia employed
100 dockers for two days to discharge. Now this work is carried
out by 12 men in a few hours!

TWO YEARS AGO THERE WERE 1000 dockers employed on the Tyne
NOW THERE ARE ONLY 400 - and more redundancies are to come!

Unemployment and redundancies among the dockers is the result
of containerisation policies being carried out by large monopolies
who are more concerned with thier private profit than the livlihood
of the workers.

For example, Lord Vesty , a multi-millionair and owner of
shipping, wharves,and a chain of meat retail shops , is closing
down his warves, putting dockers out of work , and setting up
container depots run on cheap labour.

THE PROBLEM OF REDUNDANCIES IS AFFECTING ALL WORKERS AND WE
FEEL THAT OUR STRUGLE IS PART OF THE FIGHT NEEDED BY ALL TRADE-
UNIONISTS.

We are not standing in the way of progress but we feel that
some consideration must be given to workers who are affected by
mechanisation.

WE APPEAL FOR THE SUPPORT , UNDERSTANDING , AND PATIENCE OF
ALL LOCAL TRADE UNIONISTS AND MEMBERS OF THE PUBLIC IN OUR FIGHT
FOR A SECURE LIVLIHOOD FOR OURSELVES AND OUR FAMILIES.

Produced by Tyne-Dock dockers and printed by the Strike Liaison
Committee , 143 Westeo Rd.

An example of the work of the SSTUC~trade union Strike Liaison Committee.

SOUTH SHIELDS TRADES UNION COUNCIL

143 Westeo Rd.,
SOUTH SHIELDS

TO SECRETARIES OF ALL AFFILIATED ORGANISATIONS

17 June 1972

Dear Colleague,

INDUSTRIAL ACTION

The Trades Union Council wishes to draw the attention of all branches to the following service and facilities which they offer to make available to branches involved in industrial action.

1. Strike Claimants Committee.

Recent legis lation has meant that all strike payment are likely to be deducted from any Social Security Benefits that a strikers familly may claim. As a consequence , and to protect thier funds from being plundered by the Industrial Relation Court, many unions have given up the idea of paying strike money.

As a consequence it is important that the families of strikers receive the full amount of Social Security Benefits due to them .

It has also been established that, contrary to common belief, it is possible for strikers themselves to obtain Social Security Benefits.

In both cases benefits will only be obtained with a fight, and the harder you fight the more you will get. The 1966 Social Security Act , and its amendments, which determine the basis of payments is difficult and complicated. Expert advice is needed and organised action is required by the branch.

To achieve this end every branch engaged in major industrial action is advised to set up a "Strike Claimants Committee". The Trades Union Council is prepared to assist in the setting up and operation of such a Committee , in an advisory capacity , and , in particular, the South Shields Claimants Union which is an Associate Member of the Council, is prepared to put at the service of the branch its extensive knowledge and experience.

A circular explaining the function of the Claimants Union is enclosed.

2. Strike Co-ordinating Committee

The Trades Union Council which represents over 10,000 local trade unionists is prepared , at the request of a branch engaged in industrial action, to set up a "Strike Co-ordinating Committee". The purpose of this Committee would be to promote and co-ordinate the moral, financial and organisational support of other local trade unionists .

Both of the above Committees were effective in the recent miners strike in promoting local support for their action and , in particular, in obtaining for strikers something like 5 times the amount of Social Security Benefits per head than was obtained in other areas.

Yours fraternally,

Jack Grassby
Secretary.

P.S. All affiliated branches are reminded that a Building Fund has been establshed to provide future accommodation for the Trades Union Council which is at present renting accommodation at Ede House on a limited lease. All branches are urged to make a donation to this fund.

The Trades Union Council offered direct practical support to all striking workers—

·MR FEATHER
To be sent letter

ADVISE WORKERS, FEATHER IS URGED

WORKPEOPLE should be given advice on how to organise workers' takeovers when industrial closures are threatened, according to South Shields Trades Union Council.

The council, which represents about 10,000 trade unionists in South Shields, has written a letter to Mr Vic Feather, general secretary of the Trades Union Congress, calling for "practical advice" on how to take over their workplaces.

"There is evidence that this form of resistance to future redundancies will be increasingly common and we believe that local trade union branches should be encouraged to produce contingency plans for such action," says the letter.

"We recall the futility and ignominious rejection of the conventional protests last year, which failed to prevent the closure of Palmers shipyard on the Tyne, and we are impressed by the courage and initiative of the workers of UCS in their occupation of their workplaces.

"A RIGHT"

"We call upon the General Council of the TUC to prepare and offer practical advice to unions concerning the procedures by which workers can effectively take over their place of work when threatened with closure or large scale redundancies."

Shields Gazette 26 October 1971

– and urged the TUC to give advice as to how to take over their workplaces.

PRESS STATEMENT   15TH JUNE 1973 South Shields Trades Union Council
Picket of Police Station and Court.   10.30 a.m.

This picket is in protest at the involvement of the Police and the
Courts in political action against trade unionists – particularly
against pickets and strikers.
We believe that the Police and the Law are being used as political
tools of the government against workers.

The recent action by the South Shields Police in evicting Barbours
women srikers from the local offfices of the DHSS while they were
making proper and legal application for benefits is one local
example of this abuse of police powers.
e have choosen today to protest as a gesture of solidarity and
support for the 24 Shrewsbury building workers who are appearing in
court on conspiracy charges for picketing.
his is the latest and most serious example of the abuse of police
powers and the law against strikers.
The Industrial Relations Act has been smashed. The 1875 Conspiracy
Act is now being tried in its place.

Malcolm Campbell

President.

*The SSTUC demonstrated outside South Shields Police Station and Court
expressing their support for 24 Shrewsbury building workers who were, at that time,
appearing on conspiracy charges for picketing.*

*The police were observed taking photographs of the demonstrators and a lengthy
argument developed regarding the legitimacy of their action.*

THE JOURNAL Saturday June 16 1972

A group of TUC demonstrators parade outside the police station at South Shields.

Anger at police photos

By Journal Reporter

ANGRY protesters are demanding to know why police took photographs of them during a demonstration outside a police station yesterday.

The protesters said last night they would make an official complaint to the Durham County police chief demanding an explanation for the action. They say they were unaware police were training cameras on them while they held their protest outside South Shields police station.

"And we want to know what they intend doing with our photographs. For all we know they might be for Special Branch secret files," said protest leader, Mr. Malcolm Campbell.

The row started after 20 banner - waving trade unionists paraded outside the Keppel Street police headquarters p r o t e s t i n g against what they called misuse of police power.

The demonstration was also to support the 24 Shrewsbury building workers currently facing trial on conspiracy charges stemming from picketing during their recent pay strike.

P.C. ▇▇▇ Maughan, of the town's police photographic department, was seen taking photographs with a box-type camera of groups and individual demonstrators.

A mother, passing with her daughter, stopped to talk to the demonstrators and claimed she had her picture taken.

"What right do they have to take my photograph? I haven't done anything wrong. I would like to know where those photographs are going to end up," she said.

MR PUCKERING

Shields Gazette 6 July 1973

POLICE PICS AT DEMO 'WERE JUST ROUTINE'

POLICE photographs taken during the demonstration outside the Keppel Street police station, South Shields, on June 15 were "relevant only to a comprehensive and unbiased understanding of a normal police report on an operational incident", says the Durham Chief Constable, Mr A. G. Puckering.

BY OUR POLITICAL STAFF

The Chief Constable made this statement in a letter to Mr Arthur Blenkinsop, MP for South Shields, who had written to him saying that he was disturbed to read accounts of the demonstration in the local Press.

The report in the Shields Gazette said that a police photographer took pictures throughout the demonstration. Protests had been made to him about this action and its possible implications.

Mr Blenkinsop recalled that some time ago there had been similar complaints arising from student and other political demonstrations, and certain assurances were then given. Some explanation should be given in this case.

"It certainly would not be acceptable for the police to be maintaining their own private records on occasions of this kind," said Mr Blenkinsop, "and if, indeed, a police photographer was used then some explanation is necessary."

The police claim that their photographs were 'just routine' again raised the question of the role of the police in lawful community actions.

The Youth Theatre

One theme of the South Shields Trades Union Council was to encourage alternatives to traditional employment. It supported and promoted alternative activities such as job-exchanges, co-operatives, and further education on benefits or grants. With wide spread unemployment and the collapse of the traditional apprenticeships it is not surprising that these alternative activities were wide-spread and innovative. One such venture which became entangled with the Trades Union Council was the South Shields Youth Theatre.

Photo: Lee Foster

A picture of the Pier Pavilion, South Shields in 1999 – a converted Victorian bus-shelter where some of the Youth Theatre's activities took place – all dramatic, but not exclusively theatrical.

The Youth Theatre was formed in 1966 and was composed mainly of students, 6th formers, and young unemployed. They engaged in many dubious activities, often supported by the SSTUC, and on one notable occasion they succeeded, unwittingly, in serving an audience which included the Mayor and civic dignitaries with coffee laced with police finger-print powder.

The full story of the Youth Theatre must be left to a more courageous writer. It will suffice here to say that many of its members went on to quite legitimate careers – and some to work in the professional theatre. Notably one, Edward Wilson, went on to become Director of the National Youth Theatre.

Although the Youth Theatre was not trade union based their views, and chiefly their attitude, had a close affinity with that of the SSTUC, and they contributed greatly to the spirit of that period.

SOUTH SHIELDS YOUTH THEATRE GROUP

6 Eccleston Road,
South Shields.
15th.September 1966

Mr. Jack Grassby,
13 St.John's Terrace,
East Boldon.

Dear Jack,

Please excuse this rather impersonal note but I have only one day left at the college before I go to Sunderland with the National Youth Theatre for a fortnight. As you are such an elusive character I thought it would be better to write to you rather than risk trying to see you in the college.

Last week I applied to the Youth Service Committee for a grant for the Youth Theatre Group of £100. As you are such a dedicated fighter for all that is good and right I thought it advisable to send you details for use at the next Youth Service Committee meeting so that you will not have to rely on your usual irrelevant stirrings.

You will probably find these details rather ambitious but as you know how brilliant I am I am quite sure that you will realise that the scheme is a practicable one.

The £100 we have asked for is to cover costs such as royalties, costume, properties, set construction, and the host of other things required for the productions. It may well be that the Youth Service will cut us short on this so we will have to accept what they are willing to give. The important thing is that we launched our last production at our own expense and this came somewhere in the region of £25 for a one night stand. You can appreciate our problem.

Trusting in your competence,

Kind regards,

Edward Wilson

The overture. The tone was unusual – but the subject was to become familiar.

SOUTH SHIELDS YOUTH THEATRE GROUP

<u>Proposed Youth Theatre Festival</u>   <u>Christmas 1966</u>

<u>A Note on the Festival</u>

        The Youth Theatre Festival will take place
in the town presenting a variety of arts
activities between the period Dec.19th -
Dec.30th 1966.

<u>Provisional Programme</u>

Mon. Dec.19th - Festival Opening Revue
                  built up from original material.
Tue.Dec.20th - event to be named-probably musical e.g.Folk or Jazz.

Wed.Dec.21st⎫
Thu.Dec.22nd⎬   PLAY (to be named)
Fri.Dec.23rd⎭

Sat.Dec.24th **N** THE COVENTRY NATIVITY PLAY

———————————————————————————

          Recess for Christmas & Boxing Day

———————————————————————————

Tues.**Dec 27**⎫
Wed.Dec 28 ⎬   BILLY LIAR (Waterhouse & Hall)
Thur.Dec 29⎭

                  plus Art Exhibition

Fri.Dec 30 - Festival Closing Revue

       There are other items to be fitted in e.g.recitals and
possibly talks and debates of a relevant character.The
intention of this provisional programme is to give you
some idea of what we are trying to do.

                               E.W.

*An ambitious programme – particularly as at that time, the 'Youth Theatre'
existed mainly in the minds of Edward Wilson & Co. An early example of
creative cultural constructionism?*

SOUTH SHIELDS
YOUTH THEATRE

YOUTH
THEATRE
FESTIVAL

December 19th—30th, 1966
Pier Pavilion, South Shields

SOUVENIR PROGRAMME

SOUTH SHIELDS YOUTH THEATRE

President: JACK GRASSBY.

Associates:

ARTHUR BLENKINSOP, M.P.   JOAN SHERWOOD, B.Sc.
COUN. JIM FLORENCE.   SANDRA COURTENAY.
COUN. KEN SCRIMGER.   ALAN KNOX, B.A. A.T.D.
ALEX STEPHENSON, B.A., J. P.   PAUL LAMB, A.L.A.M.
FRED G. GREY, M.A.   PETER McBRIDE, B.A.
ALEX WOODCOCK.

Director: EDWARD WILSON.

Associate Directors .... HEATHER MALCOLM, DAVID WALKER
Technical Director .... PETER MASON
Designer .... MARGARET QUIGLEY
Costume Supervisor .... DENISE KINGSBURY
Properties Supervisors .... GWEN WILLIAMS, MAUREEN HINCHAN
Art Supervisor .... MARGARET HUNTER
Lighting .... CAROL EASTLAND, KEN WILSON
Sound .... MARK REA
Make-Up .... RHONA JOHNSTON
Administrative Assistants .... JOHN WOODS, JOAN SNOWBALL
Publicity Manager .... DAVID MASON
Business Manager .... IAN J. ROWLEY
Production Assistants ..... CLAIRE EMERSON, PATRICIA BURBRIDGE
KATHLEEN SOULSBY, GILLIAN STODDART
DIANA VERNON, JANICE MASON.

In addition there are many un-named members of the Youth Theatre who have helped in this production.

Please Note: As a safety precaution, we would be grateful if patrons would refrain from smoking in the auditorium.

Monday and Tuesday, December 19th and 20th, 1966

Double Bill *The Bald Prima Donna* by Eugene Ionesco.
End Game by Samuel Beckett.

THE BALD PRIMA DONNA

Mr. Smith .... OWEN SMITH
Mrs. Smith .... BRENDA NEWCOMB
Mr. Martin .... CLIFFORD BURNETT
Mrs. Martin .... JOAN SNOWBALL
Mary, the Maid .... MARGARET HUNTER
Captain of the Fire Brigade ..... BOB HAILS

END-GAME

Hamm .... GEORGE IRVING
Clov .... PAUL THAIN
Nagg .... BOB HAILS
Nell ..,......................... MAUREEN GILPIN

Both Plays directed by EDWARD WILSON

Wednesday, Thursday and Friday, Dec. 21st, 22nd and 23rd, 1966

Blithe Spirit

by **Noel Coward**

Charles Condomine .... JOHN WOODS
Ruth Condomine ..... GILLIAN MORRISON
Elvira .... MARGARET HUNTER
Dr. Bradman .... IAN MORGAN
Mrs. Bradman .... BRENDA NEWCOMB
Mdme. Arcati .... JENNIFER ENGLISH
Edith, the Maid .... SUSAN FORD

The Play directed by HEATHER MALCOLM

Saturday and Monday, December 24th and 26th, 1966 —
Christmas Eve and Boxing Day

Rattle of a Simple Man

by **Charles Dyer**

Cyrenne .... SUSAN BAINBRIDGE
Percy .... EDWARD WILSON
Ricard .... IAN MORGAN

The Play directed by HEATHER MALCOLM

Tuesday, Wednesday and Thursday, Dec. 27th, 28th and 29th 1966

Billy Liar

by **Keith Waterhouse** and **Willis Hall**

Billy Fisher .... CLIFFORD BURNETT
Geoffrey Fisher ....OWEN SMITH
Alice Fisher ...., JOAN SNOWBALL
Florence Boothroyd .... ROSE HUNTER
Arthur Crabtree .... EDDIE STENTON
Barbara ..,................. DOROTHY SIMPSON
Rita .... SUZANNE KINCAIDE
Liz .... GILLIAN MORRISON

The Play directed by EDWARD WILSON

The choice of plays can be seen in many ways to have been a natural for that period – a case of art imitating life!

An association of local authorities, industrial organisations and individuals
to encourage, develop and promote activities in connection with all forms of the Arts in the North-East.
SUNLIGHT CHAMBERS 2/4 BIGG MARKET
NEWCASTLE UPON TYNE Telephone Newcastle 27126/7 and 27914

HW/MEG

1   25th July 1967

J Grassby Esq
South Shields Labour Headquarters
Westoe Road
South Shields

Dear Mr Grassby

I am enclosing a copy of my letter to Edward Wilson concerning the
future of the South Shields Youth Theatre.

I do hope that, in the near future, steps will be taken to put the
group on a permanent basis with adequate adult supervision.

Yours very sincerely

Heather Woodhams

Heather Woodhams

*Northern Arts, like the town council, seemed obsessed with the idea of
adult supervision – as if the Youth Theatre couldn't be trusted to act
irresponsibly themselves.*

6—Shields Gazette, Tuesday, September 26, 1967

Double blow may kill the Youth Theatre

THE South Shields Youth Theatre, founded only 15 months ago, may have to close. The theatre, which has eight productions to its credit, is facing two of the biggest problems of its short but turbulent history.

The first is the question of who steps into the shoes of 19-year-old founder and director Edward Wilson when he leaves at the end of this month. The second is the threat to the future of the theatre because of lack of funds.

Mr. Wilson, however, is confident about the future of both administration and finances 'In the long run I hope there will be one adult in charge, but to keep the theatre in momentum a production team is being established to operate on a committee basis At least half the members will be adults—people connected with other dramatic groups in the area who have helped us in the past."

EDWARD WILSON
"The future is black for us if . . ."

The Youth Theatre survived continuously on the edge of a Sartre like existential state of being and nothingness.

We'll take over Pier Pavilion —Youth Theatre

SOUTH SHIELDS Youth Theatre have offered to take over the Pier Pavilion, threatened with closure unless the Council and amateur dramatic groups can solve its financial problems. In a letter to the Town Hall today, the Youth Theatre offers to take over the Pavilion as a permanent base on lease from South Shields Council.

Shields Gazette October 1967

It would be administered, says the letter, by adult organisers with experience of theatrical production and administration, and would be hired out to other local and national drama groups.

The Youth Theatre would promise to put on a minimum number of performances with educational value at the Pavilion each year, including plays to help secondary school pupils taking GCE subjects

A dramatic gesture – a flop with the local council.

SOUTH SHIELDS YOUTH THEATRE

PATRON : JOHN NEVILLE O.B.E.

Second Season

Little Malcolm
and his struggle against the Eunuchs
BY DAVID HALLIWELL

August 15th-19th 1967

Lysistrata
of Aristophanes
TRANSLATED BY DUDLEY FITTS

August 23rd-26th 1967

PIER PAVILION, SOUTH SHIELDS Box Office : 60147

The first of these plays was claimed by the Youth Theatre to be metaphorical.

SOUTH SHIELDS YOUTH THEATRE

Patron: JOHN NEVILLE. O.B.E.

President: JACK GRASSBY.

Vice President: MICHAEL CROFT.

Director: EDWARD WILSON.

Assistant Directors	John Woods, Kathleen Bainbridge.
Technical Director	Peter Mason.
Business Manager	George Irving.
Company Manager	Joan Lee.
Publicity Manager	Tony Baynes.
Wardrobe Supervisor	Margaret McCall.
Properties Mistress	Joan Shotton.
Art Supervisor	Margaret Hunter.
Lighting	Ken Wilson.
Sound	John Tinmouth.
House Manager	Pauline Bonner.
Business Associate	**Ian Rowley.**
Production Assistants	Iain Stinson, Gill Stoddart, Gwen Williams, Bob Morton, Margaret Quigley, Mary Lee, Geoff Boyle.
Administrative Assistants	Helen Temple, Christine Hodgson. Patricia Dearden.

In addition, many un-named members of the Youth Theatre have assisted in these productions.

The South Shields Youth Theatre is affiliated to the National Youth Theatre of Great Britain and is financially aided by the North Eastern Association for the Arts.

Honorary Associates:

Arthur Blenkinsop, M.P.
Coun. James Florence.
Coun. Ken. Scrimger.
Joan Sherwood. B.Sc.
Alex Stephenson, B.A., J.P.

Alan Knox, B.A.
Peter McBride, B.A.
Paul Lamb, A.L.A.M.
Malcolm Campbell.
Sandra Courtenay.

Margaret Laybourne.
Coun. Len Harper.
Alex Woodcock.
Fred. G. Grey, M.A.

SOUTH SHIELDS YOUTH THEATRE

6 Eccleston Road,South Shields.

President		Director
JACK GRASSBY	Patron	EDWARD WILSON
	JOHN NEVILLE,OBE	

August 1st 1967

Coun.J.W.Ireland,J.P.,
233 Sunderland Road,
South Shields.

Dear Coun.Ireland,

I have been notified by the South Shields
Police of a letter written to you by Mr.David Mason,
and of certain allegations made by Mr.Mason in this
letter against **individual** members of the Youth Theatre,
and therefore,by implication,against the South
Shields Youth Theatre itself.

The Police agree with me that there are
certain factors which must be considered,not least
of which is the fact that Mr.Mason was asked to leave
the Youth Theatre on the grounds of his apparent
unwillingness to carry out his duties. The implications
of this in relation to his letter are self-explanatory.

The allegations made by Mr.Mason are so
out of proportion with reality,that the parents of one
of the individuals concerned are seeking legal advice
with a view to a possible action against Mr.Mason.
Similarly the South Shields Youth Theatre will not
hesitate to seek legal advice if any attempt is made
to defame its name in connection with these allegations.

We hope that these considerations will be
borne in mind when you draw your conclusions from
Mr.Mason's letter,and remain,

Yours faithfully,

Edward Wilson,
Director
pp South Shields Youth Theatre
Management Committee.

The police were early patrons of the Youth Theatre.

Copy for the attention of Mr. J. Grassby

233 Sunderland Road,

SOUTH SHIELDS.

3rd August, 1967.

Dear Mr. Wilson,

I thank you for your letter of 1st August and I am pleased to note your concern for the good name of the South Shields Youth Theatre. I have not, of course, drawn any conclusions from Mr. Mason's letter, being quite content to await the result of the police enquiries.

The Chief Constable makes two main points in a letter of 10th July arising from police enquiries. I quote:

(1) "the Director" (yourself) "assured my officers that the members" (of the Youth Theatre) "would be placed under more strict supervision in the future."

(2) "the time is opportune for the Youth Theatre to be managed or at least supervised by an adult."

I feel sure that if action is taken on these two issues neither of us will need to worry unduly in the future about the good name of the Youth Theatre.

Yours faithfully,

Coun. J.W. IRELAND. J.P.,
Chairman,
South Shields County Borough
Education Committee.

Mr. E. Wilson,
Director,
South Shields Youth Theatre,
6 Eccleston Road,
SOUTH SHIELDS.

233 Sunderland Road,

SOUTH SHIELDS.

3rd August, 1967.

Dear Jack,

    Arising from certain allegations made by a member of the South Shields Youth Theatre the police have been making certain enquiries.

    In view of the fact that you mentioned in the Youth Service Sub-Committee the possibility of setting up a club within the Theatre, I enclose copies of a letter from Edward Wilson and my reply. In view of the Chief Constable's remarks about supervision, I am certain that this will be the first thing to consider before we can give any financial assistance.

Yours sincerely,

J. W. Ireland.

J. Grassby, Esq.,
    239 Sunderland Road,
      SOUTH SHIELDS.

A classic example of establishment obsession with control – laced with a Pinterish threat of 'certain enquiries'.

COUNTY BOROUGH OF SOUTH SHIELDS

R. S. YOUNG, M.A.
SOLICITOR,
TOWN CLERK
TEL. No. 4321

TOWN HALL,

SOUTH SHIELDS.

My ref. LR/AGB

25th July, 1969.

Dear Sir,

X.122 - Pier Pavilion, South Shields

With reference to my letter of the 1st instant, and your reply thereto of the 3rd idem, it would be helpful if you could now advise me what steps are being taken by the Youth Theatre to meet their indebtedness to the Local Authority in respect of the use of the Pier Pavilion on previous occasions.

Yours faithfully,

R. S. Young.

Town Clerk

J. Grassby, Esq.,
President,
South Shields Youth Theatre,
Red House,
Westoe Village,
SOUTH SHIELDS.

A familiar theme.

SOUTH SHIELDS YOUTH THEATRE

4th SEASON

COCKADE

by CHARLES WOOD

PIER PAVILION

Sept. : 10th, 11th, 13th, 14th 1968

PIER PARADE. BOX OFFICE 60147

S O U T H   S H I E L D S   Y O U T H   T H E A T R E

Patron: John Neville O.B.E.
President: Jack Grassby
Vice-President: Michael Croft

Leader ... Fred Pearson

Director ....Peter Mason

Company Administrator.....................George Irving

Associate Director........................John Woods

Stage Manager.............................Iain Stinson

Costumes and Properties..................Margaret R.Hunter
                                    Marjorie Quick
Lighting and Sound.......................John Tinmouth

In addition, many un-named members have
assisted in these productions.

South Shields Youth Theatre is affiliated to the National
Youth Theatre of Great Britain and to the Youth Service
sub-committee in South Shields.

YOUTH THEATRE IN SOUTH SHIELDS

South Shields Youth Theatre was born in June of this year, though the idea was conceived much earlier, and within the first six months of its life it is producing this Youth Theatre Festival of 5 plays: surely a unique event in the history of amateur theatre.

Our first productions, 'The Bald Prima Donna' and 'The Bespoke Overcoat' were presented as a double bill on July 25th, 1966, less than one month after the groups formation. Encouragement for our further activities came from many sources. Michael Croft, Director of the National Youth Theatre of Great Britain praised the 'drive and initiative' of the young people of South Shields, and said that this was an important step in the development of a nationwide network of youth theatres. The North Eastern Association for the Arts has contributed financially to this festival, considering it to be an important addition to the cultural activities of the region.

The company is composed of around eighty young people, almost all of whom have had some part in the production of this Festival, whether acting, technical or administrative. But our concept of youth theatre is not only concerned with the production of plays for public performance. Many sessions have been spent experimenting with improvised drama and the use of original material (our end of season revue is largely the result of this). Further, recordings have been made of our production of 'The Bespoke Overcoat', and of O'Neil's 'Where The Cross is Made' and Shakespeare's 'Coriolanus' and 'Antony and Cleopatra', resulting in an increased breadth of technique and an increased dramatic imagination for the young actors involved.

When in my first programme note for the company, I spoke of 'theatre of adventure', I did not, as I think no one then did, imagine that this adventure would grow to such proportions. I hope that you will support this Festival, and in so doing, show your support for the talented young people of South Shields. I further hope that in judging our work, your consideration will be of the quality of the productions, and that you will not be influenced in either direction, by the controversy which has come to surround the Youth Theatre. The theatre members are, I assure you, more interested in the 'storms of Lear' than in the storms of official controversy.

I hope you enjoy our Festival productions, and please remember:

'The Play's the thing'.

The Youth Theatres' own version of the drama.

The Unfinished Revolution

THE FUTURE

This Festival is just the beginning for the South Shields Youth Theatre. We are intent on proving our importance as a youth group, and also as a theatrical company. When this Festival is over we shall be pressing for official recognition and support. We need your help. If you are impressed by what you have seen, TELL EVERYONE! We have argued with the powers that be for the past three months, but if we are to be successful, we need a strong patronage. Please support us and make the tough work of the last 6 months well worth while.

It was, in fact, the beginning of the finalé.

COUNTY BOROUGH OF SOUTH SHIELDS

R. S. YOUNG, M.A.
SOLICITOR.
TOWN CLERK
TEL No **4321**

TOWN HALL,

SOUTH SHIELDS.

My ref. LR/BDS/ACB

31st July, 1969.

Dear Sir,

X.122 - Pier Pavilion

Thank you for your letter of the 28th July, 1969, and I note your comments.

I note that fund raising schemes have been planned with a view to discharging the Youth Theatre's debt to the Corporation, and I await hearing from you in due course.

Yours faithfully,

R. S. Young,

Town Clerk

Epilogue.

Epilogue

The 20th century can be seen as a period of revolutionary change–in the arts, science, technology, politics and philosophy–and we can all choose our own revolutionary heroes: Picasso, Einstein, Darwin, Turin, Marx, Wittgenstein...

The events of the 60s and 70s, in what eurocentrics call 'the west', differed from events in other places and other periods in that they arose mainly from grass-root action rather than from the influence of charismatic leaders and monolithic ideologies. Indeed, the activists of that period specifically rejected the cult of elitism and promoted the role of the many. It was the conventional political wisdom that 'leaders would arise from the action'. Some did; and the slogan for the time was 'power to the people'.

The actions were then largely pragmatic and issue driven and, while some comrades surveyed the scene with revolutionary zeal, the mass of the activists remained unimpressed by the then current conventional political perspectives.

Few of those involved in these events of the late 60s and early 70s would claim that their long-term objectives had been realised. Although some local campaigns can claim to have had a limited success—heating allowances for pensioners, social security benefits for students and strikers, etc.—their success was often transient and was overturned by subsequent government legislation. Even the miners' success was to prove ephemeral.

At a national and international level some more general progressive gains might be identified: women's, black, and gay equality; environmental concerns; civil rights; and a less deferential view of establishment values – what might now be described as early manifestations of social postmodernism.

However, from a longer perspective, subsequent political events would seem to deny any construction of really radical advance. Indeed, the period can be seen as a precursor to the Reagan/Thatcher era with the ascendance of the counter-revolutionary right; the emasculation of the trade unions; the curbing of local democracy; the supremacy of market forces. Certainly some with a revolutionary perspective see this as a revolution that failed. Others see this as a period of potential revolutionary change that lost its way – a revolution not so much failed as unfinished.

Herbert Marcuse was to identify this time and these events optimistically, and prematurely, as heralding the 'New Left'. He was wrong. The new left turned out to be the Clinton/Blair 'Third Way' – a far cry from whatever it was that motivated the 60s–70s activists.

The political failure of that period might be attributed partly to a failure to identify and articulate a coherent political strategy – much less a credible unifying political philosophy. The view that radically new values and social structures would arise naturally from the struggles proved to be grossly naive and wildly optimistic.

Nevertheless, viewed from the vantage point of the late 90s, the emphasis at that time on the tactics of grass-root direct action, outside of (and often against) the establishment's power structures, can be seen to have identified an important political dynamic. (An area of possible further interest to both the existentialist deconstructionist and the evolutionary sociologist–for whom the action is more important than the issues).

The effectiveness, and indeed the necessity, of such direct action has been demonstrated in recent times in such events as the fall of the Berlin Wall and the end of the European communist states; the various civil rights movements in America and elsewhere; and, on a lesser level, the defeat of the Poll Tax in the UK.

Such events pose the classical questions of rebellion: at what point, and in what way, is action outside the established social structures (or indeed against the law) justified in a 'democratic' society which cannot (or will not) respond to perceived injustice; and how can this action be organised to give expression to popular will without allowing access to intolerance, or control by self appointed demagogues?

It might be seen that the 1969–1976 events in South Tyneside addressed these questions and attempted some innovative and creative answers. It could be chiefly in this context that these local events can be seen to have a wider relevance. In a small way, for a brief time, in an unlikely place, they were part of an ongoing social narrative.

Political theorists might debate whether or not these forms of protest represent a permanent feature of the political scene. The question arises as to whether our political structures will need to accommodate them (or indeed to encourage them) in periods of Maoist-like recurring rebellion, or whether our social structure will change so that this is no longer a necessary form of political action – a sort of democratic Utopia. (Dictatorships of the left and of the right have their own solutions.)

Some will argue that while the major economic forces (capital) remain outside democratic control the former of these options is more likely – even inevitable. The 'village Hampdens' of Gray's elegy will always be with us – the rebels and the revolutionaries.

Neal Ascherson, the political columnist, addressed this question in 1997. Writing in The Guardian about the events of the 60s–70s he said:

'Thirty years on the question is could it happen again? The explosion was totally unexpected and over so fast that terrified governments and academia of the west did not have time to understand its cause. And they still don't...

Could it happen again?

Not in the same form; not in the same words.

But, probably, yes.'

To be continued...

Acknowledgments

The activities of that period were collective actions or they were nothing. I fully recognise that while I was often the spokesperson, the projects were only possible because of the efforts and co-operation of many people.

Because of this I feel it necessary to risk offense by omission (or possibly by inclusion) by listing those responsible.

SOUTH SHIELDS TRADES UNION COUNCIL

Bernard Appleton	Ken Smith	John Boundy
Arthur Gibson	Jim Florence	Jim Berry
John Byrne	Mike Peel	Celia Pearson
Paddy Cain	Hughie Nicol	Irene Lendayou
Ron Ingoe	Doris Johnson	Maureen Tither
Kathy Brown	Iris Tate	Peter Brook
Norman Cawthorn	George Bell	John Sandercock
Stan Fox	George Mordain	Bob Growcott
Jim Slater	Malcom Campbell	Davison Brenen
Jim Rouson	Joe McAcroy	Jim Riddle
Ted Abblet	Joe Slevin	Dorothy Riddle
Brian Steele	Violet Webster	Mike Wales
Bob Stitolph	Ned Elliott	John Wakeford
Terry Devonport	Fred Pringle	George Elstob
Ivor Richardson	Jim Moore	

AND,
Peter Gillanders, Frank Mansfield, Malcolm Scott,
Stewart Smith – Journalists
Ernie Ferryhough MP, Arthur Blenkinsop MP,
Harold Tavaroges, Tony Brown – Solicitors.
Jack Smith, – Artist.
David Byrne, Deliah Slevin – Political gurus.
Keith Robison, Peter Andrews – Creatively unemployed.
Graham Perks, Ian Imrie, Ian Smith – Student activists.

ALSO, I would like to acknowledge the part played by the local and national media – often unwittingly (and sometimes unwillingly) they were nevertheless an integral part of the events. In particular I wish to acknowledge the collective work of the Shields Gazette which I have drawn upon extensively for this book and who provided at that time a real community service.

With failing memory I apologise to the many others whose names have slipped my mind but whose efforts made these events possible.

AND, FINALLY, FOR THEIR HELP IN THE PRODUCTION OF THIS BOOK:
Lee Foster; for his patience and design skills.
Dave Temple; printer, for his professional advice.
Paul Gray and Mark Houlsby; for their editing and advice.
John Temple and Ian Malcolm; for local Labour Party history.
Bill Gray; for his advice about everything.
Dave Johnston; for his tolerance and support.
The Lipman – Miliband Trust; for their financial support.

About The Author

Jack Grassby was born in South Shields in 1925 and has lived and worked on Tyneside apart from a period of service in the Royal Navy.

He studied electrical engineering at the then Sunderland College of Durham University and worked for several years in the electronics industry. He taught for some 25 years in the local colleges of further and higher education.

He served on many trade union and education bodies at local and national level and was, for seven years, a member of the national executive of his professional union

From 1964 to 1969 he was secretary of the joint South Shields Labour Party and Trades Union Council.

On his retirement in 1988 he took up art and has had several solo exhibitions. His latest work is a form of conceptual art based on quantum physics.